AR-15 SKILLS & DRILLS

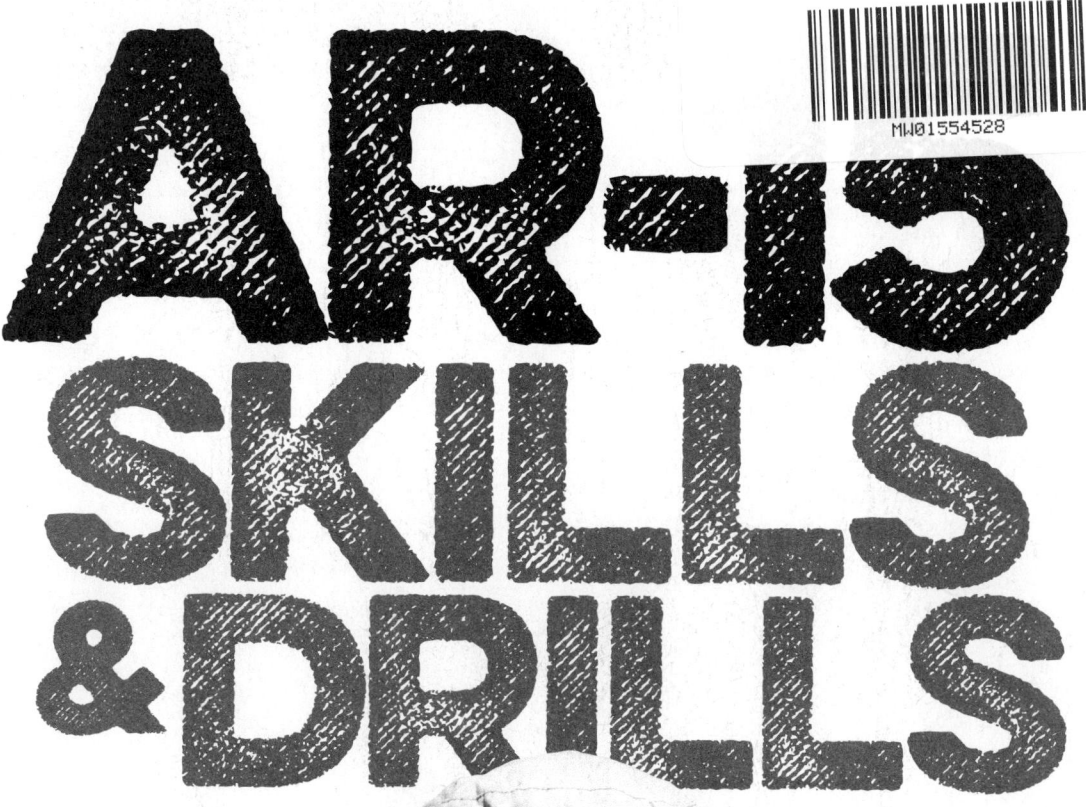

Learn to Run Your AR Like a Pro

Tiger McKee

Copyright ©2017 F+W Media, Inc.

All rights reserved. No portion of this publication may be reproduced or transmitted in any form or by any means, electronic or mechanical, including photocopy, recording, or any information storage and retrieval system, without permission in writing from the publisher, except by a reviewer who may quote brief passages in a critical article or review to be printed in a magazine or newspaper, or electronically transmitted on radio, television, or the Internet.

CAUTION: Technical data presented here, particularly technical data on the handloading and on firearms adjustment and alteration, inevitably reflects individual experience with particular equipment and components under specific circumstances the reader cannot duplicate exactly. Such data presentations therefore should be used for guidance only and caution. F+W Media, Inc., accepts no responsibility for results obtained using this data.

Published by

Gun Digest® Books, an imprint of F+W Media, Inc.
Krause Publications • 700 East State Street • Iola, WI 54990-0001
715-445-2214 • 888-457-2873
www.krausebooks.com

To order books or other products call toll-free 1-800-258-0929
or visit us online at www.gundigeststore.com

Cover photography by Al Reese,
Langston, Alabama

ISBN-13: 978-1-4402-4720-0
ISBN-10: 1-4402-4720-X

Cover Design by Dave Hauser
Designed by Dane Royer
Edited by Corrina Peterson

Printed in The United States of America

10 9 8 7 6 5 4 3 2 1

RELATED TITLES FROM GUN DIGEST

GUNSMITHING THE AR-15: THE BENCH MANUAL

GUN DIGEST GUIDE TO THE MODERN AK

GUN DIGEST BOOK OF SUPPRESSORS

www.gundigest.com

THIS BOOK IS DEDICATED TO MY WIFE,
GRETCHEN, WHO HAS PUT UP WITH A LOT
OVER THE YEARS TO SUPPORT MY
TEACHING AND SHOOTRITE.

ACKNOWLEDGEMENTS

Thanks to all the guys who helped me get here. Clint Smith gave me the opportunity to study and teach with him. The instructors at Thunder Ranch helped me become a better teacher. Hal Herring, friend and author, helped me to become a better writer. There are numerous people who have supported us in a multitude of other ways. There's no way to list everyone. You know who you are, and I couldn't have made it without you.

A big thank you goes to the Shootrite instructors. There aren't very many of you, but each of you has played a vital role in what Shootrite is and will be. Shootrite is great because of the sum of its parts.

The folks at Gun Digest get praise for entrusting me to write this work, and then putting it together so it makes sense. My first book was self-published. Gun Digest took a leap of faith and invested time and money into this project.

Thanks to God, for providing me riches beyond what I deserve.

CONTENTS

INTRODUCTION 6

1 | SAFETY 8

2 | PARTS & OPERATION OF THE AR 12

3 | SLINGS 50

4 | READY POSITIONS 60

5 | CARRY MODES 63

6 | STANCE 82

7 | ADMINISTRATIVE MANIPULATIONS 88

8 | FUNCTIONAL MANIPULATIONS 106

9 | MARKSMANSHIP 128

10 | TACTICAL USE OF YOUR EYES 133

11 | FIRST SHOTS 137

12 | ZEROING THE AR 140

13 | TRAINING, PRACTICE & LEARNING 147

14 | DEFENSE FUNDAMENTALS 156

15 | TARGET ZONES 161

16 | DATA BOOK 168

17 | MOVING 170

18 | FIRING POSITIONS 188

19 | USING COVER 209

20 | LOW-LIGHT CONDITIONS 232

21 | TRANSITION TO HANDGUN 243

22 | CLEANING 249

23 | PRACTICE TOOLS 258

24 | VESTS, CHEST RIGS & PACKS 265

INTRODUCTION

This book isn't about the history and development of the AR-type weapon, building an AR or performing modifications. There are plenty of good sources for that information already out there. It's also not a "tactical" book, although it does include subjects like using cover, working in low-light conditions and the fundamentals of responding to a threat. These are skills that you need, but learning to apply them for defensive or combative purposes is beyond the scope of this book.

AR-15 Skills & Drills is about the techniques you need to operate the AR platform safely and efficiently, regardless of your application. Whether you're hunting, competing or using the AR for defensive purposes, the same skills are used to manipulate the AR efficiently and shoot it accurately.

To learn anything takes practice, performing the same skills over and over until eventually you learn them. We'll discuss how to operate the AR so that you know *what* to practice, but equally important *how* to practice, providing a solid learning curve and the greatest return from your time and money invested. Some sections of this book describe how to perform certain actions, while other sections list specific drills that include applying the skills and techniques discussed in previous chapters. There are a variety of ways to practice; the only limit is your imagination. Just keep in mind that anything and everything you do should be performed safely. Safety is your number one concern any time you're working with firearms.

This book is not intended to be a substitute for training under a qualified instructor. Yes, one of the ways we learn is by reading and studying a subject. A book can tell you how, why or when to perform a certain action. What it *can't* tell you are all the ways you can do it wrong or an alternative approach if a technique doesn't work for you, or watch to make sure your finger comes off the trigger while reloading. Often you'll be doing something wrong and you won't even be aware of it. Cultivating the correct skills is mandatory and this book will help you with that, but eventually you need to attend training under a qualified instructor.

Although this book focuses on the AR-type rifle and carbine, the same skills apply to a variety of firearms. The safety or magazine release may be in a different location, but the same techniques apply regardless of what type semi-auto you're working with.

Keep in mind that there are different ways to accomplish the same task, and various schools of thought on how to operate the AR. This book presents a way of doing things, but it isn't an absolute or the only way. Your specific application of the AR may call for different techniques or operating principles. Becoming proficient with a firearm is an art; everyone's artwork will be a little different.

The AR is one of the best firearms ever produced. In the early days it experienced some growing pains, but it has served our military faithfully for decades now, with no end in sight. Today's AR is reliable, simple to operate, and accurate. There is a huge industry that supplies accessories for the AR, and its modular design allows users to customize it to suit any purpose. You can do almost anything with an AR. But first you need to know how to operate it safely and efficiently. I hope this book helps with learning your AR.

A NOTE ABOUT VERBALIZING TO LEARN

Every technique we perform is a series of actions or steps chunked together and applied in the correct sequence. To learn a technique, or to modify an existing skill, the sequence is broken down into individual steps. You have to go step by step, performing the proper sequence so you get predictable results from your actions.

The problem is that our brain always wants to get ahead of the body; the mind is on step five while the body is performing step two. Your body tries to catch up by going fast. When you try to go fast to catch up, things start going downhill. Steps are left out of the sequence. Your performance is poor, and improper repetitions are detrimental to learning. A good technique to use is verbalizing your actions, saying each step out loud as you work through the sequence. This helps you focus, consciously thinking about each step of the process, and it slows the mind down to the speed that your body can perform the required actions.

Reloading is a perfect application and example of this learning technique. Just remember this tool, saying your actions, can be applied to any skill or technique.

You're shooting and the AR runs empty, the bolt locking to the rear on the empty magazine. Step one is getting your finger off the trigger and out of the trigger guard. (See the Functional Manipulations section for details on reloading.) You say out loud, "Finger off the trigger!" Next, "Old mag out!" Press the mag catch to release the empty mag. "New mag in!" Once the fresh mag is in the receiver, "Bolt release!" Press the bolt release to chamber a round.

After some practice and repetitions you can start to shorten your verbal cues. Instead of saying "old mag out" you cut it down to "mag out." Eventually you reach the point where you're not saying it out loud, but you're still thinking about this action at a conscious level. After plenty of repetitions this action begins to become a subconscious action. The mind says, "Reload" and the subconscious mind takes over to perform the sequence. This is the point we want to be at with all our skills.

Learning or modifying a skill takes time and repetitions. In the beginning you have to walk. You can't be concerned with the outcome; the mind is only focusing on the task at hand. The brain doesn't like to walk, so you vocalize the actions to keep the mind and body together functioning at the same pace. Later you run, which the brain enjoys. At some point you begin to fly. A conscious cue prompts the subconscious to perform the task efficiently. •

CHAPTER 1
SAFETY

THE FIRST AND FOREMOST concern when working with any firearm is safety. Consistency, which is the theme with all gunhandling skills, is mandatory. Consistently applying the four basic safety rules ensures safe handling of the firearm regardless of the application. It only takes a fraction of a second for your mind to wander, for a distraction to occur, and you've opened the door for trouble to enter.

I still find it amazing that the majority of gun owners are not aware of the basics of firearms safety. Even those who have been shooting all their lives sometimes don't understand the four basic safety rules, the reasons for them, and how to incorporate them into their gunhandling.

RULE 1
TREAT EVERY FIREARM AS A LOADED FIREARM.

The key to Rule 1, and the same is true for the other three rules, is consistency. Applying Rule 1 greatly reduces your chances of making a mistake. Inconsistency — usually treating it like it's "loaded" but then sometimes handling it like it's "unloaded" — leads to trouble. Sooner or later you'll get confused. Mistakes with firearms are embarrassing at best; often times they are tragic.

You have to make Rule 1 a part of your life, and not just when you're the one handling the weapon. You're standing in a group at the range when someone pulls out their new favorite firearm to show it off. At the same time they're waving the muzzle around, pointing it at everyone. You need correct that problem before it becomes a tragedy. While at the range the gentleman next to you sets his .45-.70 buffalo rifle on the bench, pointing it at you in the process. "Please don't point your rifle at me," you ask. "Don't worry," he replies, "she ain't loaded." Pack your gear and come back another day.

There are no exceptions to Rule 1. If you don't believe me do a search on the web under "shot with unloaded gun." (2,790,000 hits in .32 seconds.) People are constantly shooting themselves and others with "unloaded" weapons.

Firearms were originally designed for fighting. Later people figured out you could use them to put meat on the table, for competition and for just plain fun or recreation purposes. No matter what you use them for, firearms are lethal weapons and should be treated as such. The first and foremost thing in our mind when handling firearms is safety. Even in a defensive confrontation, you, as a good guy, still have to be fighting safely. The first rule means you always apply the three following rules anytime there is a firearm present. Again, consistency is the key.

RULE 2
NEVER POINT THE MUZZLE AT ANYTHING YOU'RE NOT WILLING TO DESTROY.

Firearms have one job, launching projectiles out of the barrel. They have no mind and don't care what direction they are pointing. Your job is to make sure the muzzle is always pointing in a safe direction.

"Safe" is normally with the muzzle of your firearm pointing down. (This is especially true for the AR, which has a free-floating firing pin. We'll discuss what that means later.) Even when pointing the muzzle down, be aware that bullets can/will bounce off a surface. Make sure there is a backstop capable of stopping a round or a clear area in front of where the muzzle is pointing in case a negligent discharge were to occur.

Ultimately the environment determines what is a

THE FOUR SAFETY RULES

These four rules are found in numerous variations, but they all mean the same thing.

RULE 1	TREAT ALL GUNS AS LOADED
RULE 2	NEVER POINT THE MUZZLE AT ANYTHING YOU'RE NOT WILLING TO DESTROY
RULE 3	FINGER OFF THE TRIGGER UNLESS YOUR SIGHTS ARE ON THE TARGET AND YOU ARE READY AND WILLING TO SHOOT.
RULE 4	BE SURE TO IDENTIFY YOUR TARGET, AND WHAT'S SURROUNDING AND BEYOND THE TARGET.

safe direction. I'm on the second level of a building, with a wooden floor separating me from the people in the building's lower level. Pointing it at the floor may not be a good idea because the bullet could easily penetrate the wood. I can point it at the wall, because the brick exterior would stop a round.

I'm not a big fan of pointing the muzzle up. What goes up comes down. If a negligent discharge does occur the bullet flies off into the sky. When it drops it can injure or kill. In Los Angeles, from 1985-92 one medical center treated 118 people due to falling-bullet injuries. Thirty-eight of the people died from their injuries. (http://www.abc.net.au/science/k2/homework/s95523.htm)

Tactically, pointing the muzzle up is not a good idea because if the threat gets in tight and close, where we know most confrontations take place, they can pass and trap the muzzle or jam it into your head.

Keeping the muzzle pointing in a safe direction sounds simple, but it only takes a fraction of a second for this rule to be broken. The AR is attached to your body in several locations. The stock is in the pocket of the shoulder and normally both hands are holding it. When the body moves the carbine follows. Something draws your attention, you look to the side, and at the same time the rest of your body begins to follow. Suddenly your muzzle is pointing in an unsafe direction. Or, you're pointing the muzzle in a safe direction when someone unaware walks in front of you. You have to be paying attention so you can lower the muzzle down and avoiding sweeping or covering them with your carbine.

On a range Rule 2 is pretty easy to apply, but again always keep an eye on those around you. In a defensive situation, when mayhem is breakin' loose all 'round, it gets complicated quickly. You're moving, the threat(s) are moving, bystanders are freaking out running everywhere or frozen in place. Even though you're in a fight you still have to practice muzzle discipline.

Until you identify your target and decide that it's time to fire, keep muzzle pointing in a safe direction.

RULE 3
FINGER OFF THE TRIGGER UNLESS YOUR SIGHTS ARE ON THE TARGET AND YOU ARE READY AND WILLING TO SHOOT.

In concept this is pretty simple. When the sights are off target your finger is off the trigger. Regardless of the type firearm the ultimate safety mechanism is your finger working in conjunction with the brain. This should be common sense, but the biggest safety issue with people and firearms is Rule 3.

Rule 3 is violated for several reasons. First, the AR is designed so that, when holding it, having your finger on the trigger feels natural and comfortable. Also, some people believe having their finger on the trigger will allow them to shoot quicker. This isn't true, and only makes you a danger to yourself and those around you. Properly handling a firearm means the majority of the time when it's in your hands the finger is off the trigger. If you don't practice this habit you'll end up with your finger on that trigger at the wrong time, especially under stress.

When it's not on the trigger the proper location for the finger is high on the receiver, clear of the trigger and trigger guard. From this location it takes a mental decision and physical action to place your finger onto the trigger. Simply taking the finger off the trigger but leaving it inside the trigger guard isn't enough. You get startled, stumble, or someone shoves you and suddenly the finger is applying pressure to the trigger. Avoid positioning your trigger finger on the mag release, which can lead to dumping your mag unintentionally.

On the other side of the coin, when the sights are on target your finger is on the trigger. If you have a sight picture, you're aiming at the target, which means you've made the decision that you're going to fire a round; otherwise the sights shouldn't be on target. The sights are on target so your finger is on the trigger. This doesn't mean you have to be pressing the trigger, but if you wait until it's time to shoot to place your finger to the trigger just that little bit of motion will move the sights. Getting into a rush to get your finger on the trigger also greatly increases the chances you'll slap or jerk the trigger to fire as opposed to pressing it smoothly. Sights off the target, finger off the trigger. Conversely, sights on target, finger on trigger.

With today's weapons, due to the design and materials of which they are constructed, they don't go bang unless something presses the trigger. Being owner and master of that weapon means it doesn't fire until you've decided it's time to shoot. Knowing when to have the finger off and on the trigger is a mandatory, fundamental part of safe gunhandling.

RULE 4
IDENTIFY YOUR TARGET, AND WHAT'S SURROUNDING AND BEYOND THE TARGET.

Rule 4 applies any time you are shooting. Identifying your target is mandatory prior to firing a shot, whether it's on the range, taking game meat or in a violent confrontation. You also must know what's surrounding and beyond the target to ensure a safe path for any errant rounds.

On an established firing range confirming your target is easy. There are proper backstops to trap rounds, even if the bullet bounces off something, or goes high or to the side. There are no bystanders around your target or neighbor's housed behind them. On a range everything is controlled to provide a safe environment.

Shooting on an improvised range requires more care. A couple years ago near here on Christmas day a shooter was zeroing a new rifle by firing at a cardboard box on top of a hill. The round went through the box, over the top of the hill and traveled 590 yards before striking and killing a man in his backyard.

Pay attention to your bullet's path. Bullets, especially high velocity rifle rounds, can travel a long distance before losing their energy and falling to ground. (Depending on angle of trajectory a .308 round can easily travel 2-3 miles or more.) With rural developments popping up all around, you better make sure what direction you're sending that round.

Rule 4 applies when hunting. Make sure what you are shooting at is your intended target. Never fire at movement, sounds, or something you think might be game. In a self-defense situation Rule 4 is absolute. First, you locate and identify your target, in this case a threat. You have to be able to justify, both legally and morally, your reason for firing. Never fire on noise or movement. Every year people shoot family, friends and non-threats because they lost control and shot without identifying their target.

Even though it's a fight you're responsible for every round fired no matter where it ends up. Bullets will penetrate multiple sheetrock walls, traverse a parking lot, or bounce off an object and zing out in a different direction. It would be a rare situation when you don't have to be concerned with errant rounds. You may have to move to obtain a clear angle of fire or position a backstop behind the threat. The angles can change suddenly. You have a clear field of fire but then a bystander takes a couple of steps putting themselves between you and the threat. The bad guy moves, using a bystander for cover.

As owner of a firearm you memorize these rules. They apply any time a firearm is present. You have to pay attention to what you do, and you have to watch everyone around you. These rules apply at home, on the range, during hunting or competition and especially during an armed confrontation.

PROPER GEAR

Another important aspect of safety is making sure you're using the proper gear when training and practicing. Eye and ear protection is mandatory. You need to wear a hat, which keeps hot brass from landing between your eyes and the eye protection. A shirt with a high tight collar, or a bandana worn around the neck keeps hot brass from going down your shirt. Rifle brass is very hot and it will burn, so keep everything covered and protected. When working on different positions, elbow and knee pads are needed to ensure you don't injure anything when dropping into position. If you're going to be doing a lot of manipulations it's a good idea to wear a pair of thin gloves, which will protect your fingers yet still allow you to feel what's going on as you work the AR. •

CHAPTER 2
PARTS & OPERATION OF THE AR

EUGENE STONER WAS a genius when it came to ergonomics, and the AR-type rifle and carbine are among the most user-friendly designed firearms ever produced. All the parts necessary to operate the firearm are in just the right place, and it works well for right- or left-handed shooters. However, even though it's a well thought out design, in order to learn how to use the AR efficiently you have to know what each part does and the best way to manipulate it.

For purposes of our discussion the terms strong, dominant or primary hand refer to the hand you use most; a right-handed person's strong or primary hand is the right one. The support hand for a right-handed shooter is the left hand, and for left-handers it's just the opposite. Each hand has specific tasks to perform. On some operations there are options, but after you determine what works best consistency is the key.

Start from the beginning and learn how to manipulate the AR without needing to see it. Your ultimate goal is to be able to operate the AR while

On the civilian AR the selector, or "safety," has two positions – "Safe" and "Fire."

keeping your eyes on something more important, such as the target. Also, this creates the skill necessary to manipulate the AR in dark or low-light environments. In the beginning it takes real effort not to look at the AR as you work with it. There may be times when it's necessary for you to glance at it to locate something, but eventually you'll learn where everything is and develop the ability to operate it through physical confirmation.

SELECTOR LEVER, OR "SAFETY"

The AR has a "selector lever," which most everyone calls the safety. On the semi-auto civilian version of the AR there are two positions – "Safe" and "Fire."

When the selector is in the "Safe" position the trigger cannot be pressed. In the "Fire" mode the trigger is unlocked so that it can be pressed to fire. Constant manipulation of the safety, engaging and disengaging it, makes you a safer shooter, ensures the AR will fire when you press the trigger and also serves as a partial systems check for the AR.

Operation of the safety, disengaging and engaging it as appropriate, must become habit. Unless the sights are on target the selector is in the "Safe" position, or engaged. Every time you come up on target the safety is disengaged, switched to the "Fire" position. When you come off the target the safety is engaged. The key is consistency, manipulating the safety the same way every time you work with the AR.

Having the safety "on" makes you safe. (I know, this should seem obvious, but some people have strange ideas.) The first thing you do when picking up the AR up is to go into a Low-Ready position and ensure selector is in the "Safe" position. If the safety won't engage you may need to cycle the charging handle, resetting the hammer so the safety can be engaged. Remember to perform this action without looking, keeping the eyes up as discussed previously, physically confirming the safety is engaged.

Every time you come up on target you disengage the safety, switching it to the "Fire" position. This action must become habit in order to ensure that whenever you come on target the selector is flipped to the "Fire" position. I've seen numerous shooters that will be inconsistent with manipulation of the safety, and many times they'll be on target pressing the trigger with all the strength they can, but it won't fire because they forgot to flip the safety off. Manipulating the safety must become a habit that you perform without having to consciously think about it.

Some people think having to disengage the safety will slow them down in firing. This definitely is not the case. It takes longer to get the sights on target than it does to flip the safety off. As the muzzle comes up to the target the safety is depressed. In the "Fire" position the safety is vertical, running up and down.

After firing you come off the trigger, off the target – for example into a Low-Ready position – and engage the safety. There may be times when the safety won't engage. This is because the hammer hasn't been reset and indicates a malfunction that requires attention. Just because the safety does engage doesn't mean there isn't something that needs attention – for example the AR is empty and needs to be reloaded – but when it won't engage there is definitely a problem to address.

After engaging the safety the digit that is used to disengage the safety – which digit depends on whether you're a right- or left-handed shooter – is positioned back on top of the safety where it's ready to depress it again.

Right-handed shooters use the right thumb to disengage the safety.

The right thumb also engages the safety. This will normally require you to reposition the hand slightly to flip the safety up. As soon as the safety is on, reacquire the proper grip with the hand and position the thumb back on top of the safety where it's ready flip it to "Fire" the next time you're ready to shoot.

Left-handed shooters can use the left thumb or the trigger finger to disengage the safety. Which digit you use is dictated by hand size and/or personal preference. When using the thumb to disengage the safety, the thumb can either stay on the left

Right-handed shooters use the right thumb to manipulate the safety.

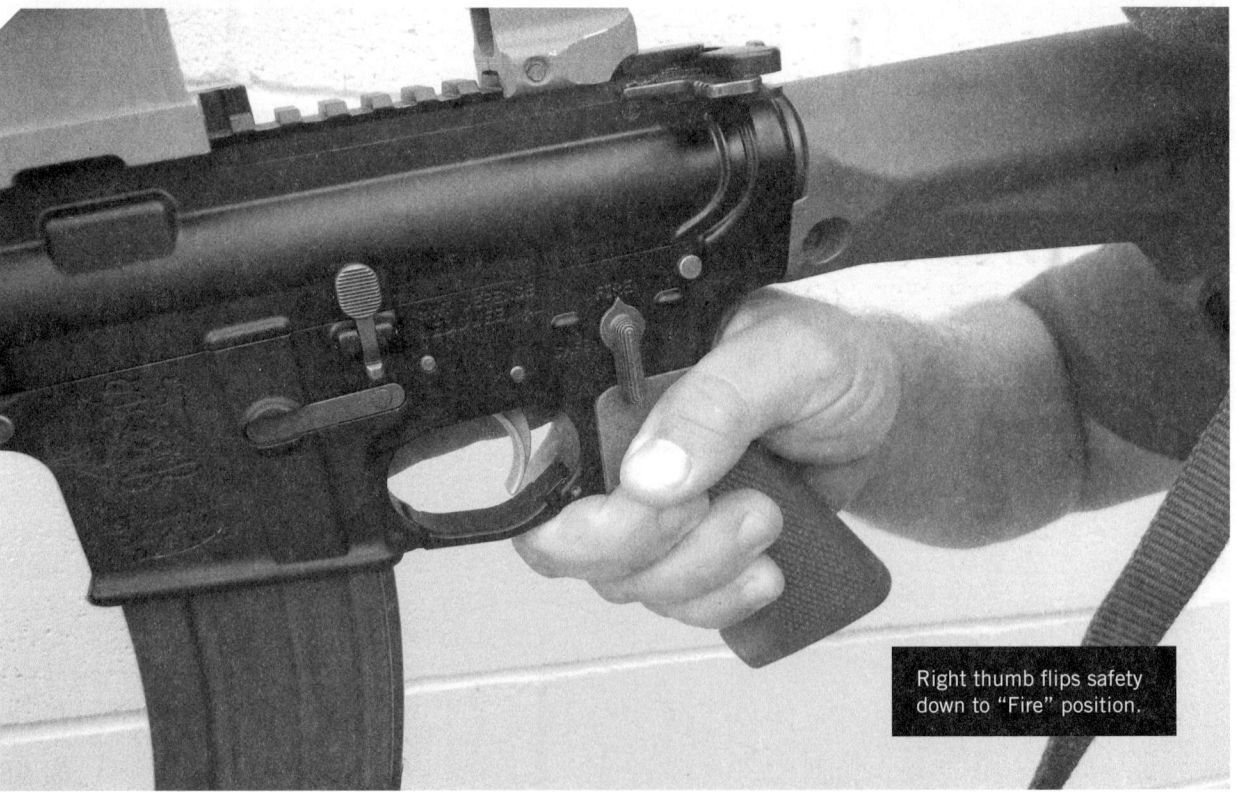

Right thumb flips safety down to "Fire" position.

Right-handed shooters also use the thumb to engage the safety.

side of the receiver or you can transition it over to the right side of the grip for more control.

Some left-handed shooters will use the trigger finger to flip the safety to "Fire," keeping the thumb on the right side in a standard type grip.

To engage the safety, left-handed shooters can use the left thumb or the trigger finger.

Again, after engaging the safety reposition the thumb or trigger finger back on top of the safety, where it's ready to flip the safety off. Left-handers may need to do a little experimenting to determine what works best. Once you decide what works best for you then start developing consistency, habitually doing it the same way every time.

Manipulation of the safety is something that must be consistent. For this action to become habit, operating safety without conscious thought, you have to practice. In the beginning, especially for those who have a lot of time behind a pistol that doesn't have a thumb safety, working the safety requires constant attention at a conscious level. Verbalizing this action will help with the learning process. You're coming up on target. You say out loud, "Safety off." After shooting you say: "Off the trigger, off the target, safety on."

CHARGING HANDLE

The charging handle is used to manually cycle the bolt group, such as when loading, unloading or clearing malfunctions. Cycling the charging handle is almost an art in itself. It's important to perform

Left-handed shooter using thumb to disengage safety.

Left-handed shooter using trigger finger to flip safety to "Fire."

Left-handed shooter can use their trigger finger to engage the safety.

this action properly; otherwise it creates friction and wear on the handle, making it more difficult to cycle. Improperly cycling the handle twisting or torquing it, can permanently bend it out of shape. Once it's bent the bolt group can't slide back and forth and the AR ceases to function. Incorrect technique can also break the charging handle, again taking the AR out of action.

Cycling the charging handle is broken down into three steps, and each one is critical. Right-handed shooters normally use the left or support hand to cycle the handle. You want to maintain a firing grip with the strong hand as much as possible.

Step 1: Position the thumb in the center of the back edge of the handle.

Step 2: Use your first finger to unlatch the handle, releasing it from the receiver.

Step 3: Cycle the charging handle by pulling it straight to the rear. Pull your thumb (which is on the center rear section of the handle) back, tracking it to the rear using the centerline or top of the stock as a guide. The action to cycle the handle should occur in the elbow, not the shoulder. Using the shoulder to cycle it will twist the handle as you pull it. Working it with the elbow helps keep everything in a straight line.

Once the handle has reached full travel to the rear, release it completely, letting it snap forward with full spring pressure. Do not let your hand "ride" the handle forward, as this will retard the action and create problems. The bolt needs that momentum to strip rounds from the mag, feed them into the chamber, and seat fully into battery or to extract a round from the chamber and eject it cleanly.

Shooters who find it difficult to support the AR using only the strong hand on the grip can use an alternative method, holding the handguard with the support hand and cycling the charging handle

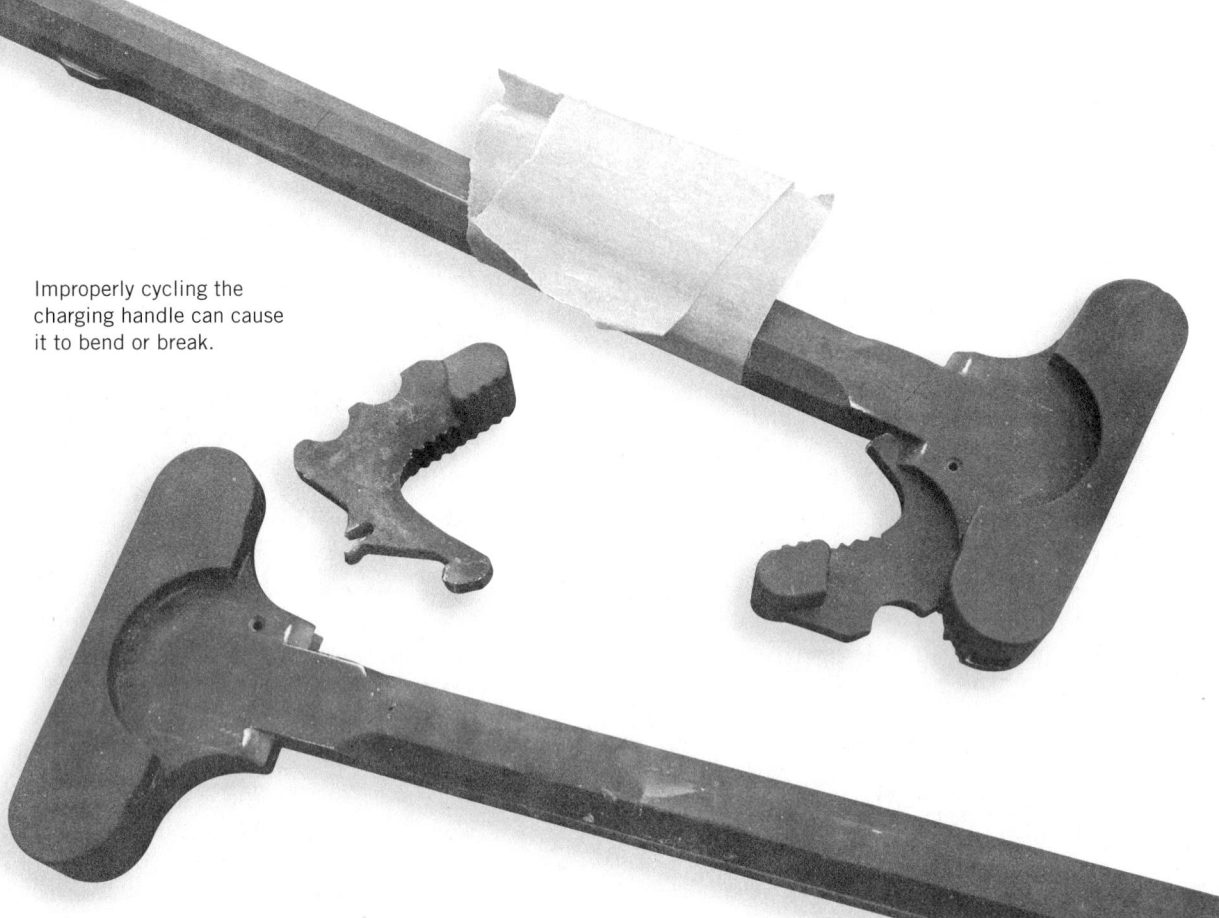

Improperly cycling the charging handle can cause it to bend or break.

with the strong hand. With this technique the support hand has most of the AR's weight. For this technique a right-handed shooter will position the first two fingers of their right hand on each side of the handle — what we call "snake fangs" — and the thumb is positioned on the back center section of the handle.

Left-handed shooters have a few different options. Traditionally, lefties use the right hand to cycle the action. The thumb is on the center back section of the handle. The first two fingers of the right hand are used as "snake fangs," with the first finger on the left side of the handle, unlatching it from the receiver and the second finger on the right side of the handle. Pull straight to the rear, again using the elbow joint to cycle the charging handle.

You can also install an ambidextrous charging handle, which has a release on both sides of the handle and allows left-handed shooters to use the same technique a right-handed shooter uses when cycling the handle with the support hand.

Even if you do have an ambi charging handle, you still need to know how to cycle a standard type handle in case you have to use an AR that isn't set up like yours.

A third option for lefties is to use the left hand, the strong or dominate hand, to cycle the action. The right hand holds the handguard, supporting the AR, and the left hand comes off the grip to cycle the action. While this technique isn't traditional, it does work well for shooters who have problems supporting the rifle with just their strong hand on the grip. Left-handed shooters should experiment with the different options until discovering what works best.

The charging handle is also used to perform a "chamber check," confirming the condition of the chamber, or to manually lock the bolt to the rear. To check the chamber pull the handle slightly to

To cycle the charging handle the thumb is centered on the back and first finger hits the latch.

Pull the thumb straight back down the centerline of the stock.

Once the handle reaches full movement to the rear release it completely, letting it snap forward.

It may be easier to hold the AR with the support hand and use the strong hand to cycle the charging handle. Here a left-handed shooter is using the strong hand to cycle the action.

Using the two first fingers of the strong hand to cycle the action.

An ambidextrous charging handle will allow a left-handed shooter to use a "right hand" technique to cycle the action.

the rear to inspect the chamber for loaded or clear. For chamber checks I prefer to use the strong hand on the charging handle. This segregates the actions. When cycling the charging handle, an aggressive action, I use the support hand. To check the chamber or engage the bolt catch I use the strong hand on the charging handle.

For example, a right-handed shooter uses the left hand to cycle the action, working it aggressively as described above. To perform a chamber check or lock the bolt to the rear, which are not aggressive actions, I use the right hand to pull the charging handle slightly to the rear, with the left hand on the handguard to support the carbine.

For left-handed shooters it may be a little different, depending on which technique works best for cycling the action.

Consistency is the key, and once you determine what works best, stick with it.

You also use the charging handle to manually lock the bolt to the rear. This will require you to pull the charging back with the strong hand, while bringing the support hand back to engage the bolt catch, pressing the bottom of it once the bolt is all the way to the rear.

There are a variety of different types of charging handles. Your application may determine what you need. For example, with a traditional type optic you'll probably need a charging handle that is wider in order for you to be able to get the proper grip on it for manipulations.

MAGAZINE CATCH

The mag catch – commonly called the "magazine release" – does just that. It catches or locks the mag in place. Pressing it releases the mag, allowing it to be removed or dropped from the magazine well of the receiver. Right-handed shooters use their trigger finger to press the mag release.

Left-handed shooters bring their support hand – the right hand – back, cupping it around the mag-

Left-handed shooter using the support hand to cycle the charging handle.

Right-handed shooter using strong hand to pull charging handle back to check chamber.

Left-handed shooter using strong hand to pull the bolt back to check the chamber.

Right-handed shooter manually locking the bolt to the rear.

Left-handed shooter locking the bolt to the rear.

A wider handle will be necessary if you have optics that extend past the charging handle's location.

well, and use the right-handed thumb to press the mag release.

A properly adjusted mag release should drop the mag when it's pressed. This is also dependent on having good magazines, which should seat and lock in the AR easily and drop free without having to be pulled from the magwell.

BOLT CATCH

The bolt catch locks the bolt assembly to the rear. The magazine runs empty and the follower engages the bolt catch, locking the bolt to the rear. Or, you pull the charging handle to the rear and manually engage the bolt catch to hold the bolt group to the rear. The bolt catch is also used as a bolt release. You use the charging handle to manually cycle the bolt group – loading or unloading and clearing malfunctions. Whenever the bolt is locked to the rear – reloading an empty rifle – you chamber a round by using the bolt release.

Manually locking the bolt to the rear is one of the few times the strong hand comes off the grip of the AR, unless you are using one of the alternative methods where you're holding the AR with the support hand and using the strong hand to cycle the action. (The other time is when performing a "chamber check," which is discussed in the Administrative Manipulations section.) The support hand comes back, cupping the magwell in a position when you can press the bottom of the bolt catch. The strong hand comes off the grip to pull the charging handle to the rear.

Once the handle is all the way to the rear you use the support hand to press the bottom of the bolt catch, which locks the bolt to the rear. After locking the bolt open push the charging handle forward and latch it in place.

The bolt catch is also used as a bolt release. You're firing and the AR runs empty, bolt locked to the rear. Once a new, loaded mag is in the receiver – see the section on Empty Reloads – you press the top of the bolt catch, releasing the bolt to chamber a round.

Right-handed shooters use their trigger finger to press the mag catch to release mag.

Left-handed shooters use their right thumb to press the mag catch.

CHAPTER 2: PARTS & OPERATION OF THE AR

A right-handed shooter will release the bolt by pressing with the left hand thumb. Left-handed shooters will normally use their trigger finger to release the bolt.

For left-handed shooters who don't have a lot of strength in their trigger finger, the left hand thumb can be used, but this isn't as efficient as using the trigger finger because it requires much more movement of the left hand in order to reacquire a firing grip after releasing the bolt.

Releasing the bolt in this fashion is ergonomic, efficient, and the way the AR is designed to function. You can maintain your cheek-weld on the rifle while keeping the muzzle on the target, ready for follow-up shots after reloading if necessary. The more you mess with the charging handle the more chance there is you'll create a problem. For example, shooters will cycle the charging handle to release the bolt, but allow their hand to ride the handle forward, slowing the bolt assembly down enough that it doesn't strip a round off the mag or chamber it correctly. This is especially true with a fully-loaded magazine because it takes a lot of force to strip those first few rounds out of the mag.

Learn how to use the bolt catch to lock the bolt to the rear and also to release the bolt. That's the way the AR rifle is designed to operate and it's ergonomic, which translates into efficient and quick actions. This may seem like a small matter, but when time counts it's the small things that make a big difference.

FORWARD ASSIST

Most ARs have an external forward assist, but this wasn't always the case. The original design didn't have an external forward assist, but the Army was adamant that the AR be modified so that there was a way to externally ensure the bolt was seated and in battery. Stoner, the AR's original designer, was

Right-handed shooter locking the bolt to the rear.

Left-handed shooter locking the bolt to the rear, bringing the support hand back to engage bolt catch.

Right-handed shooter using right thumb to press bolt latch to release bolt.

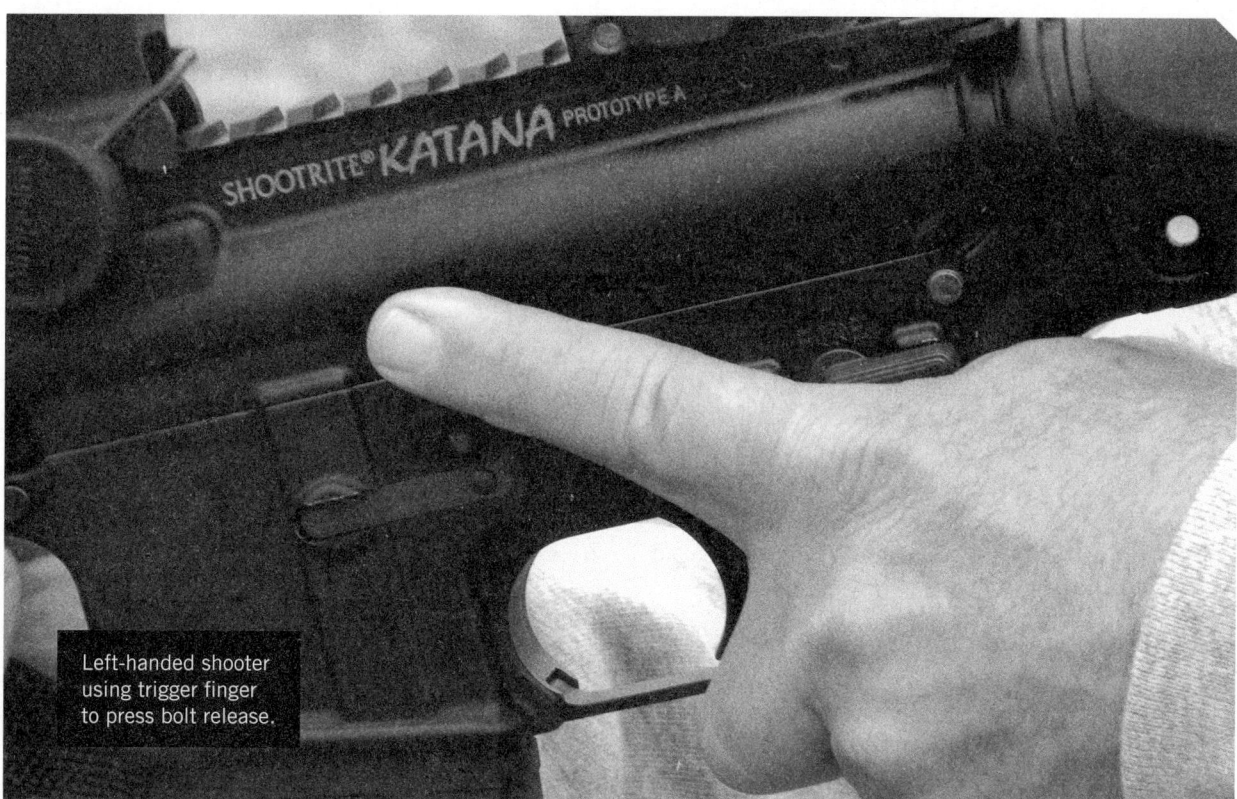

Left-handed shooter using trigger finger to press bolt release.

Using the bolt release is easy even when wearing gloves, or with cold, slippery hands.

against this feature. During testing he never saw a situation where a forward assist or external bolt closure would have made any difference. But, the Army had to have it so it was added.

I teach people to ignore the forward assist and never use it. Think about it along these lines: If the bolt won't go into battery naturally, there is some type of problem. Banging or forcing a round into the chamber by using the external forward assist is probably going to create a worse problem.

Instead of banging or jamming on the external forward assist, use the concave cutout on the right side of the bolt carrier as a forward assist. Right-handed shooters will normally use the first or middle finger of their left hand to press the bolt carrier forward to seat the bolt. Left-handed shooters will normally use the thumb on the right hand.

When the bolt won't seat by applying pressure with the finger or thumb you have a problem, such as a bad round or something in the chamber. Unload and start over again. Using the external forward assist to force the round into the chamber may create a malfunction or stoppage, such as a case from a fired round that sticks in the chamber. We'll learn how to fix this, but it's better to avoid it in the first place.

DUST COVER

The AR has a dust cover. Use it. The dust cover is manually closed, and opens automatically once the bolt cycles. Any time it's possible, such as after checking the chamber or after a string of fire, it's a good idea to close the dust cover. This keeps foreign matter from getting into the working components of the AR.

Right-handed shooters bring the support hand back, cupping it around the mag well, and use the

The original upper did not have an external forward assist.

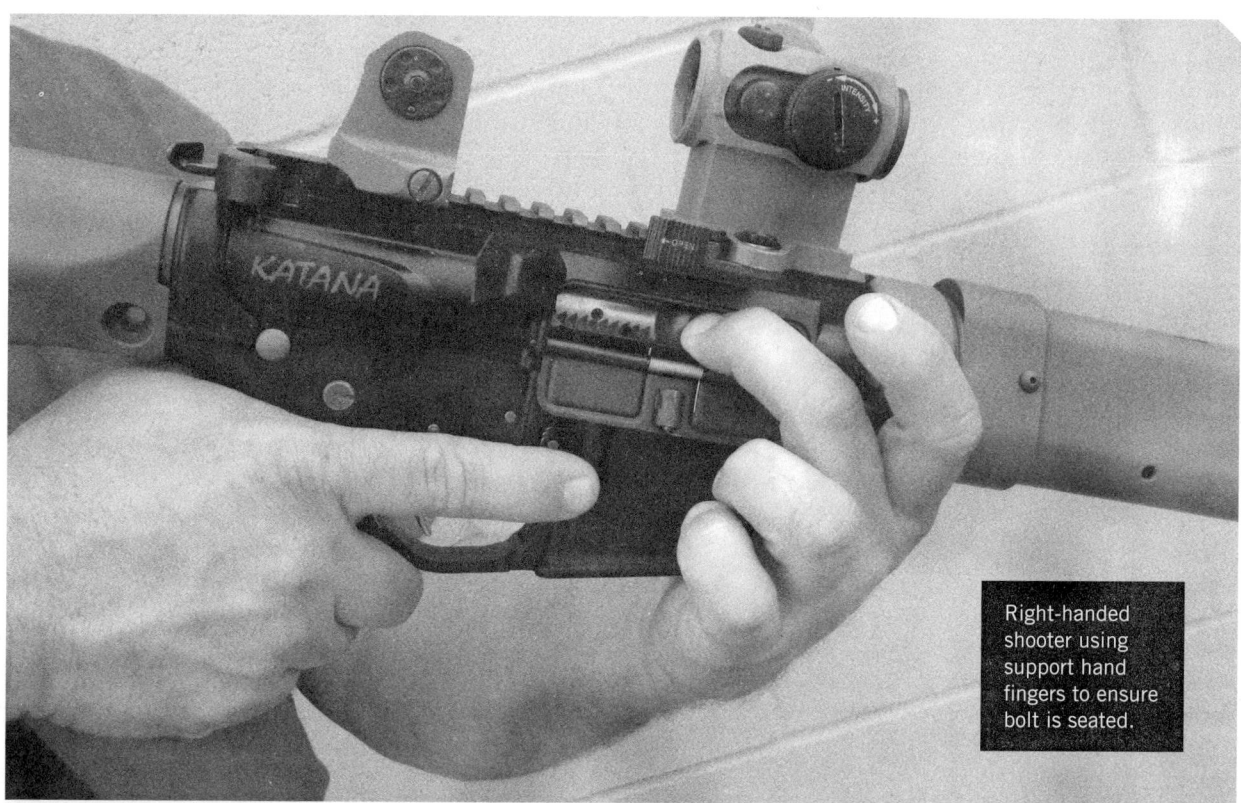

Right-handed shooter using support hand fingers to ensure bolt is seated.

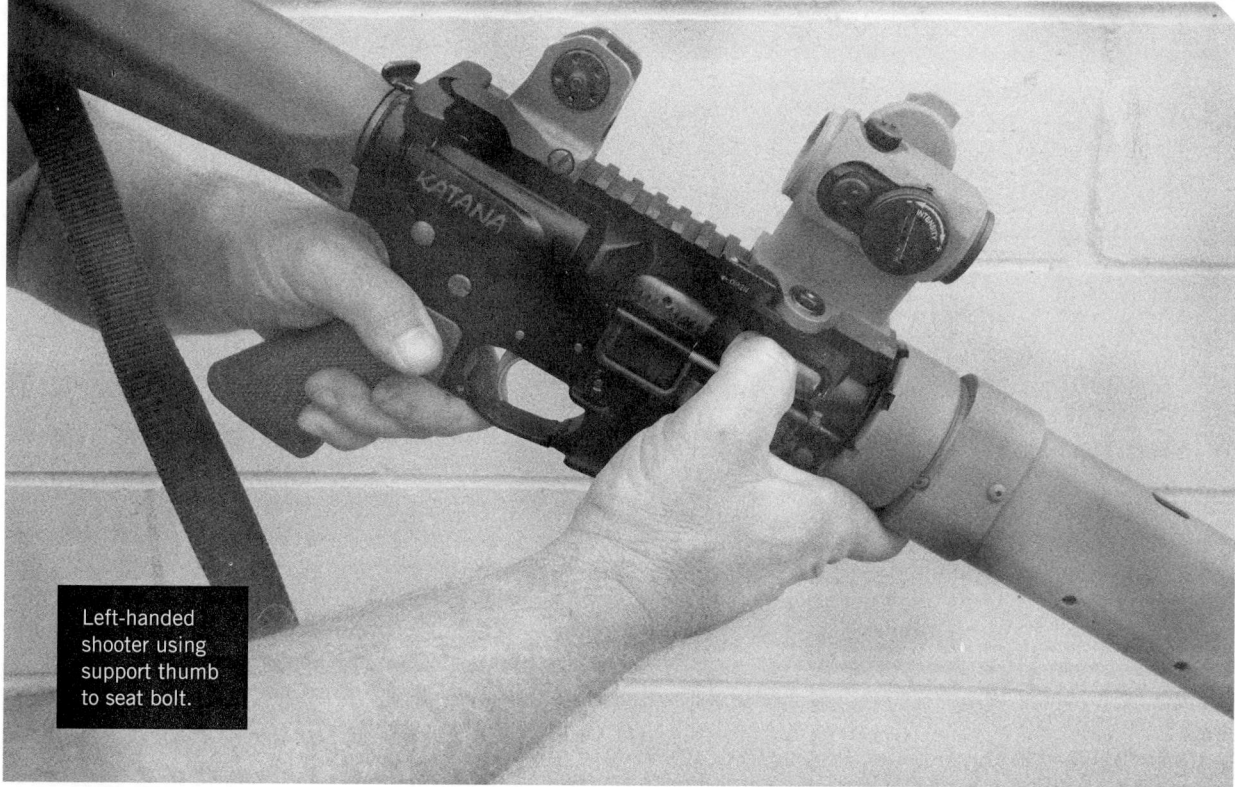

Left-handed shooter using support thumb to seat bolt.

Right-handed shooter closing dust cover.

Left-handed shooter using support hand to close dust cover.

first finger of the left hand to close the cover. Left-handed shooters use the thumb of the right hand.

You can use your strong hand, but this requires taking if off the AR's grip, and you want to maintain a proper grip whenever possible. This action should be performed consciously, until eventually the act becomes a habit and occurs at a subconscious level.

SIGHTS

Understanding the basics of how the original or iron sights on the AR work is necessary for zeroing the sights, adjusting them so the rounds are hitting where you are aiming, shooting accurately, and compensating for the difference between the sight alignment or sight picture and the actual impact of the bullet due to the offset between the sights and barrel. Knowing how the standard sights work will also help you when working with a red-dot or traditional optic. Also, regardless of what type optics you use it's a good idea to having a set of backup sights in case your optic fails.

It is my opinion that all new shooters should start out using standard sights, learning how to apply the basic fundamentals before working with some type of optic. As mentioned, using them helps develop your fundamental skills, and there's no golden rule that says you'll always have your AR. These same principles apply to other types of firearms as well.

There are a couple of variations of "standard" sights. For simplicity we'll call them A1 and A2.

The main difference is in the rear sight. The A1 rear sight has adjustment for windage, intended for use in zeroing only. The A2's rear sight is adjustable for windage, with a knob used to make adjustments in the field as you fire, for example to compensate for wind at long distance. The A2 also has a dial for adjusting elevation to compensate for bullet trajectory when firing at longer distances.

There are also small differences, such as the size and shape of the front sight, the size of the holes in the rear "peep" sight, and whether the front sight has four or five cutouts in it for the sight adjustment tool.

The AR rear sight, a peep sight, has a large and small aperture that you can flip between. The large aperture is normally for close range work. The smaller aperture is used for extended distances, pro-

The A1-style sight has adjustment for windage only. A sight tool or bullet tip is used to adjust it.

The A2-type rear sight has adjustment for windage, but also adjustment for elevation for extended distances.

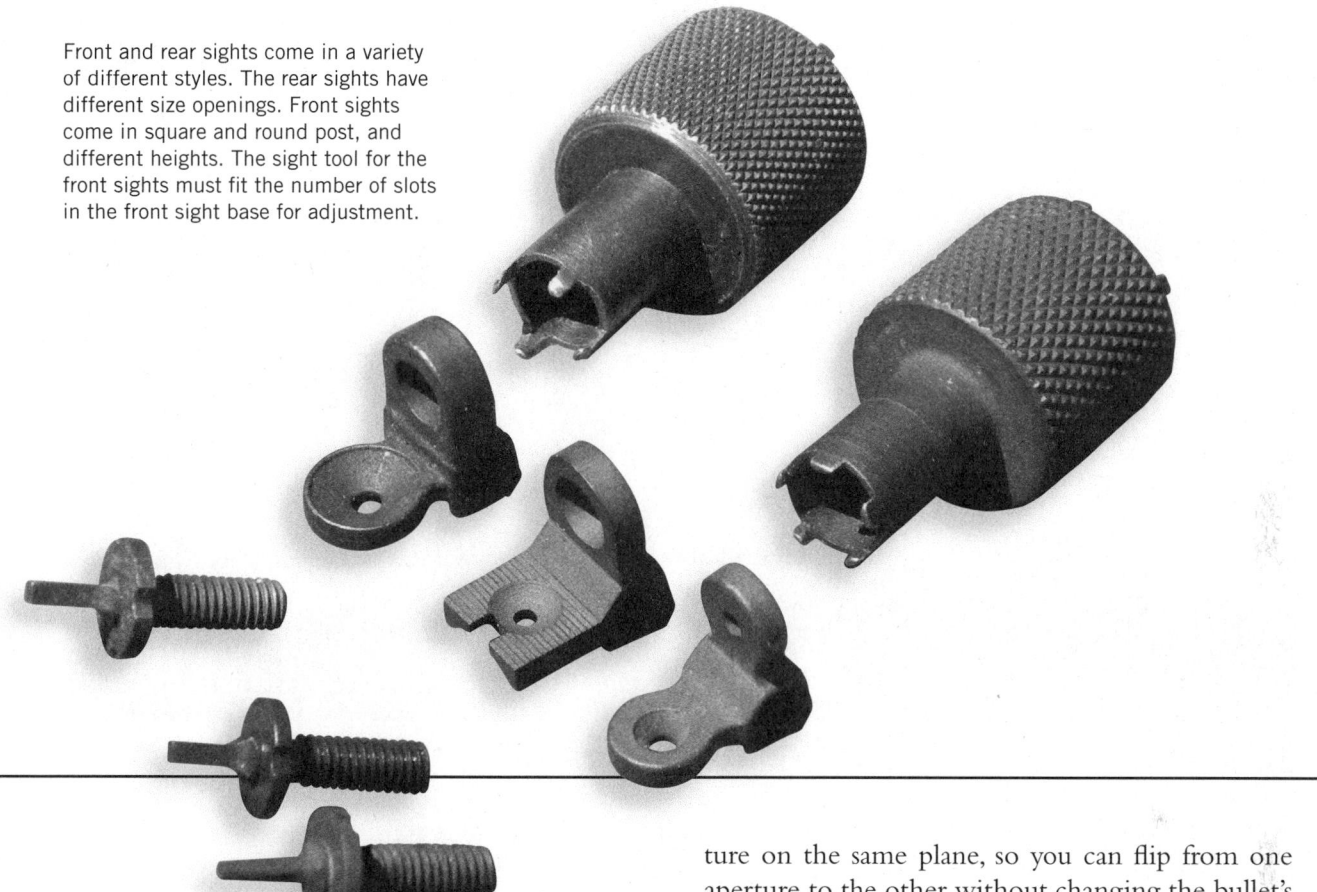

Front and rear sights come in a variety of different styles. The rear sights have different size openings. Front sights come in square and round post, and different heights. The sight tool for the front sights must fit the number of slots in the front sight base for adjustment.

viding a more precise sight picture and raising the bullet's point of impact to compensate for bullet drop. Flipping from one to another will change the point of impact of your bullet. (It depends on the type sight as to the actual size of the apertures, the distances you use them at, and the amount of compensation it provides.)

I personally prefer to shoot all the time with the smaller aperture. It doesn't slow my times down and for my eyes it gives me a lot better accuracy. But, in low-light conditions the larger aperture works better. To be able to flip back and forth between the large and small aperture without changing the bullet's point of impact I install a rear sight from XS Sights. This rear sight has the small and large aperture on the same plane, so you can flip from one aperture to the other without changing the bullet's point of impact.

When you start looking at aftermarket parts the list gets really long. There are a variety of different size and shape front sights. Some are very thin, made specifically for High Power competition. You can get front sights with tritium or light gathering fiber rods. There are rear sights specifically made for High Power competition, with true 1/4 minute adjustments; one click moves the bullet's point of impact 1/4 inch at one hundred yards. You can get rear sights with different size apertures, with tritium, and as mentioned the XS sight with the small and large aperture on the same focal plane.

The AR's front sight is used to adjust for elevation when zeroing. On A1 rear sights there is no elevation adjustment. With A2-type sights the rear sight should be on its lowest setting, such as 6/3 or 8/3 – depending on what generation the sight is –

On the A2-type sights and later mods, the rear drum should be on the 8/3 or 6/3 setting for zeroing.

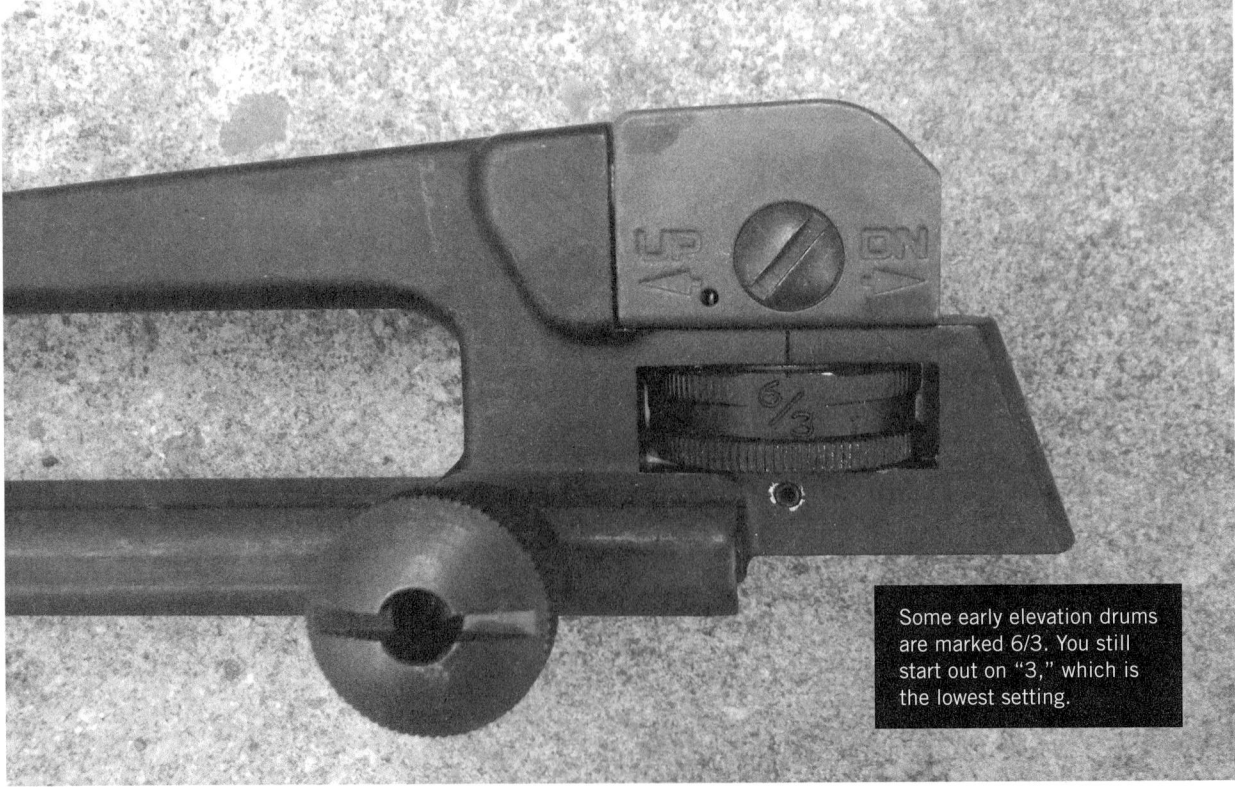

Some early elevation drums are marked 6/3. You still start out on "3," which is the lowest setting.

with three being the starting point for zeroing and six or eight – one full revolution – raising the sight for firing at eight hundred meters.

The large aperture is used, starting with it centered in the rear of the sight base. The front sight is adjusted for elevation. Turning the front sight clockwise lowers the sight, which raises the bullet's point of impact. The rear sight is used to adjust windage. Turning the rear sight knob clockwise moves the rear sight right, which moves your point of impact right. (For full details on zeroing and adjusting sights see the section on Zeroing.)

Another factor that you have to consider with the AR is the offset between the sights and the barrel. This becomes a factor in zeroing the AR, and once zeroed you have to compensate for the difference between your point of aim, where the sights are holding on target, and your point of impact, where the bullet will actually strike. This is especially true at distances closer than twenty-five yards, and also applies to optics, both red-dot and traditional scopes.

Compensating for this offset means once you move in closer than twenty to twenty-five yards you have to start aiming high to place the bullet where you want it to hit. To hit the center of a one-inch dot, I have to aim about two and one half inches above that point. As the distance increases, the difference between the point of aim and point of impact start to decrease, until reaching the distance that the AR is zeroed. For example, with a one hundred yard zero the point of aim and point of impact are the same. As you move closer they start to separate, with the bullet hitting lower than your point of aim.

In the beginning don't get to consumed with

You can see the offset here, with the front sight being about two and one-half inches higher than the bore of the barrel.

With a one hundred yard zero your point of impact will be about two and one-half inches low. To put the shots where you want them you will have to aim high.

modifying your sights. Start with what you have, and learn to work those. At some point you may discover that a different type sight is best for you, or that the factory sights are fine. Think about your application, your specific needs, and then test and experiment under a variety of different conditions until you discover what works best.

FURNITURE

The grip, handguard and stock are called "furniture." As with all other parts for the AR there is a variety of choices available. One of the great features of the AR is its "modular" design. With a little knowledge, and sometimes a few specific tools, it's easy to swap out components such as the handguards, grip and stock. In the old days you had two choices when it came to furniture – the A1 or A2. Today's shooters have a variety of different grips for every type application or personal preference you can think of.

The grip is a small part when you consider the big picture, and it doesn't make any difference in the way the AR operates. But, making sure the AR "fits" is an important consideration, and having a grip that fits your hand, positioning the trigger finger in the right place, will make training and practice a lot more productive. Having a grip with an extension on the front to smooth out the sharp edge between the grip and trigger guard will make training and practice more comfortable.

The type grip you need depends on hand size

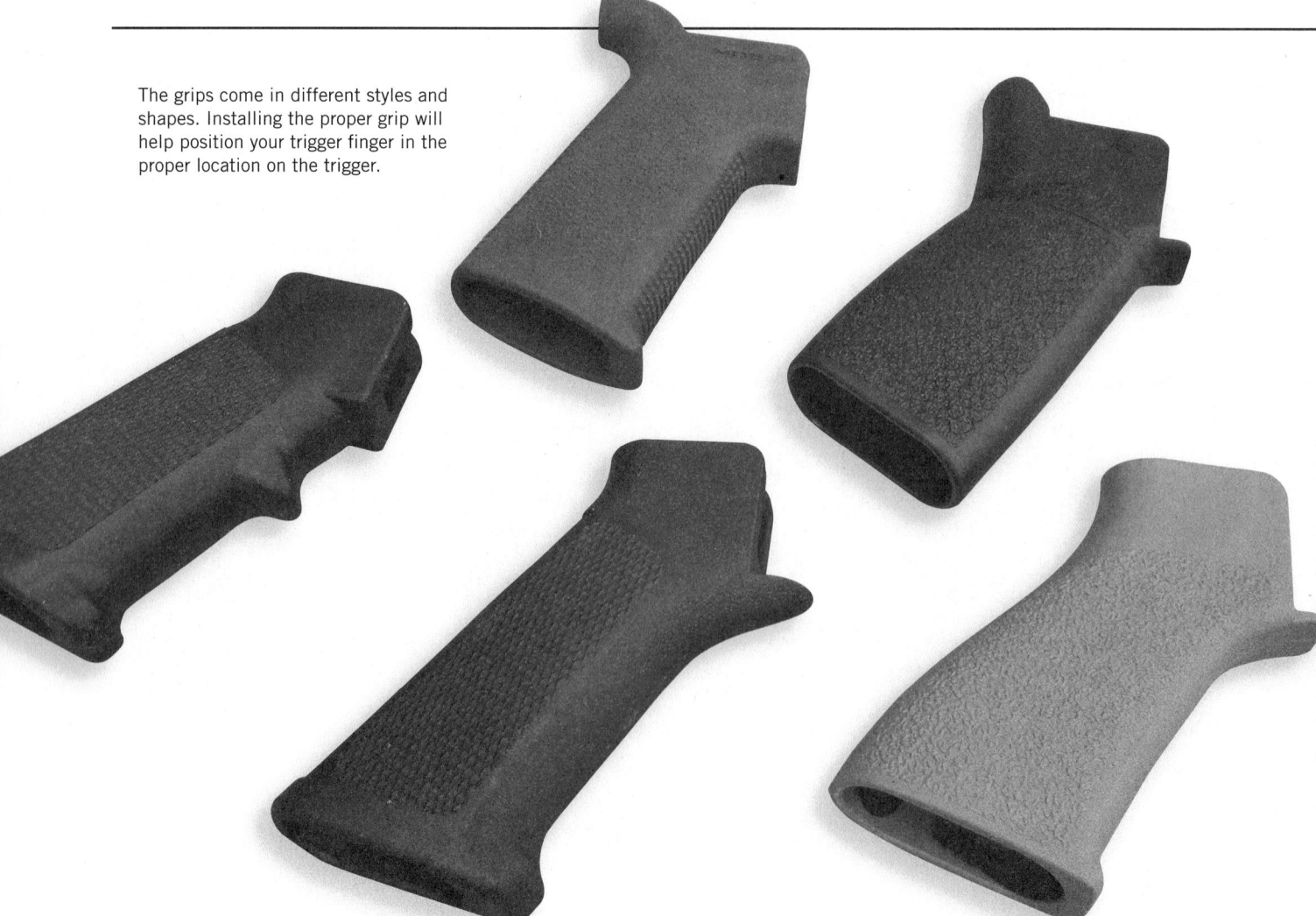

The grips come in different styles and shapes. Installing the proper grip will help position your trigger finger in the proper location on the trigger.

and intended application of the AR. Grips with extended back straps will help with larger hands, moving the hand more to the rear so you can get the trigger finger properly located on the trigger. A grip with a different angle may be more comfortable in prone, if that's where you do most of your shooting. Having an extension on the grip that smoothes out the area between the sharp edge of the trigger guard and grip makes it more comfortable during training and practice.

The handguard is another part that has seen lots of innovation in the last few years. Today you have an almost endless choice, and it's a simple matter of installing the type handguard you need for your anticipated use of the AR. In the beginning I wouldn't worry about getting caught up in exactly what type handguard you need. To make that decision you need to spend time behind the carbine, training and practicing, learning how it operates. At the same time you're figuring out what type accessories you need, such as a flashlight, and where they need to be located. Or you swap out for a free-floating handguard, which isn't connected to the front of the barrel.

Handguard length is determined by what length gas system you have: Rifle, Mid-Length or Carbine.

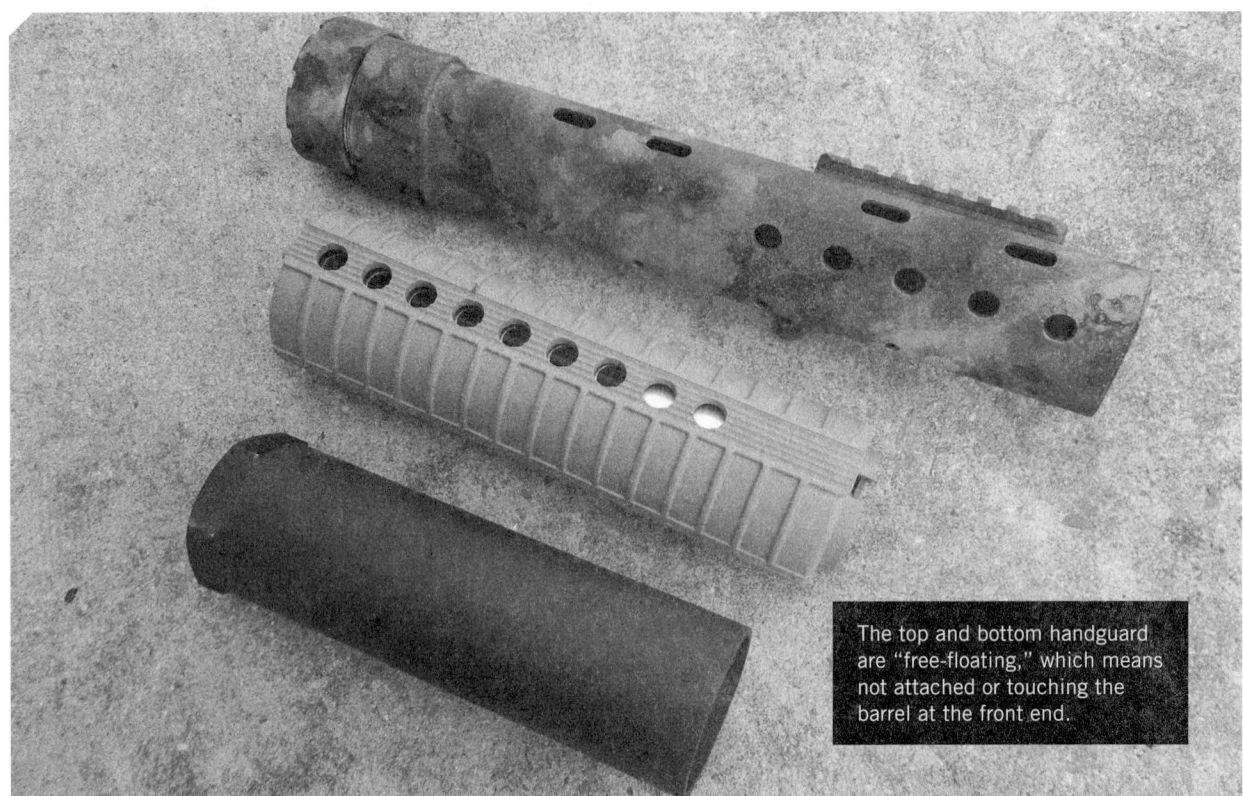

The top and bottom handguard are "free-floating," which means not attached or touching the barrel at the front end.

Once you've learned the fundamentals and how to operate the AR you can start thinking about what type handguard you need.

To make things easy handguards are broken down into two types – standard and free-floating. The standard type handguard has a mount that attaches and supports the front of it on the barrel. Free-floating handguards don't use this front mount.

STOCKS

To keep things simple we're going to break the stocks down into two categories: Fixed and Adjustable. These two categories have numerous variations; one could fill a book just listing all the different type stocks available. "Fixed" means there's no adjusting the "length of pull," the stock is one length. With an "adjustable" stock the length of pull can be changed.

There are advantages and disadvantages with each type. Having the ability to adjust the stock is good if different size shooters are working with the same AR, to compensate if you're wearing bulky clothing, or if space is an issue for storage. One of the disadvantages of adjustable stocks is seen during a Type IV malfunction – a case stuck in the chamber. Before slamming the back of the stock against something to generate enough force to strip the case out of the chamber you have to collapse the stock, otherwise it can bend the extension/buffer tube, break the receiver where the tube is attached, permanently collapse the stock or a combination of any combination of the above. After clearing the stoppage you have to extend the stock. Adjusting the stock while clearing a malfunction consumes extra time. (This procedure is described in the Malfunction section.)

One problem I often see with adjustable stocks is shooters wanting to run them too short. Shortening the length of pull and shoving the head forward prevents you from being able to cycle the charging handle without first having to move the head out of the way and then reacquiring a cheekweld after

There is a wide variety of stocks available. The two main categories are fixed and adjustable.

With adjustable stocks, be careful about running them too short, which will cause you to dip the head down, and also make it difficult to cycle the charging handle efficiently.

running the charging handle. I prefer to be able to cycle the action while maintaining and cheekweld and sight picture. The less motion required the more efficient you're working the AR.

With a fixed stock you don't have to worry about collapsing or adjusting it. The length of pull is good for most shooters, and the way it attached to the receiver is a little bit stronger than the adjustable stock.

My favored stocks, whether adjustable or fixed, come from MagPul. The length of their fixed stocks is normally an ideal length, and they are designed so that you can add spacers to the rear of the stock to make it longer if necessary. Their adjustable stocks are sturdy. Both fixed and adjustable stocks come in different variations. They allow you to add spacers to fine tune the stock's length. Most versions have a wider comb – the top of the stock – that provides a good positive and consistent cheekweld.

The AR will work fine with standard military-type furniture. Don't feel like you immediately have to start swapping out parts. Practice with what you have, then if your needs require it you can change out parts to meet your requirements. With the AR's modular design it doesn't take much to swap out parts, so don't be afraid to experiment. At the same time don't hesitate to go back to the "old" if the "new" doesn't work like you thought it would.

(For detailed information on the different type grips, stocks and handguards check out the variety of books offered by Gun Digest on the AR.)

MAGAZINES

Although technically not a part of the AR, the magazines are a critical component and deserve a lot of attention. First off, the magazines must function properly. A good mag seats and locks into the receiver smoothly, feeds rounds into the chamber reliably, and drops free of the receiver when the bolt catch is pressed to release the mag. Some ARs are particular. For some reason there may be one type magazine that simply doesn't work in your AR. Don't spend a lot of time worrying about why this is, just find the type magazines that do work and buy a bunch of them.

For purposes of this book we're looking at 20- and 30-round mags. There are other options out there, for example SureFire's 60-round mags function great, but this isn't something you would need for general-purpose use, training or practicing.

First, we want to learn how to tell the position of the mag in your hand without having to look at it. The front section of the mag is flat. The rear has a hump or raised section running down it. The top is easily distinguished from the bottom, again based on feel. Once you have this skill you can grab the mag, immediately tell what its orientation is, and reposition it in the hand if necessary.

Although today you mostly see the 30-round mags, I'm still a fan of the 20-round magazines. Being shorter means less weight and a smaller profile, both of which I think are important considerations. Twenty-round mags are held with the first finger of the support hand running up the front of the mag and thumb and other three fingers holding the sides down low.

You should position your hand on the lower part of the magazine – both 20s and 30s – otherwise as you seat it into the receiver you'll have to lower the hand, repositioning it in order to lock the mag in. With a 30-round mag you grip it low, but like a soda can, with the fingers and thumb around the mag, or you can position the thumb on the side of the mag, gripping it between the fingers and heel of the hand.

Loading the AR mags is a simple thing, but loading the correct number of rounds is very important. When the magazine is locked into the receiver, the bolt carrier depresses the top round down into the magazine. If there are too many rounds in the mag you'll have to bang on the mag to get it seated. Put way too many rounds in it and the mag won't seat no matter how hard you try. Even if the bolt is locked to the rear, say during an empty reload, if there are too many rounds in the mag the bolt may not have enough spring pressure to strip off and load a round into the chamber.

After testing a variety of magazines and carbines we've decided that the magic number for 30-round mags is 25 rounds. With 25 rounds the mag should be easy to seat and lock into the receiver. Yes, you might get away loading a few more rounds in the

Mags come in a a lot of different styles. Find what works best in your AR by testing them.

You hold 20-round mags much like you do a pistol magazine, with the first finger on the front of the mag. 30-round mags are held low, using the thumb and fingers grasp the mag, ensuring a good grip and control.

Don't worry about modifying your AR too soon. After learning how to work with it, you can make educated choices on how you need to make changes.

mag, but I'd rather err on the safe side, ensuring the mag will be easy to lock in place. For 20-round mags load 18 rounds.

In the beginning don't worry about trying to configure your AR exactly how you think it should be. Attend training and learn how to operate it properly. Practice, in all type environments, so you know what you need. Then, after actually learning how to operate the AR you can start modifying it to fit your application.

SPARE PARTS

The AR should be simple and lightweight. You can carry it all day and the next if necessary. The carbine is individually maintained. This means you know how to clean and inspect it, and if necessary replace small parts. The AR is great for this because understanding how the weapon operates, knowing the indicators for problems, and replacing parts is easy due to its design. The parts you need are affordable and easy to remove and replace. Having

There are many reference sources available on the AR, how it works and what you need to modify and maintain it.

your AR down because you don't have a $3.00 part on hand isn't a good thing.

First, get a book, or several, on the how the AR works and the tools and parts needed to maintain or modify one. The military manuals are a great reference. Gun Digest also offers a variety of books on this subject. The 'net is another great resource, just be careful because not everything on there is right.

It is good practice to keep small parts on hand. Look up a schematic on the AR, especially the bolt group and trigger assembly. Then get the small parts, such as detents, springs, pins and gas rings, that go on the bolt and all other pieces so you have spares.

In my opinion it's also a good idea to have a complete spare bolt assembly on hand. That way, if something does break all you have to do is put in the new bolt group and then later replace a spring or pin on the other bolt. In order to ensure the bolt will work in your AR, it needs have the head spacing checked. Usually there's no problem, but checking this spacing will prevent a dangerous situation if you do come across a bolt that doesn't space out right. You can purchase the gauges to check the spacing, or a gunsmith shouldn't charge much to check it for you.

Keep in mind you're looking for true "mil-spec" parts. Not all parts sold today that are advertised as mil-spec meet the true definition of that term. Just because its dimensions are correct doesn't mean it's made from the proper material or properly hard-

Having spares for all the small parts that may break allows you to get your AR up and running again without ordering or finding parts.

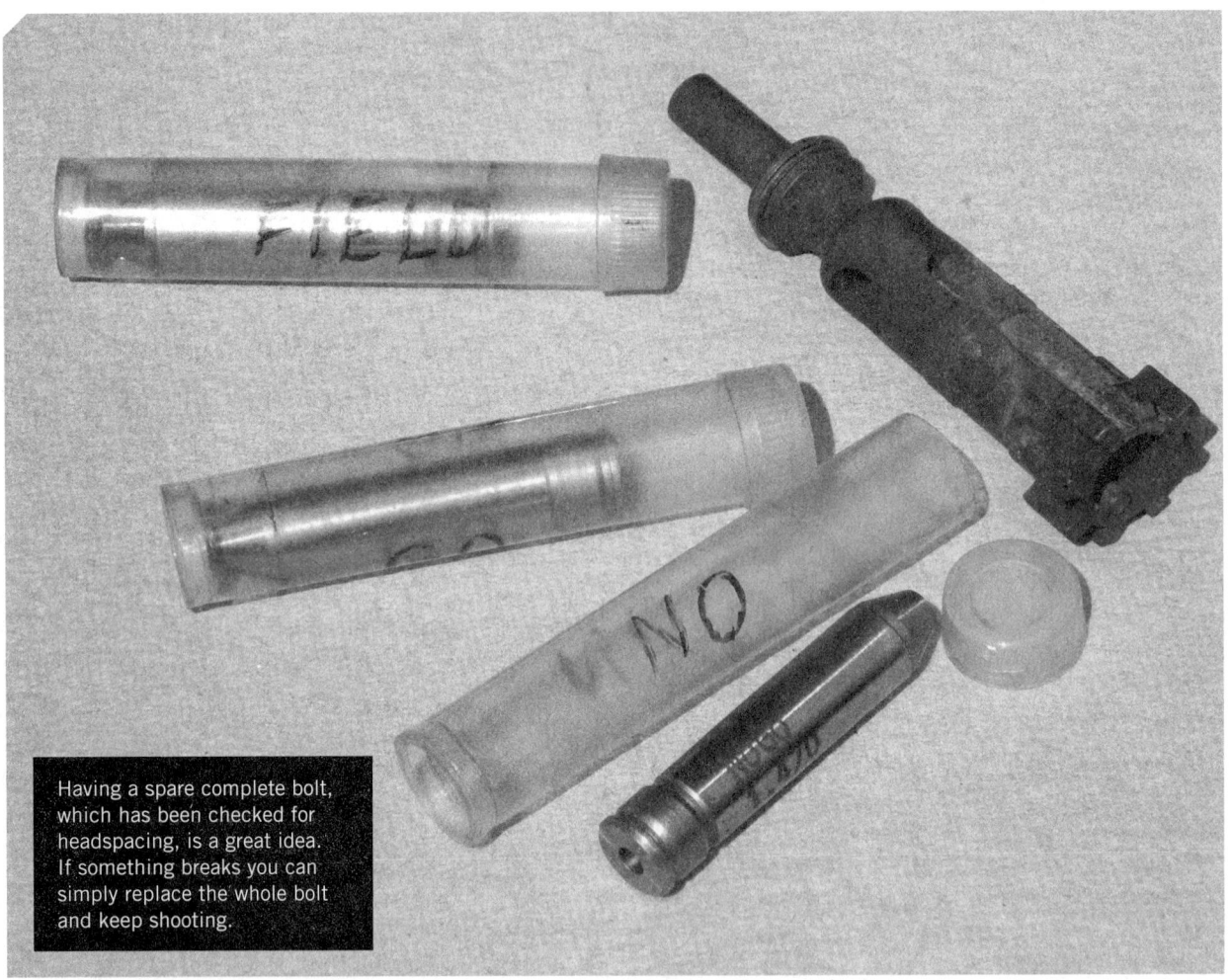

Having a spare complete bolt, which has been checked for headspacing, is a great idea. If something breaks you can simply replace the whole bolt and keep shooting.

ened. With the rise in popularity of the AR, more companies than ever produce AR components. Some of these companies produce well-made parts. Some of them produce explosions waiting to happen. Some used to make car parts and then decided to get into making bolt carriers for the AR. Make sure any parts you buy come from a solid company, and even then check the specs to ensure they meet all your requirements.

Again, one of the great features about the AR is that the parts you need are small and easy to carry. Spare parts for the bolt group, including a spare extractor and ejector and springs for each, gas rings, cam pin, firing pin, and a spare firing pin retaining pin, are mandatory. All of these parts can be oiled up, put in a zip bag and into the storage space in your stock. I also like to have hammer, trigger and disconnector springs, and pins for the hammer/trigger. These may be too big for the stock's storage area, but they are easily carried in your range bag.

Remember batteries. You need spares for your red-dot and flashlight. My handheld and weapon lights use the same batteries, so this simplifies things. Rotate your batteries. I use my spares to replace the ones that go down, then put new spares in my kit.

Having the spare parts you need isn't expensive, and they are easily replaced when needed. Again, having them on hand means if you have a problem you won't need to wait to order one. •

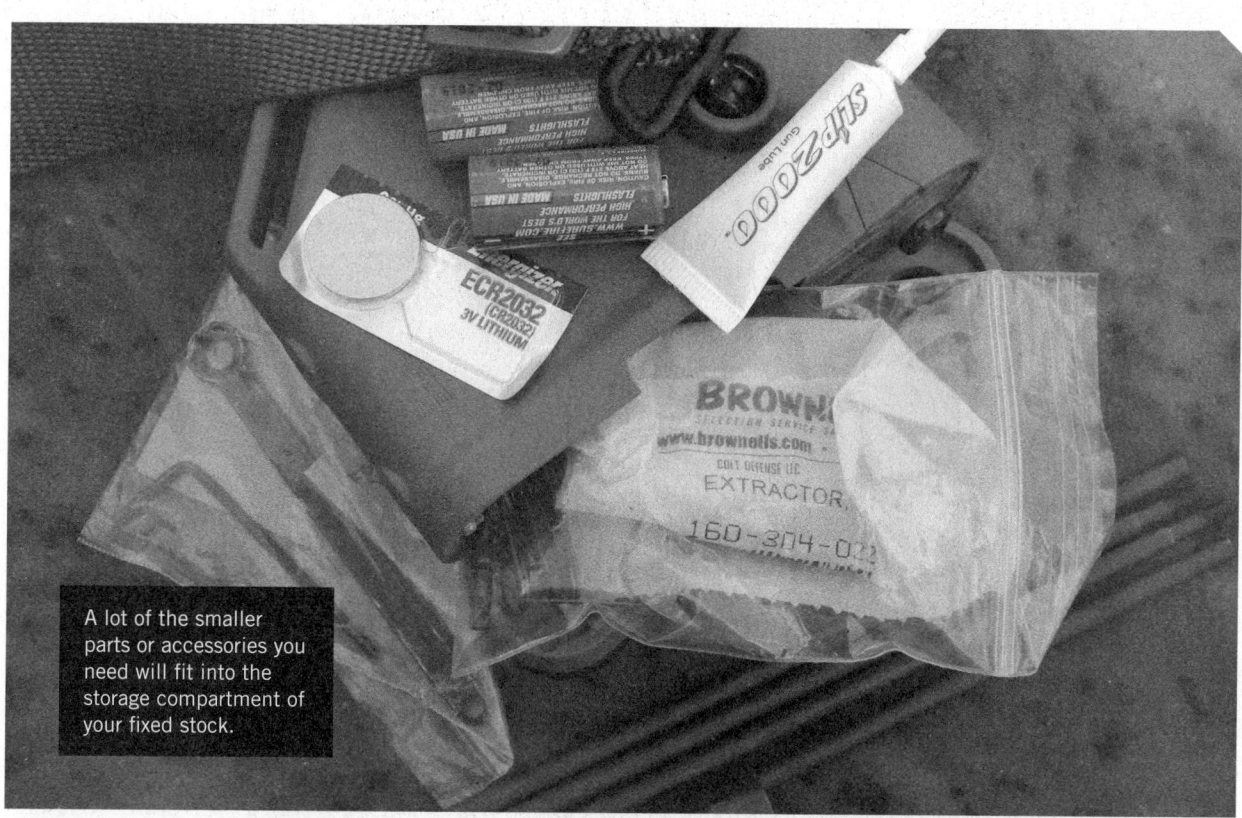

A lot of the smaller parts or accessories you need will fit into the storage compartment of your fixed stock.

With a little knowledge, some special tools and the parts, almost anyone can correct a problem with the AR.

CHAPTER 3
SLINGS

THE SLING FOR your carbine is like the holster for your pistol; it's a mandatory piece of equipment. It's also one of the most misunderstood pieces of equipment. There are a variety of slings and while it may seem simple, choosing the right sling can get complicated. Application and personal preference determine what sling is best for you. Also, keep in mind that you can always swap slings, changing out to fit what you are doing.

I highly recommend starting off with a simple two-point sling. Set up correctly, a two-point sling design will do everything you need, without being too complex. After working with the AR and learning how to use it, you can start experimenting with the various type slings, making an educated decision on what you need or what is required for your specific application. (For details on using the sling and the different carry modes, see the section on Carry Modes.)

SHOOTING SLINGS

Shooting slings are traditionally made of leather. The support arm is looped through the sling to create a more stable firing position, but only when the support elbow is resting or braced against something. For marksmanship this is a definite advantage. (Jeff Cooper was a major proponent of shooting slings and devoted a whole chapter to this in "The Art of the Rifle.") The competition sling takes time to loop up, and is normally reserved for matches, such as NRA High Power competition. The exception to this is the Ching Sling, designed by Eric Ching, which is very quick to loop into, however you rarely see them in use on ARs.

If you are going to work with a shooting sling, looping it up for stability and accuracy, you need to remember that this puts force on the handguard, pulling it downward enough to affect shot placement. With a standard-type handguard the front fits into a handguard

A leather shooting sling is used for slinging up around the arm for stability in positions where the support arm is resting on or braced against something.

"cap," which is around the barrel just behind the front sight base. The sling is connected to the handguard. Applying downward pressure to the sling pulls the barrel down. For example, with my stock AR HBAR, looping up in the sling will lower the point of impact, where the bullet hits the target, by about six inches at one hundred yards.

In order for this pressure not to affect your shot placement you need a free-floating handguard. This type handguard isn't attached to the front of the barrel. This way any pressure on the handguard doesn't affect the barrel or your point of impact.

CARRY SLINGS

A simple carry sling, or "two-point" sling, is a great choice for general-purpose use, self-defense or patrol officers. When adjusted to the proper length the two-point sling is extremely versatile. It can be used for "African" carry, slung on the support side of the body with muzzle down, or "American" carry, on the strong side of the body with muzzle up. The sling can be looped over the neck to free up both hands, "scramble" carry, or around the neck and body, in "tactical" fashion. Add a quick-release buckle so you can get free of the sling quickly if necessary and you've got a good thing going.

TACTICAL SLINGS

I use the term "tactical sling" for any sling that is designed to be worn around the body, looped over the neck and underneath the support arm. While most people think this is a new thing, the U.S. cavalry used something similar in the mid to late 1800s to free up their hands for riding. Today's versions are broken down into three types: single, two-point and three-point slings.

The advantage of tactical slings is that, with the rifle slung, you have both hands

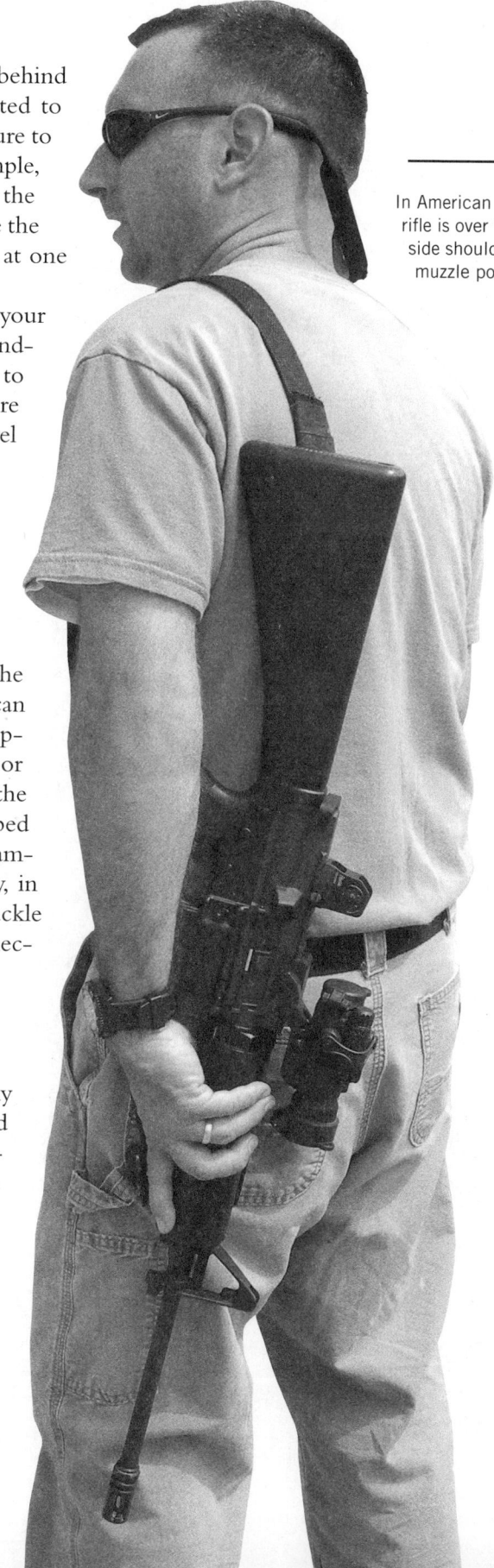

In American carry the rifle is over the strong-side shoulder with the muzzle pointing up.

In American carry the rifle is over the strong-side shoulder with the muzzle pointing up.

For a quick hands-free mode you can loop the sling over the neck. With the sling adjusted properly you can still fire the AR.

free and the rifle is readily accessible for immediate use. Transitions to the pistol are simplified. Lower the rifle down with your support hand while presenting the pistol, and then with the rifle hanging you have the use of both hands for operating the pistol. Any time you need both hands free, to climb a ladder or take control of a suspect, you don't have to worry about what to do with the rifle. Plus, I've found that it works really well when I'm taking the dogs for their evening walk. I can control the dogs on their leash and still have access to my rifle.

The single-point sling attaches both ends of the sling to one point on the carbine, usually right behind the grip, forming a loop that goes around the body. The sling should fit tight to the body, so most come with an adjustment strap.

The advantage of a single-point sling is that it is easy to attach and detach from the carbine. For example, when it's time to gear up you loop the sling around your body, then connect it to the AR. Once you're done, perhaps ready to set the carbine in the rack, you unsnap the sling to release the carbine, leaving the sling looped around your body.

There are a couple of issues to be aware of, however, that I consider to be disadvantages of the single-point sling. With the sling attached to the rifle right behind the grip, sometimes the sling gets in the way of your hand acquiring a proper grip or manipulating the safety. There is only one attachment point, so when the rifle is hanging and you don't have the strong hand gripping and controlling the carbine it will flop around and move about freely. When the AR is hanging on your body the weight will seek the lowest point, so the sling will rotate around the body, which causes

The two-point sling, if adjusted to the correct length, can also be used as a "tactical" sling, looping it around the neck and underneath the support-side arm.

The single-point sling loops around the body and attaches to the AR in one location.

the AR to hang too low. The stock is lower than the shoulder, requiring more movement to get into a firing position. The muzzle is low, so if you go into a kneeling position you have to take extra care to make sure the muzzle doesn't dig into the ground. Firing with the muzzle blocked is dangerous and will damage your AR.

As with every piece of equipment there are advantages and disadvantages. You have to train, practice and experiment under all types of conditions until you discover what works best.

The two-point "tactical" sling is basically the same as the two-point carry sling, only normally it'll have features such as a slide buckle for quick adjustment of the length. The two-point sling is the most versatile, and will do about anything you need. The sling attaches at two points, normally the rear of the stock and the front of the handguard, creating a large loop. Once the sling is looped around the body you adjust the length so the stock is just below the pocket of the shoulder. You don't want it too long, which will allow too much movement when the AR is hanging, and you don't want it too tight, because that will restrict movement and the firing positions you can use. (The Carry Mode section goes into detail on the various carry or slinging techniques you can use.)

Three-point slings attach to the rifle at the front of the handguard, on the rear on the stock – similar to a two-point sling – and then have another section of sling that runs between these two sections that provides quick adjustment. For me this extra section of sling gets in the way of manipulating the AR, inserting or removing the mag, and sometimes gets caught between the strong hand and grip.

SLING TIPS

For slings other than a traditional Shooting sling, which is pretty much a standard setup, there are some tips that make life easier. I prefer the T-2 webbing, which is what the military has been using since the early 1970s, in the one and one-quarter inch width. This material has shear strength of 4,500 pounds, and it isn't slippery like the nylon material found in most slings, so it will "cling" to your shoulder when the AR is slung or hanging on your body. The extra one-quarter inch width makes it more comfortable when the AR is hanging on your body, as opposed to a one-inch width sling that will bite or cut into the body with the weight of the AR.

Most slings use tri-glides to buckle loop the sling through to hold the sling in position. I highly recommend using metal tri-glides so they don't break. Once the sling is adjusted to the proper length, run the tail of the sling material thru the tri-glide one extra time. This stops the sling from working loose,

Looping the sling back through the tri-glide an extra time locks it in place and ensures it won't slip loose.

and is cheap insurance compared to the expensive damage I've seen to rifles and optics when slings come undone and rifles drop from high distances.

Mounting locations are another factor to consider. I attach the front end of the sling to the bottom of the handguard, usually as far forward as possible.

Where you position your hand will vary according to the firing position you're using, so having the sling mounted forward prevents it from getting in the way of the support hand. Attaching the sling to the bottom of the handguard, as opposed to one side or the other, allows you to grip the sling in the fist when bracing on something for stability. (Gripping the sling in this mode is a part of what's traditionally been called a "Hawkins" firing position.) With it attached to the side of the handguard, any pressure or tension on the sling will twist or pull the rifle to that side.

The rear of the sling should be mounted to the side of the stock – left side for a right-handed shooter. With the sling on the side of the stock, the rifle will lay flat against the body when slung or hanging, instead of wanting to flop around, as it will when the sling is attached to the bottom or toe of the stock. A lot of stocks have a loop attached to the toe of the stock to run the sling through, but mounting it to the side of the stock is much better.

When the rifle is in "transport" mode, sitting in my truck or in the house, I loop an elastic hairband over the handguard and thread the sling back and forth through it. This keeps the sling out of the way and a quick jerk releases it when needed.

The sling should have a have a quick disconnect buckle, especially the tactical slings that loop around your body. There are times when you need to get free of the rifle and don't have time to unloop or work the sling off your body. For example, a Type IV malfunction is an empty case stuck in

There are a lot of advantages to having the front of the sling attached to the bottom of the handguard, and as far forward as possible.

Attaching the front of the sling to the bottom of the handguard works well for the "Hawkins" position, where you're supporting the front of the handguard by holding the front of the sling.

Attach the rear of the sling to the side of the stock so the AR will hang flat against the body when slung.

the chamber. In order to clear the chamber you slam the stock against a solid object – usually the ground – while pulling charging handle to the rear. Since most tac-slings hold the rifle tight against your body, you'll need to disconnect yourself from the rifle to perform this clearing procedure. Being tied to the rifle is also a problem when your rifle gets caught or hung on something. A soldier once wrote to tell me how his rifle became caught on a helicopter skid, leaving him hanging in the air by his sling. Plus, if you are injured in your strong hand or arm, being tied to the rifle can make it difficult to operate the rifle with the support hand.

An adjuster to vary the length of the sling is a good idea for carbines that may be used by different size people. A six-foot-tall person is going to need more sling than someone who is five and a half feet tall. The quick adjuster allows you to sling up and then pull the sling to tighten it to the proper length.

Your sling should also be versatile. A sling that loops around the body should be capable of being used as a simple carry sling if necessary, for times when you don't have a chance to loop it around your body. The key is to practice, using a variety of carry and sling techniques in order to discover what works best for you. •

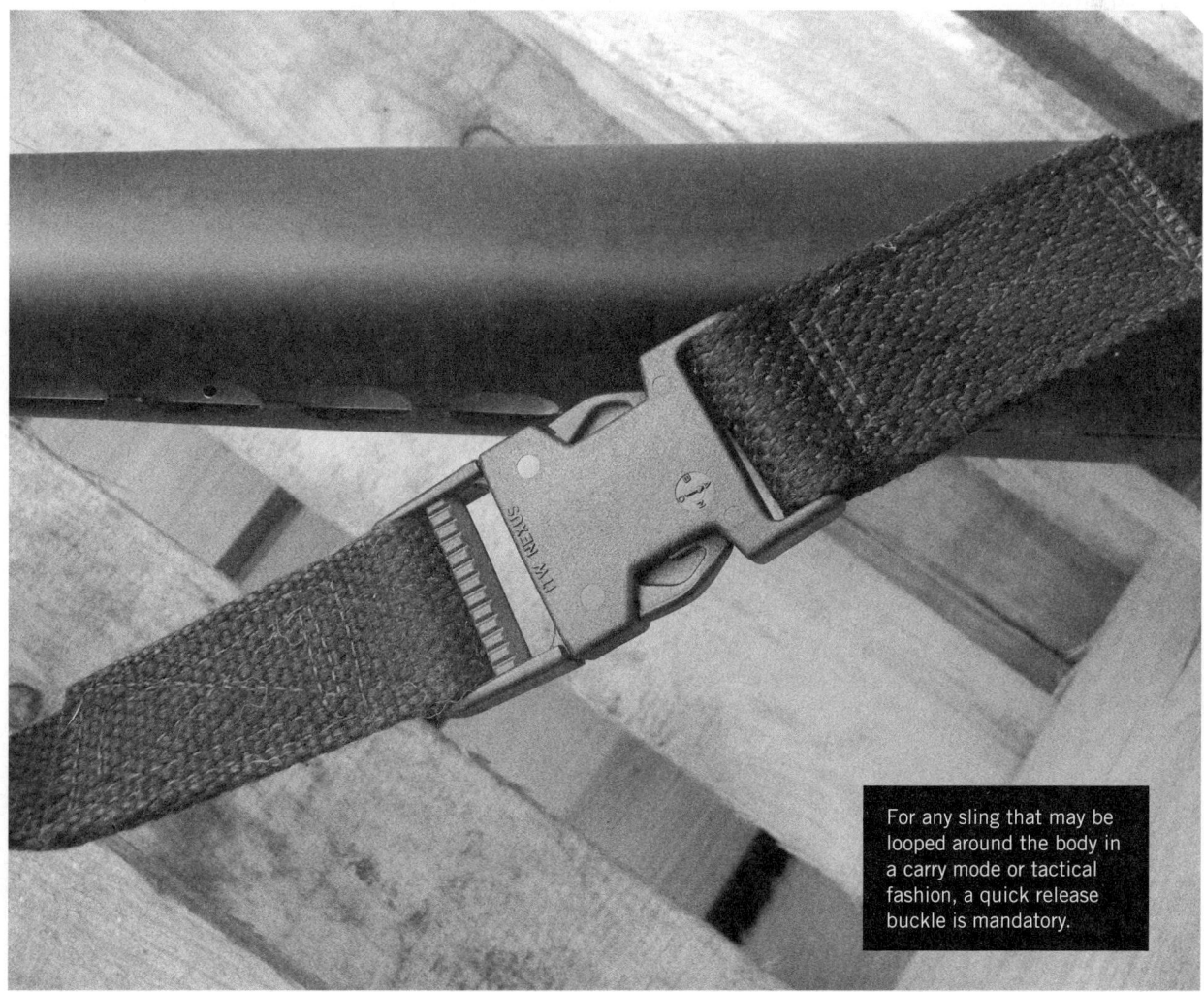

For any sling that may be looped around the body in a carry mode or tactical fashion, a quick release buckle is mandatory.

CHAPTER 4
READY POSITIONS

A **"READY" POSITION** is the term used for when you are holding/handling the AR. The traditional ready positions are "low" and "high," which refer to the location of the muzzle. The "cross-body" ready – everyone has different names for this and similar ready positions – is with the rifle flattened against the body and the muzzle pointing outboard of the support side foot. There are other types of ready positions, but these are the three we'll focus on.

LOW READY

The low ready position is the one most often used for the AR. The heel of the stock is in the pocket of the shoulder, the muzzle is pointing down and the body is relaxed. The safety is on and trigger finger is indexed clear of the trigger and trigger guard. The dominant hand is gripping the AR, ready to disengage the safety, and the trigger finger is indexed, off the trigger and clear of the trigger guard. Support hand is on the handguard. You are ready to come on target to fire. Low ready is the position used for administrative manipulations, such as loading and unloading.

The height at which you hold the muzzle depends on safety – making sure a negligent or unintentional discharge bullet would be stopped or trapped – or on what you need to see. For example, if searching for a target the AR, muzzle, and hands and arms are low enough so they don't block you from seeing, identifying and engaging a target.

To fire from the low ready you bring the muzzle up, with it pivoting on the stock in the shoulder. As you come up the safety is disengaged. Once you're on target you place the finger on the

The low ready position is the one most used for tactical situations. The stock is in the shoulder, and the arms, hands and muzzle are low enough so they don't block you from being able to see what's important.

trigger. (This doesn't mean you have to be pressing the trigger, but the trigger finger is there and ready to press once you decide it's time to fire.)

After firing you come off the trigger, off the target – lowering the muzzle, again with the AR pivoting at the stock – and engage the safety.

HIGH READY

Holding the rifle at low ready for extended periods of time can get tiring; the support arm is holding most of the AR's weight. For situations when you have to hold the rifle for long periods of time and don't have to worry about a threat popping out from around a corner or any type of close quarters action, the high ready works well.

The stock is held about waist level with the muzzle out in front of you at eye level. Finger is off the trigger and safety ready to disengage. Once you have located your target and are facing it, the stock comes up to the shoulder. The muzzle maintains alignment with the target, so the AR is basically pivoting at the muzzle, with the muzzle holding between the eyes and the target as you come up. While coming on target the safety is disengaged, and once on target finger goes to the trigger.

After firing you come off the trigger, off target – by lowering the stock down and with muzzle at eye level – and engage the safety.

CROSS-BODY READY

The cross-body ready is used for situations when the low ready isn't low enough and the high ready is too high. For example, you have to move in and around people. For these situations we teach a cross-body ready, which positions the carbine as though it were hanging from a tactical type sling except you're holding the carbine with both hands. The stock is up by the strong side shoulder and the AR is flat against the chest with the muzzle pointing just outside the support side foot. With the cross-body ready you can work safely, with muzzle depressed, around and near people or objects that may contain people. When a target is located you face it, bringing the carbine up into a firing position, controlling the muzzle and keeping it "down range." As you come up safety comes off, and once on target the finger is on the trigger. •

The high ready is used when having to hold the AR for long periods of time, but you are not worried about someone getting in close. Good examples of use for the high ready are hunting or working in a large open area.

DRILLS

Ultimately you need to be able to flow from one ready position to another. You never know what the situation or environment will call for. Practice coming on target from each ready position. Start in one ready position, come on target, and then come off target going into a different ready position. Simply practice flowing from one position into another ready position. The best way to practice this is by first using dummy weapons, and then going to the range to confirm you're efficiently acquiring the target.

On the range, work from the different ready positions coming onto the target and firing. When you have a partner, work in a coach and shooter format. Flow from one position to another. Have your partner call the drill, such as "Up" or "Threat Front." Efficiently come onto target from whatever position you are in to engage the target. There are a variety of different ways to practice the ready positions, both dry and live fire.

Cross-body ready is for working in tight quarters, or when you need the muzzle depressed so you don't have to worry about sweeping or covering people as you move.

CHAPTER 5
CARRY MODES

THERE ARE MANY varieties of carry modes and slings. You should be familiar with different carry techniques so that you can use the one that best fits the situation and environment you're working in. Part of this decision is also based on sling choice, or the sling you need may be dictated by your application. For purposes of this book we're going to focus on four basic carry or sling techniques: African, American, scramble carry and the techniques for using a "tactical" sling, the term I will use for slings that loop around your body, usually over the neck and underneath the support arm.

Regardless of how you have the AR slung, remember Safety Rule 2; you always have to be aware of what direction the muzzle is pointing. When it's time to retrieve gear off the ground or move around, you have to pay attention to the muzzle, keeping it pointing in a safe direction.

AFRICAN CARRY

"African" carry is with the carbine slung over the support-side shoulder and muzzle pointing down.

This is a great way to carry, especially for general-purpose use of the AR. African carry provides you with the ability to easily control the carbine and present it efficiently. The muzzle is pointing down, which is safe, and it creates a low profile, which could be a factor depending on the situation. African carry positions the AR on the support side, so you can still get to gear on your strong side, such as the pistol.

To sling in African carry hold the carbine normally, with dominant hand on the grip and support hand on the handguard. Bring the support hand back and grab the rear of the sling in your fist. Lower the muzzle down and loop the sling

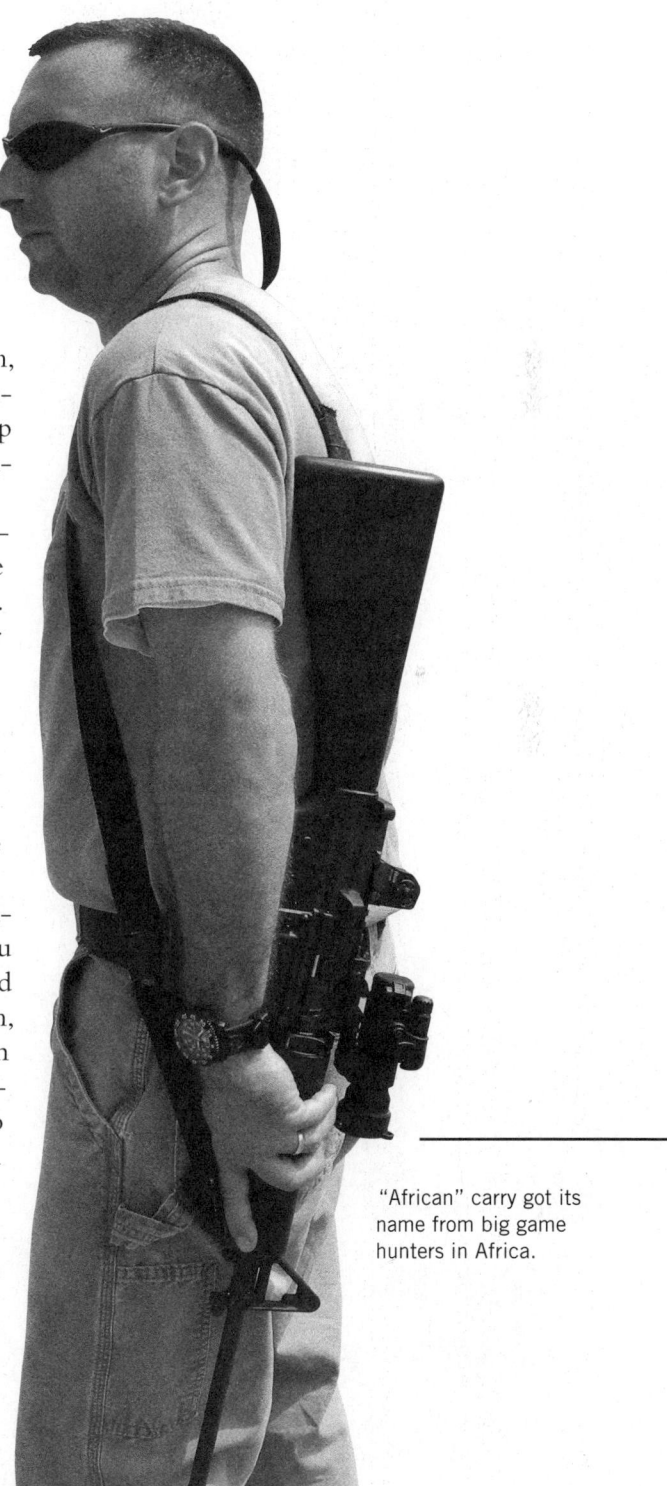

"African" carry got its name from big game hunters in Africa.

over the support shoulder.

The ideal sling length should position the mag well of the carbine just about belt level or a little lower. While slung, keep your support hand on the sling, near the chest, or on the handguard so the carbine doesn't slip off the shoulder.

A big part of presenting the carbine, bringing it into a ready position or onto target, is controlling the muzzle. Start by bringing the support hand down to the area on the AR where the handguard meets the receiver. Twist the hand so palm is outward with thumb pointing to the rear and slip the hand between the receiver and your body. Grip the receiver or handguard, lift the AR up slightly and bring the muzzle up, pointing it downrange in a safe direction.

As you bring the muzzle up rotate the AR counterclockwise – for right-handed shooter – and as soon as possible the strong hand acquires its grip. The entire time the muzzle is pointing downrange. Bring the stock up and position it into the shoulder assuming a low ready position, or you're on target and ready to fire.

Once you're in low ready you can manipulate

Bring the support hand back and grab the rear of the sling in a fist.

the AR, or if conditions call for it go into the high ready position.

Regardless of the technique or sling you're using, when you have a chance, pick up the loose part of the sling so it's not dangling down to get caught on objects, such as tree limbs, shooting benches or doorknobs and such.

I use the pinky finger of the support hand to pick up the sling, that way the sling doesn't get between my hand and the handguard. With practice this presentation sequence can become a smooth, fluid action.

AMERICAN CARRY

In "American" carry the AR is slung on the strong-side shoulder with the muzzle up.

To sling the weapon, the support hand grabs the front of the sling in a fist. The strong hand, on the AR's grip, lowers the stock down and then releases the carbine once it's vertical, hanging muzzle up and stock down. Straighten out the strong arm and feed it between the sling and rifle using the support hand to move the rifle onto the strong-side shoulder.

While slung the strong hand holds onto the sling,

Loop the sling over the shoulder.

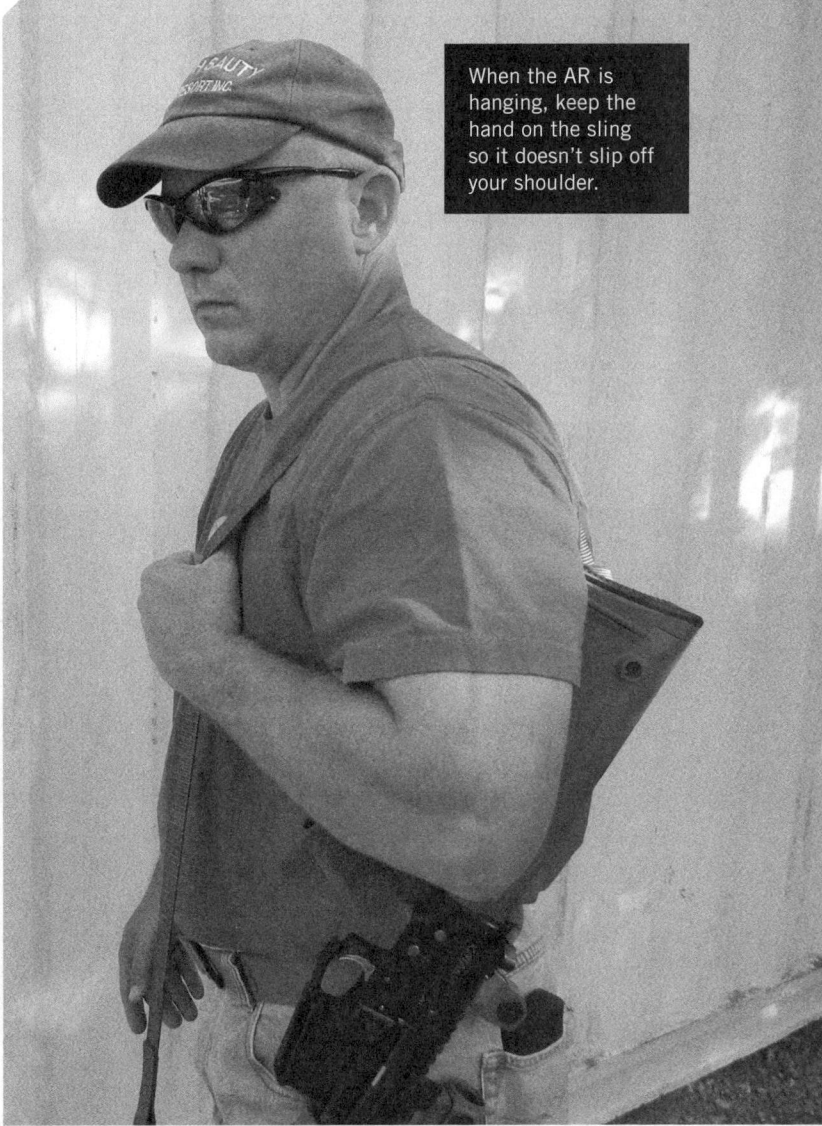

When the AR is hanging, keep the hand on the sling so it doesn't slip off your shoulder.

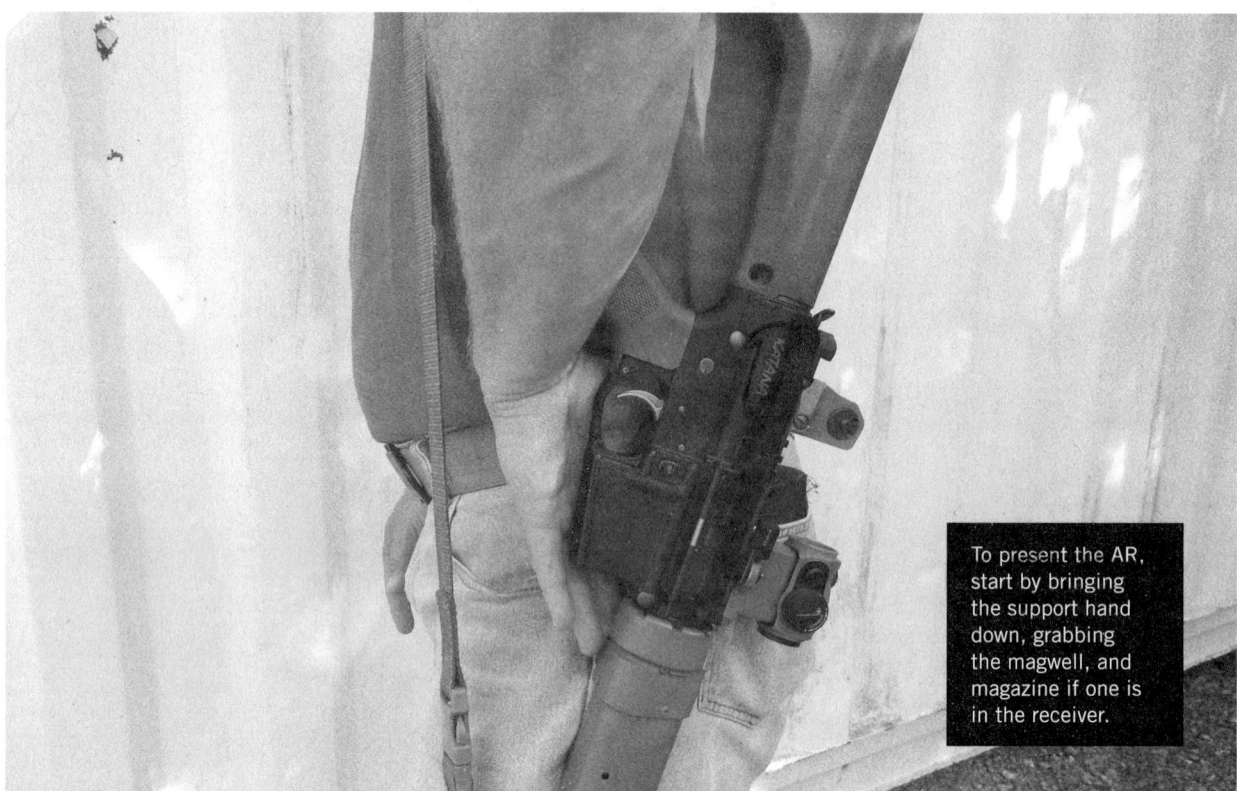

To present the AR, start by bringing the support hand down, grabbing the magwell, and magazine if one is in the receiver.

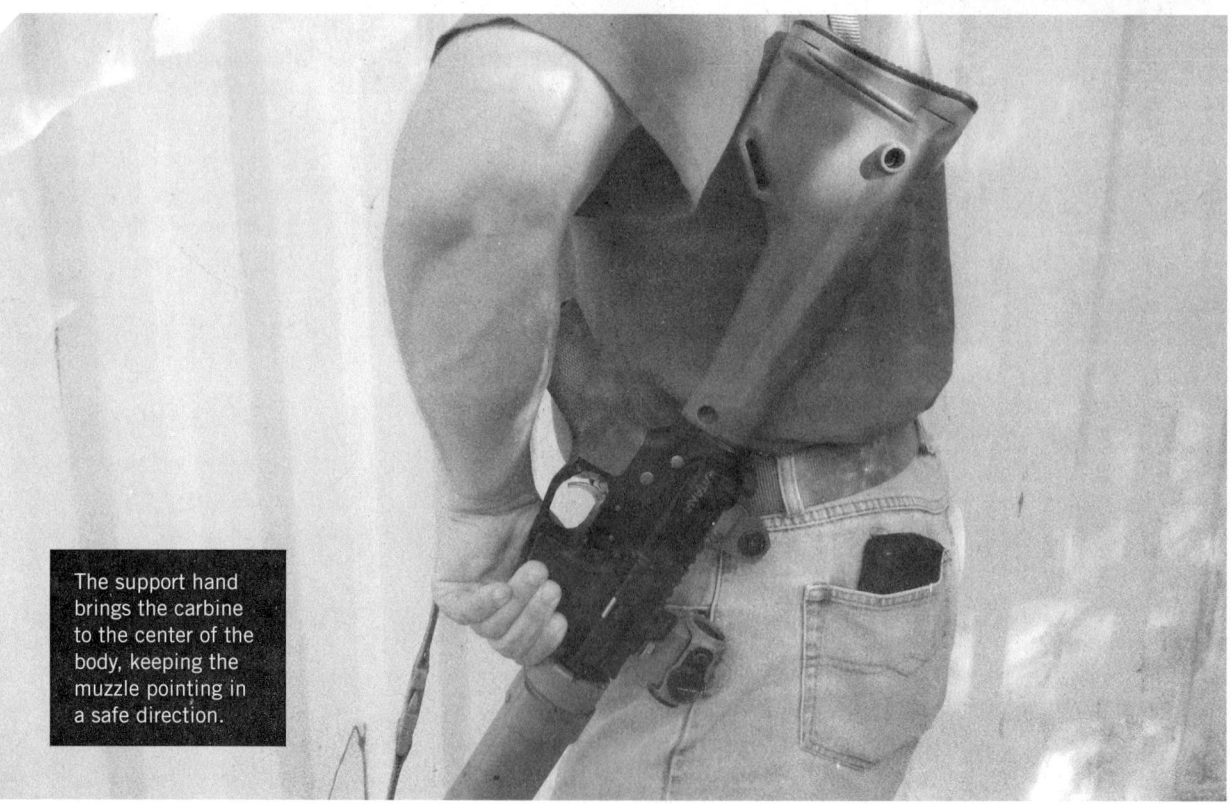

The support hand brings the carbine to the center of the body, keeping the muzzle pointing in a safe direction.

CHAPTER 5: CARRY MODES

As soon as possible, the strong hand acquires a grip on the carbine.

Pick up the sling so it's not hanging down to get caught on door knobs, tree limbs or other obstructions.

up high near the chest, to keep the AR from slipping off the shoulder.

To present the rifle, the support hand comes between the strong arm and body, underneath the armpit and acquires a grip on the AR's handguard.

Lift the AR up slightly, to take the weight off the sling, and straighten out the strong-side arm, pointing it toward the target. The support arm moves the AR forward, toward the target.

The entire time you are controlling the muzzle, keeping it in line between your eyes and the target. Once the AR is in front of the body, the strong hand drops down to acquire a firing grip and you're bringing the stock up into the shoulder. As you're bringing the stock up you're keeping the muzzle in line with the eyes, so that once the stock is in the shoulder the sights are on target. From this position you go into the ready position needed at that time.

SCRAMBLE CARRY

For situations where you need both hands free, simply loop the sling over the neck in what I call "scramble carry." This is a temporary or short-term sling mode and isn't something you use for long periods of time. From the low ready position, bring the support hand back and grab the rear of the sling, about one-third of the way from the stock. Take the hand and loop this part of the sling over the neck. Once the sling is looped over the neck the support hand goes back to the handguard, and using both hands lower the carbine down. While the rifle is hanging, the strong hand stays on the AR's grip to control the muzzle and you're keeping the thumb or

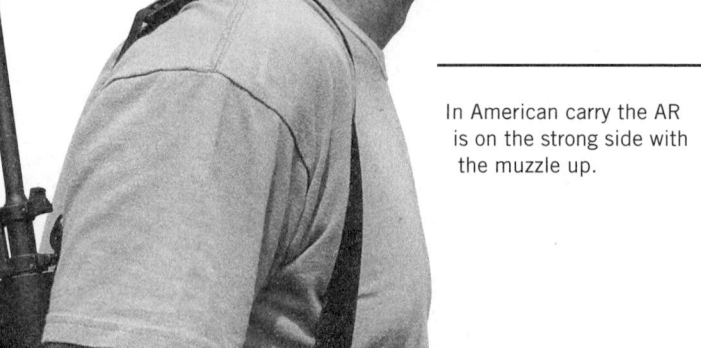

In American carry the AR is on the strong side with the muzzle up.

To sling in American carry, start by gripping the front of the sling with the support hand.

Slip the sling over the strong-side shoulder.

GunDigest.com

Make sure the sling is actually over the shoulder before letting the AR hang.

While the rifle is slung, the strong hand holds the sling in place to prevent it from slipping off the shoulder.

CHAPTER 5: CARRY MODES

To present the AR the support hand goes between the sling and body to grab the handguard. The strong arm is straightened out so the sling can slip off the arm.

The support arm is moving the AR forward, controlling the muzzle.

The strong hand acquires a grip and the muzzle is staying in line with the body.

Once complete you're in a low ready or on target, ready to fire.

finger that operates the safety underneath the selector to make sure it doesn't get bumped or switched to "Fire" as you're moving around. With the sling adjusted to the proper length, the stock will be just below the pocket of the shoulder and you should still be able to mount the AR into a firing position.

Now you have both hands free to climb a ladder or perform other such tasks. Remember, this is a temporary sling mode. All the weight of the AR is on your neck, and it doesn't take long before it starts to get tiring. As soon as possible you should unloop the sling from around the neck. This is done from the low ready position, muzzle down and stock in the shoulder. The support hand grabs the sling and takes it over the head, unlooping it from around the neck.

When looping the sling over the neck, or using any other sling that attaches the carbine to your body where it's hanging in front of the chest, there are several factors to consider. While the carbine is hanging on the body, keep the strong hand on the carbine's grip to control the muzzle, and thumb or finger underneath the safety to ensure it doesn't get disengaged. You may need to take the strong hand off the grip to perform a task, but as soon as possible return it and make sure the safety is engaged. Of the negligent discharges I've seen on ranges, about half of them occurred when the shooter was wearing some type of vest or chest rig. The carbine was allowed to sling about freely, and at some point the safety bumped against the vest and was disengaged. Then the shooter moved, twisted, kneeled or some other similar movement, the trigger bumped against part of their gear and the AR went "bang." In the inci-

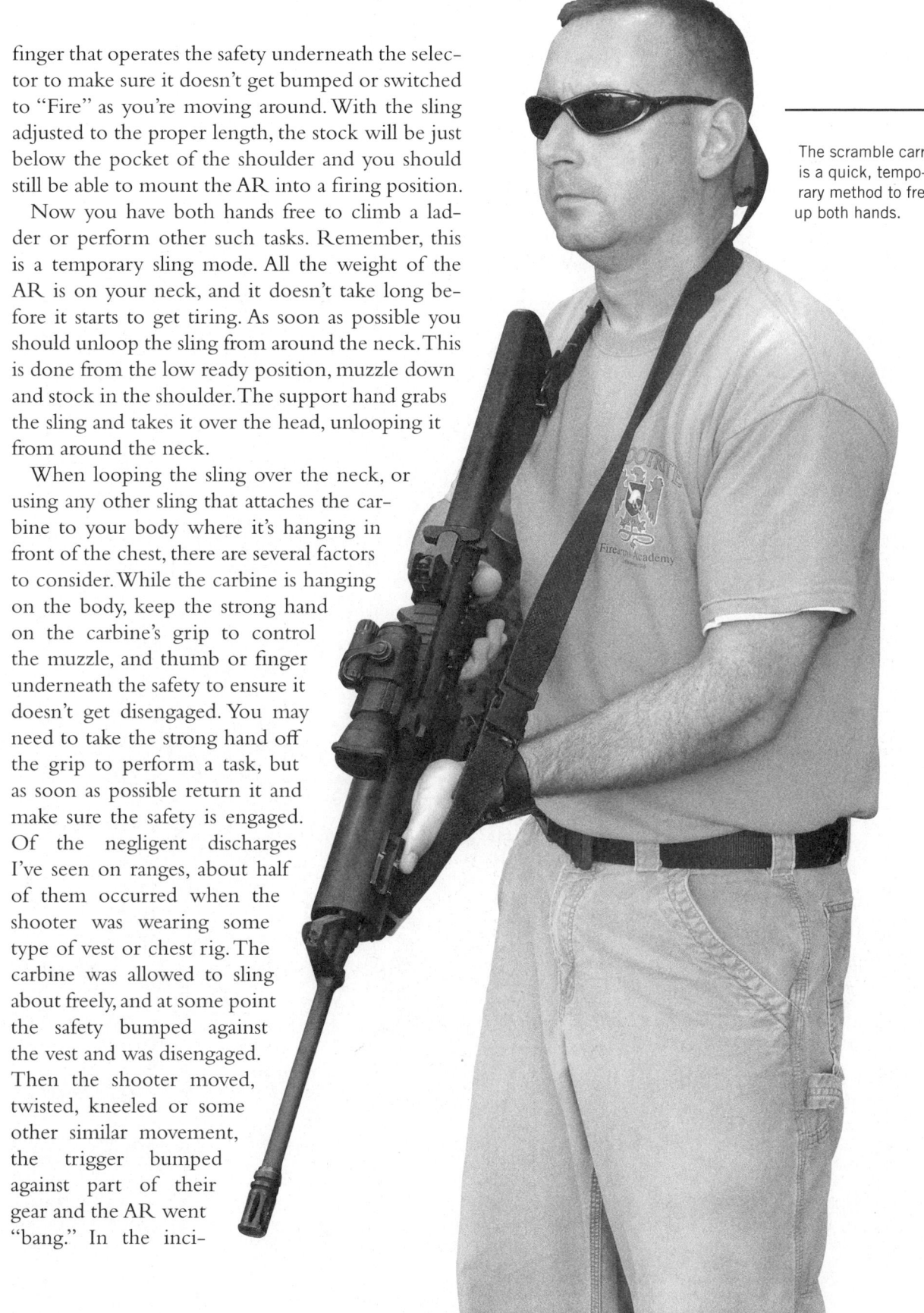

The scramble carry is a quick, temporary method to free up both hands.

dents I've seen no one was injured; luckily there was nobody standing near them and the muzzle was pointing outboard, away from their legs and feet. But, this negligent or unintentional discharge can easily injure or kill. Control the muzzle and keep the safety on.

The other discharges I've seen occurred when someone decided to manipulate the carbine while it was slung. Never perform any manipulations with the carbine hanging or slung around your body; while slung or hanging you can't use the correct techniques to manipulate the AR. Using improper techniques means you're opening the door for trouble. Whenever you need to do anything to the AR, go to the low ready position, using the correct and proper techniques for the task you need to perform.

The support hand grabs the sling to loop it over the neck. Make sure to control the muzzle.

The strong hand stays on the grip, controlling the muzzle and ensuring the safety stays engaged.

With the sling adjusted to the proper length you should still be able to come up into a firing position.

TACTICAL SLINGS

I use the term "tactical sling" for any sling that loops around the neck and underneath the support-side shoulder. When using a tactical sling, or a two-point sling looped over the neck and underneath the support arm, the AR is "slung" by letting it hang. To sling the AR, go to the low ready position and use the support hand to loop the sling around your body. The strong hand is on the AR's grip, controlling the muzzle and keeping it pointing in a safe direction. I normally loop the sling over the neck first and then run the support arm through the sling. With the sling under the support arm the AR will hang to that side, so when hanging you have access to your pistol, which is on the strong side of the body. The sling should be adjusted so that the stock is just below the pocket of the shoulder and there is enough slack in it that you can come up into a firing position without the sling restricting your movement.

As mentioned above, the strong hand should stay on the AR's grip, controlling the muzzle and ensuring the safety or selector lever stays in the "Safe" position. To come up on target the support hand grasps the handguard, bringing the muzzle up in line with the target and into a firing position.

If you're going to carry the AR with the sling looped around the body it's important you have a quick-disconnect buckle. This way you can quickly shed the sling and get the carbine free from the body.

Tactical slings normally loop over the neck and underneath the support arm.

To loop into a tactical sling, start by looping it over the neck and then run the support arm through the sling.

The tactical sling positions the AR to the support side when hanging, so you have access to the pistol on your strong side.

The sling should be adjusted so you can manipulate the AR or assume different firing positions.

A quick disconnect buckle allows you to get free of the carbine when it's looped around the body, which may be needed for a variety of reasons.

RETRIEVING

Regardless of the carry mode and what type sling you're using, when it's time to retrieve something off the ground make sure to control the muzzle. Safety Rule 2, keeping the muzzle pointing in a safe direction, still applies. To pick up something off the ground while the AR is slung, you need to squat or kneel down while at the same time controlling the muzzle to ensure it's not pointing in an unsafe direction, covering part of your body, or digging into the ground, which can obstruct or clog the barrel resulting in the barrel splitting the next time you fire a shot.

If at any time you feel like there may be something stuck in the barrel, flash hider or muzzle break, do not fire until clearing it. This means unload, then split the receivers and remove the bolt group. Now you can safely run a cleaning rod through the barrel and out the muzzle to clear out the obstruction. Again, firing the AR with a clogged barrel or obstruction in the muzzle will cause damage to your weapon and create an unsafe environment for you and anybody in the vicinity. •

DRILLS

> Learn to work with these various carry modes. You must be able to smoothly present the AR to the ready position or onto target, safely, which means controlling the muzzle the entire time. Dry practice is the best way to learn. When you're practicing don't worry about speed. In the beginning practice step by step, pausing at each to ensure it's correct before going to the next step. Eventually the steps will flow from one to another, providing a smooth, flowing presentation into a ready position or directly onto the target.

Regardless of how you have the AR slung, when it's time to retrieve something off the ground you need to squat or kneel down, keeping the muzzle pointing in a safe direction and making sure it doesn't hit the ground where it can get an obstruction caught in the barrel.

With a tactical sling the muzzle will normally go to the outside of the support leg when you kneel or squat down.

CHAPTER 6
STANCE

THERE ARE DIFFERENT schools of thought when it comes to stance and how you position and hold the AR. I lean towards traditional techniques, especially when first working with an AR. Later, after you have a good grasp of the fundamentals, you can start experimenting with different approaches.

A proper stance provides the platform for the AR. The stance should create balance and stability for accurate shooting. A good stance puts your body mass behind the weapon, assisting you in recovering from recoil – a component of accuracy and/or follow up for additional shots. The proper stance allows you to move in any direction necessary, which is a major part of using the AR for self-defense. The proper stance should be as relaxed as possible, relying on bone support more than muscle tension. Obviously muscles are involved, but bone support is always more consistent than muscle tension. In the beginning your goal is to be as machine-like as possible, assuming the same stance, consistently, over and over.

Start with the feet shoulder-width apart. (These instructions are for right-handed shooters; left-handed shooters will simply do the opposite.) The left foot is pointing toward the target. Position the right foot slightly behind the left foot, and pointing outboard slightly – roughly about a 20-degree angle. For most people the toes of the right foot should be slightly behind the heel of the left foot, again with the feet shoulder-width apart. You don't want the feet too close together, which reduces stability, or too far apart, which requires you to shift your weight completely over to one foot or the other to move.

Bend the knees slightly and lean forward at the waist. Ideally you're looking for about 60 percent of your body weight on the left or lead leg. This weight distribution puts the body's mass in behind the rifle to assist in recovering from recoil. I normally lift the heel of my right foot slightly, which helps transition the weight to the left leg and also preps me for moving quickly if necessary.

Positioning the feet and legs in this way means the hips and torso are at a slight angle to the target,

A proper stance is the foundation for everything else.

The feet should be shoulder-width apart, with the strong-side foot slightly behind the support foot.

which is perfect for mounting the rifle into a firing position. With the rifle attached to your body in four locations it's important to have the upper body indexed on the target. Think about it along these lines: The body actually aims the firearm, and then we use the sights to confirm it's aiming exactly where it needs to be.

This is the same stance I use for handguns. Keeping things simple, with one stance for the AR and the same for handguns, makes it easier to be consistent. Consistency is the key to success. (I also use the same stance for empty-handed fighting or using edged weapons. For shotguns the same stance is used, except with more aggression, transferring more weight to the lead leg and moving the rear or strong-side leg farther back.)

The strong hand is on the AR's grip. In a ready position the hand is relaxed. When you're on target the strong hand applies slight pressure, pulling to the rear and taking out any slack that may be there due to body tissue or clothing. This rearward pressure seats the stock into the shoulder's pocket. This rearward pull also prevents the stock from bouncing back and forth in the shoulder when firing.

The upper body is leaning slightly forward, and the support hand should just cradle the handguard.

The support hand should simply create a cradle for the handguard to rest in. Normally my fingers and thumb are not applying any gripping pressure; the more pressure you grip with the more movement will transfer from your body to the muzzle. The elbow is underneath the hand, using as much bone support as possible as opposed to muscle tension. (Again, we're looking at traditional techniques and this will vary some once you start working different positions or adding accessories such as a vertical grip.)

The design of the AR makes it a little different when it comes to mounting and positioning the stock in the shoulder. The barrel of the AR is in line with the stock extension, or buffer tube, and the stock fits over this tube. With this design, the "heel" of the stock – the top part of the back section of the stock – is higher than a traditional stock, which is normally lower than the barrel and bolt assembly. This means that only the toe of the stock, roughly the bottom half of the stock, is positioned in the shoulder pocket.

Having the toe of the stock in the shoulder pocket means when you come up on target you're

The stock should be positioned in the pocket of the shoulder, with only the "toe," or bottom part of the stock, in the shoulder.

You should practice until assuming a good, aggressive stance becomes "natural."

bringing the sights up to eye level as opposed to bringing the eyes down to the sights. We want to take advantage of our natural tendency to bring things up to eye level, such as the sights on the AR; positioning the stock in the right location of the shoulder is critical.

The first step is ensuring the toe of the stock, the bottom corner, is in the actual pocket of the shoulder. To find your shoulder's pocket raise the strong arm up high. Take your support hand, with thumb pointing forward, and come right underneath your jaw, positioning the edge of the hand on the collarbone. Slide the hand outboard until you feel the collar bone dip below the deltoid muscle. This is the pocket of the shoulder, where you want position the toe of the stock.

The stock should be high in the pocket, with only about the bottom half of the stock, the toe, in the shoulder pocket. To test for the proper height bring the muzzle up to obtain a sight picture. You shouldn't have to move or reposition the head, and once you have a cheekweld the sights should be in alignment with your eye. If you have to bring the head down to get on the sights, the stock should be moved up higher in the pocket. Leaning your head over to the side to acquire the sights tells you the stock is to far outside, past the shoulder pocket.

Having the stock too low, or outside the shoulder's pocket, will force you to dip the head down to get a sight picture.

The exact positions/locations of these index points will vary for each individual. Work on dry practice, coming up on target, hitting the cheekweld, and obtaining a sight picture until you discover the right combination. Then, striving for consistency, practice assuming a firing position until it becomes natural, automatic and requires a minimal amount of movement in your body. Dry practice is the best way of getting in the repetitions necessary to learn and perform consistently. •

DRILLS

Make it a habit that every time you're working with the AR to do so using the proper stance. Remember the stance is the foundation for everything else. Consistency is the key. Initially you have to consciously think about assuming the proper stance; eventually it should become habit.

CHAPTER 7
ADMINISTRATIVE MANIPULATIONS

MANIPULATIONS OF THE AR can be divided into two categories – administrative and functional. The admin manipulations include loading, unloading and verifying the status of the firearm, whether it's loaded or unloaded. The functional manipulations are reloading and clearing malfunctions, the actions that keep your AR running.

Manipulation of the AR must be done safely, always your number one concern, and efficiently, which is definitely critical when using the AR for defensive confrontations. Consistency is the key. Using the proper techniques, regardless of the situation, ensures you're operating the AR safely and provides predictable results from your actions. Also remember that every time you handle the AR it's a learning opportunity. Make sure every repetition is a good one, using the proper techniques, as opposed to varying the way you operate the weapon, which could be unsafe and doesn't promote learning.

The administrative manipulations are important for several reasons. First, you want to make sure you're performing these actions safely, again the primary concern

All Admin manipulations are performed in the low ready position, with stock in the shoulder and muzzle pointing downward.

The "free-floating" firing pin of the AR strikes the primer every time a round is chambered. A faulty round can cause the AR to fire while loading.

when operating any firearm. Second, the functional manipulations are all based on the same techniques you use for loading and unloading. Each time you load or unload, you're getting repetitions that apply to all the other manipulations.

While manipulating the AR, both the admin and functional manipulations, get into the habit of keeping your head and eyes up. You want to get to the point where you can operate the AR without needing to see it, relying on physical confirmations as opposed to visually confirming your actions. The only time you want or need to look at the AR is when visually checking the chamber to see if it's loaded or unloaded. (Regardless of the AR's condition, we're still applying Safety Rule 1, treating it like it's loaded.) All other actions are performed by physical confirmation. This allows you to work the AR while maintaining visual contact with your target, an important consideration for self-defense, and/or manipulate the weapon in dark or low-light environments.

The administrative manipulations are performed in the low ready position: stock in the shoulder, muzzle down, safety on and finger off the trigger and clear of the trigger guard. (During *any* type of manipulation your finger should be off the trigger and clear of the trigger guard.) Having the stock in the shoulder gives you more control of the rifle. You keep the muzzle pointing down for safety. The AR has a free-floating firing pin, which means every time the bolt goes forward, such as when loading, the firing pin goes forward, striking the primer of the round being chambered. Normally this strike does not have enough force to ignite the primer, unless you have a faulty round with a high or sensitive primer. If this is the case the rifle will fire while loading. Keep the muzzle pointing in a safe direction, which is usually down. During the administrative manipulations the safety is always engaged, and it's a good habit to check every so often to ensure the selector lever is in the "Safe" position.

The admin actions always start with the magazine. You're inserting the mag, removing it, checking to ensure the mag in the rifle is loaded or confirming there isn't a magazine in the mag well. The administrative manipulations end by checking the chamber, ensuring it's either loaded or empty, and shutting the dust cover to keep foreign matter from getting in the works.

LOADING

Loading, as with all administrative manipulations, is performed in the low ready position. The muzzle is down, your finger is off the trigger and clear of the trigger guard and safety is on. Keep your eyes up, learning how to load without looking at the weapon.

The support hand acquires the new magazine. Bring the mag up and index it to the mag well. I normally index the back of the magazine against the back of the mag well. This is a very positive index that is easy to feel, as opposed to trying to stick the magazine straight into the mag well.

Or, you can index the front of the mag with the front of the mag well, the same way you do an AK or M14. Sensitivity is key to obtaining this index. Force will not work. Once you have the magazine indexed, align the mag with the mag well, seat it aggressively, and then tug on the mag, pulling it down to ensure it's locked in place. A lot of times you may think the mag is seated, but when you tug it will

Indexing the back or front of the magazine to the mag well is much easier than trying to stick it straight in.

Tugging on the magazine ensures it's seated and locked in.

After locking in the mag, cycle the charging handle one time to load a round into the chamber.

The "press" or "chamber" check confirms you have a round chambered. I prefer to do a physical confirmation.

The support hand indexes the magazine.

CHAPTER 7: ADMINISTRATIVE MANIPULATIONS

come out. Tugging, pulling down on the mag after seating it, provides you with a physical confirmation that it's locked in place.

Once the mag is seated, cycle the charging handle one time. (See the section on the Charging Handle for the proper technique used to cycle the charging handle.) After cycling the charging handle to load the chamber, you perform a chamber check to ensure the AR is loaded. You've gone through all the proper actions, but you won't know for sure if there's a round in the chamber unless you check it.

Left-handed shooters will perform the same sequence, using the appropriate techniques. Index the magazine. Seat and tug to ensure it's locked in, and then cycle the charging handle.

The final step is performing a chamber check, and then shutting the dust cover. There are a few different options to confirm the chambered round. You can do a visual check, a physical confirmation, or you can check the top round on the magazine before and after loading. To visually check the chamber the support hand holds the handguard. The strong hand comes off the grip, pulling the charging handle slightly to the rear. This allows you to look, visually confirming there is a round chambered. As soon as you've checked get the eyes up again. Release the charging handle so it snaps forward, and reacquire your firing grip with the strong hand.

The support hand comes back a little farther to press the bolt carrier forward to make sure the bolt is in battery. (See the section on Forward Assist for details on this action.) The final step is to shut the dust cover, again using the support hand.

You can also perform a physical confirmation.

Cycle the charging handle to chamber a round.

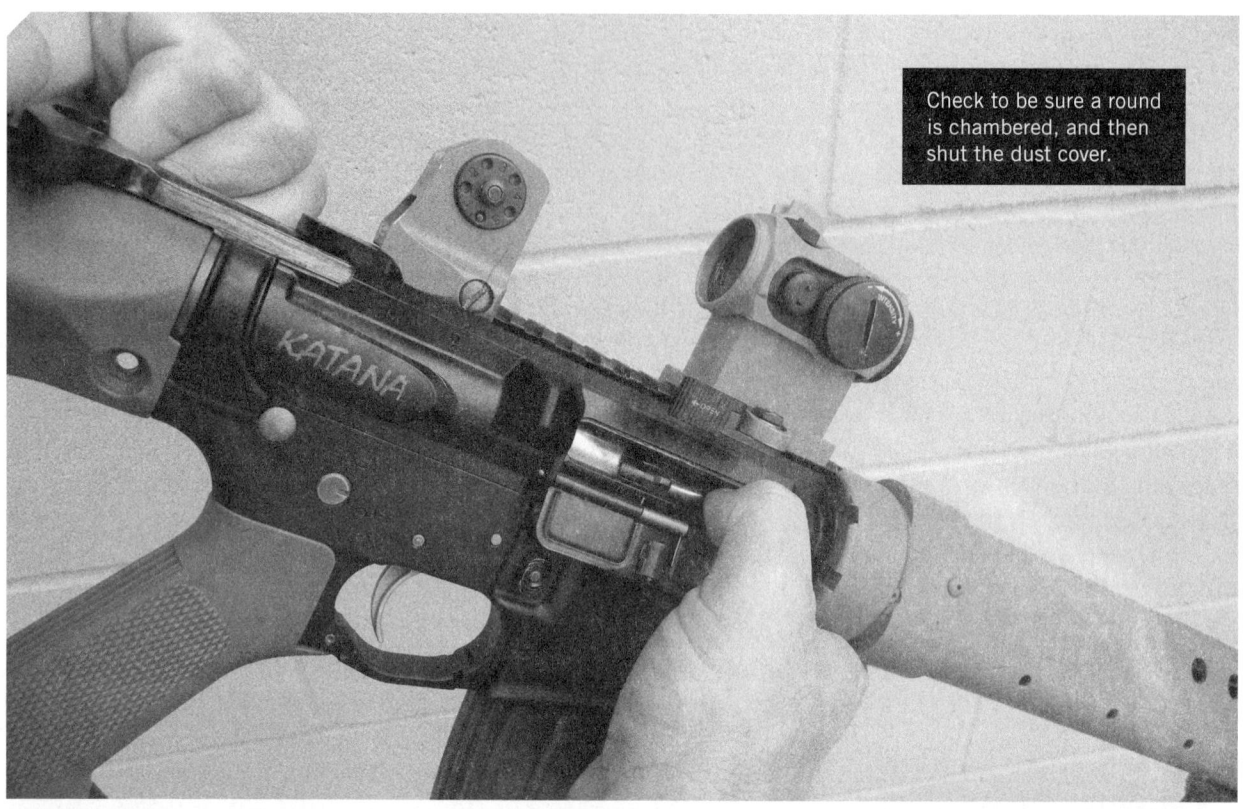

Check to be sure a round is chambered, and then shut the dust cover.

You can do a visual check of the chamber to confirm whether it's loaded or empty.

After performing a chamber check, always make sure the bolt is seated. I use the concave area in the bolt carrier to pres the bolt forward.

The technique is the same as described above, except that you bring the support hand farther back, cupping it around the mag well so that you can feel for the round as you pull the bolt to the rear. Right-handed shooters will normally use the first or second finger on the support hand to feel the round. Left-handed shooters will use their thumb, which will be positioned on the right side of the receiver. After physically checking the round release the charging handle, make sure the bolt is in battery and shut the dust cover.

The third option to check the chamber is actually done using the magazine, checking the position of the top round in the magazine before and after loading. The top round in the mag will be high, either on the right or left side of the magazine. Prior to inserting the magazine feel to see which side the top round is on. After loading you remove the mag and feel to ensure the top round has swapped sides. In other words the top round was on the left side, and after loading the top round is on the right side. This tells you that a round is chambered.

For loading I normally like to do the physical confirmation, using a support hand to feel the round, again keeping my head and eyes up as much as possible. But, if I'm wearing thick gloves and I can't get a finger in the ejection port, I visually check it. I'm not a big fan of checking the top round on the mag because this means you have to reposition your hand to feel for the round, then remove the mag, feel again, and then reinsert the mag into the AR.

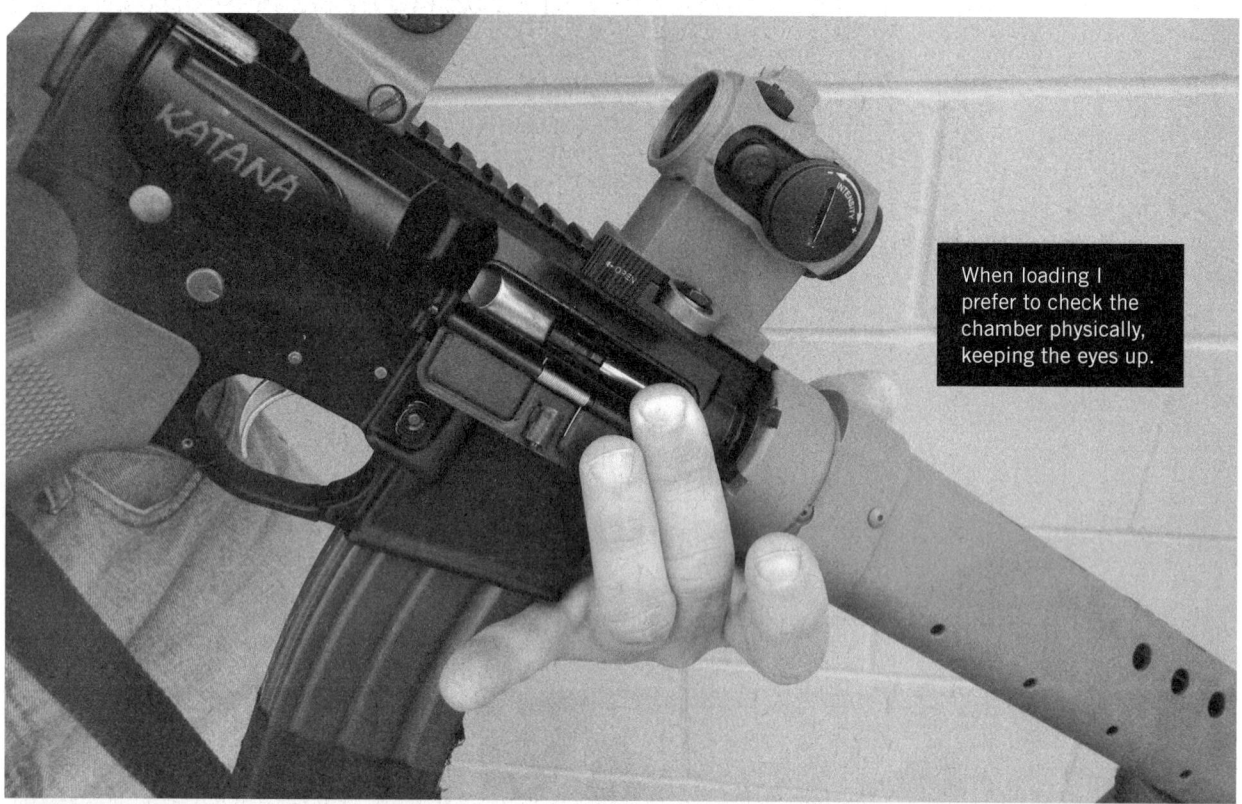

When loading I prefer to check the chamber physically, keeping the eyes up.

Left-handed shooter using the support hand to physically confirm a loaded round.

CHAPTER 7: ADMINISTRATIVE MANIPULATIONS

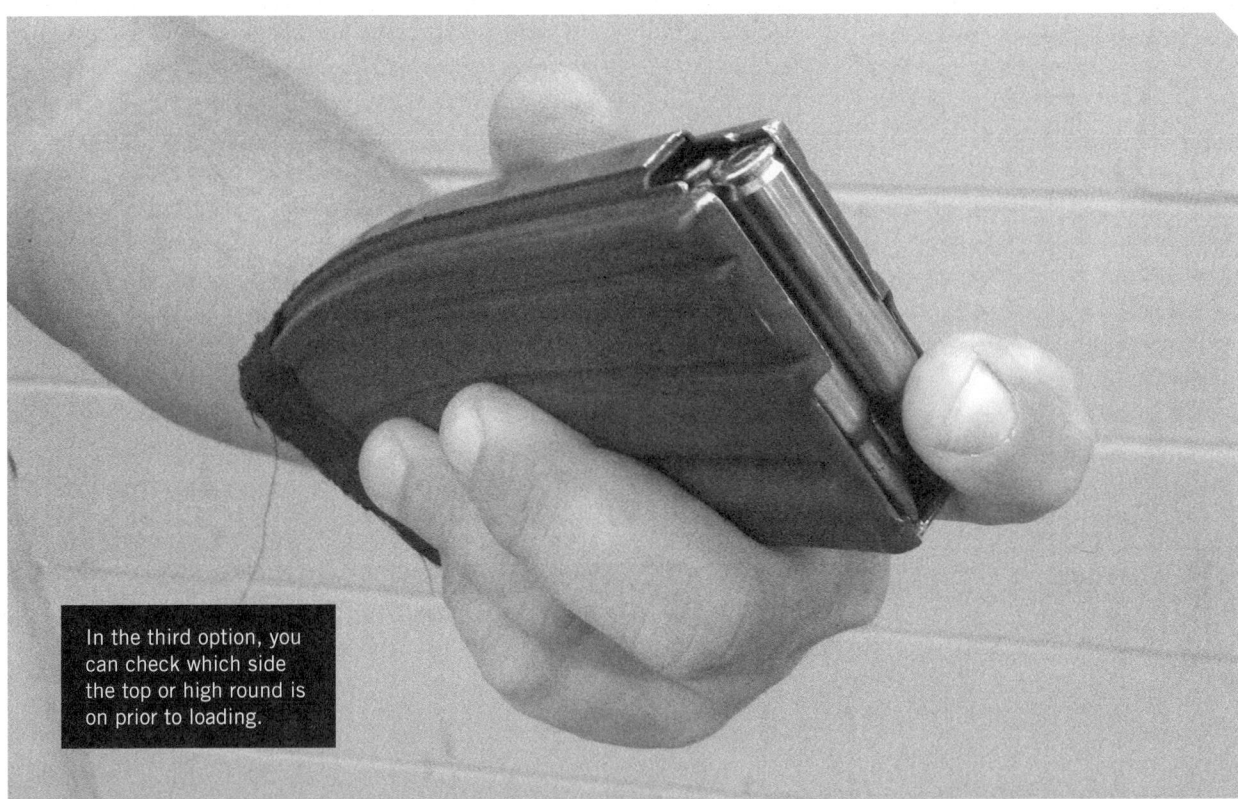

In the third option, you can check which side the top or high round is on prior to loading.

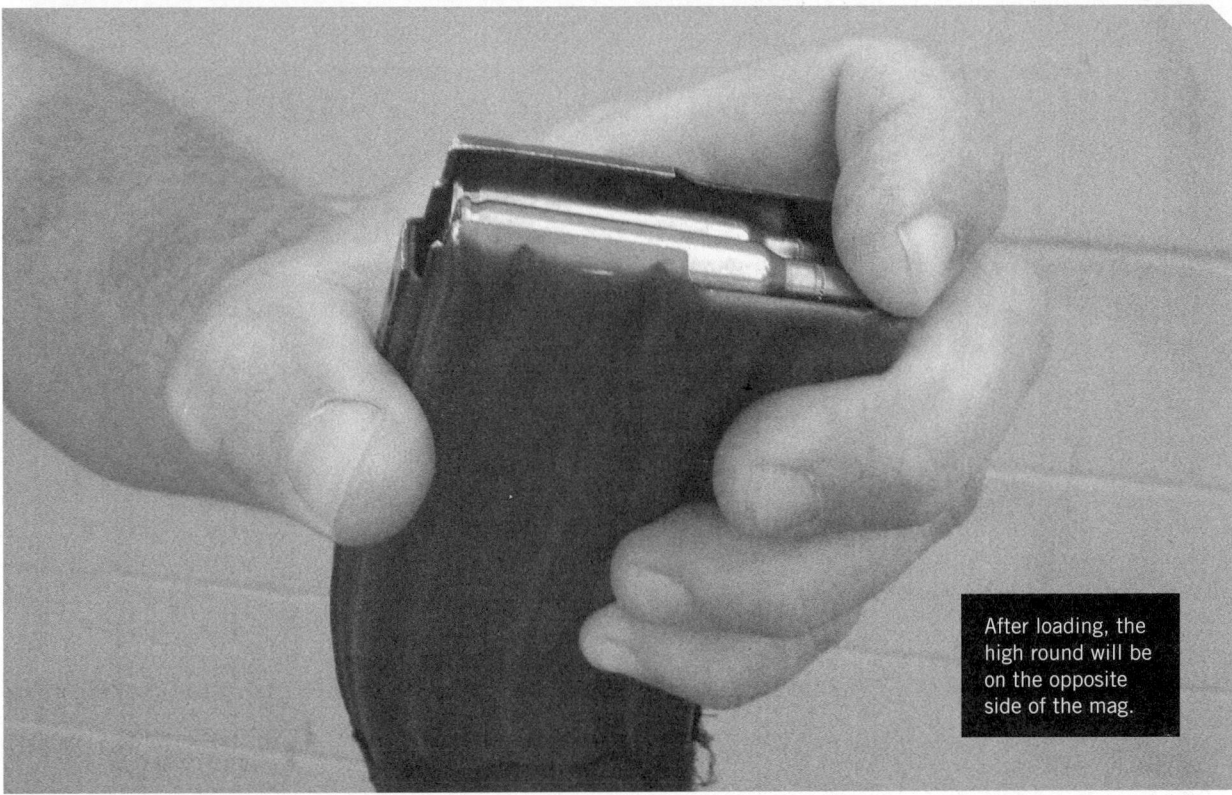

After loading, the high round will be on the opposite side of the mag.

CONFIRMING LOADED

There may be situations when you retrieve the AR and it's supposed to be loaded, but you have the time or need to confirm this. As always, go to the low ready position. Again, this is an administrative action so it begins with the magazine. Remove the mag, make sure it's loaded, and put it back into the AR, tugging to ensure it's seated. Perform a chamber check as described above to ensure there's a round in it. Finish by shutting the dust cover.

UNLOADING

Unloading is performed in the low ready position and the process begins by removing the magazine, the source of ammo. Press the mag release, remove the mag with the support hand, and retain it in the support hand while performing the rest of the actions required to unload the AR.

Holding the mag with the support hand while cycling the charging handle and performing other actions may be awkward at first, but you'll see how this comes into play later for clearing malfunctions. (Basically every time you unload you're getting practice clearing what we call Type III malfunctions.)

After removing the mag you'll need to position it in the hand in a manner that will allow you to hold it and cycle the charging handle, assuming you're using the support hand to cycle the charging handle. Right-handed shooters will tilt the magazine at a downward angle while bringing the thumb forward toward the first finger. This allows the thumb and finger to cycle the charging handle as you normally would. Left-handed shooters will normally

Unloading begins by removing the magazine.

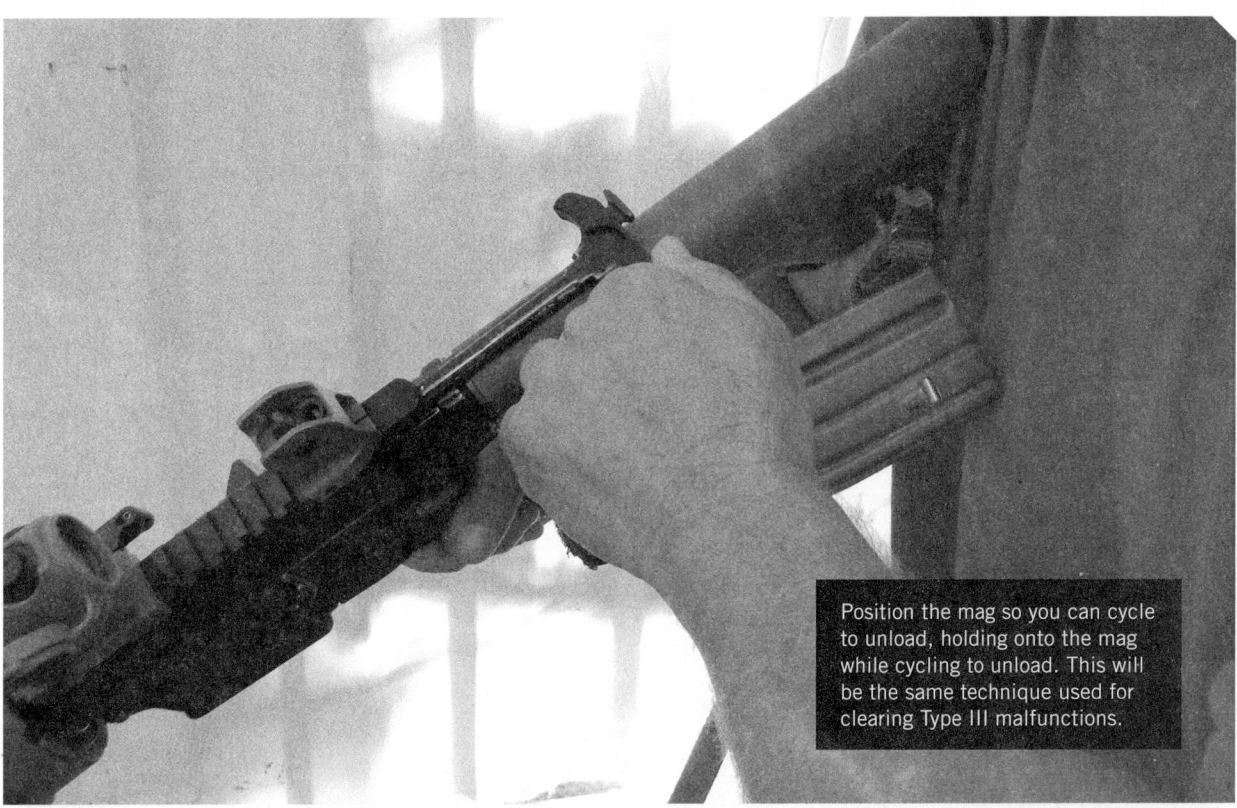

Position the mag so you can cycle to unload, holding onto the mag while cycling to unload. This will be the same technique used for clearing Type III malfunctions.

Left-handed shooter using support hand to cycle while holding magazine.

hold the mag with the bottom two fingers of the right hand, freeing up the thumb and first two fingers to cycle the charging handle.

If you're using the strong hand to cycle the charging handle, the support hand is holding the magazine while also gripping the handguard to support the weight and control the muzzle. This is similar to the technique used to lock the bolt to the rear.

Cycle the handle three times. Why three times? Because this is the same way you'll be clearing Type III malfunctions. The goal is to have one set of skills that apply to a variety of operations. There's the consistency thing again. This keeps things simple, safe and efficient. Plus, cycling the action three times ensures it's clear, or in the case of a malfunction you're clearing out all the trash or after cycling three times you'll know a different type action is required.

It may be easier to use the support hand to hold the weight of the AR and use the strong hand to cycle the charging handle.

Right-handed shooter visually checking to ensure chamber is clear.

After cycling three times you're going to perform a visual chamber check, as previously described. When loading I prefer to do a physical confirmation; you're feeling for a round that is captured and pulled back by the bolt. The way the AR's ejection port is positioned in relationship to the chamber it's impossible to actually stick a finger into the chamber, as you would with a bolt-action rifle. The only way to ensure the chamber is empty with the AR is to look inside the ejection port at the chamber.

The support hand goes to the handguard, still holding the magazine, and you use the strong hand to pull the charging handle to the rear, which allows you to visually check and confirm the chamber is actually empty. This is about the only time you should need to actually look at the AR. Everything else is performed by physical confirmation.

After confirming the chamber is clear, let the charging handle and bolt snap forward and close the dust cover. It's also not a bad idea to confirm that the safety is on. Now you can secure the mag the support hand is holding.

UNLOADED CONFIRMATION

Any time you pick up an "unloaded" AR you want to check it, confirming that it is truly unloaded. This action is performed in the low ready, and as with all administrative manipulations it starts with the mag and ends by checking the chamber and shutting the dust cover. It's not very "tactical," but using the proper technique is safe, and remember every repetition is a learning repetition.

The support hand comes off the handguard and you stick your fingers in the mag well. This gives you a physical confirmation that there is no magazine in the receiver. Yes, you can look, but remember we're trying to learn how to operate the AR

Left-handed shooter visually checking the chamber for clear.

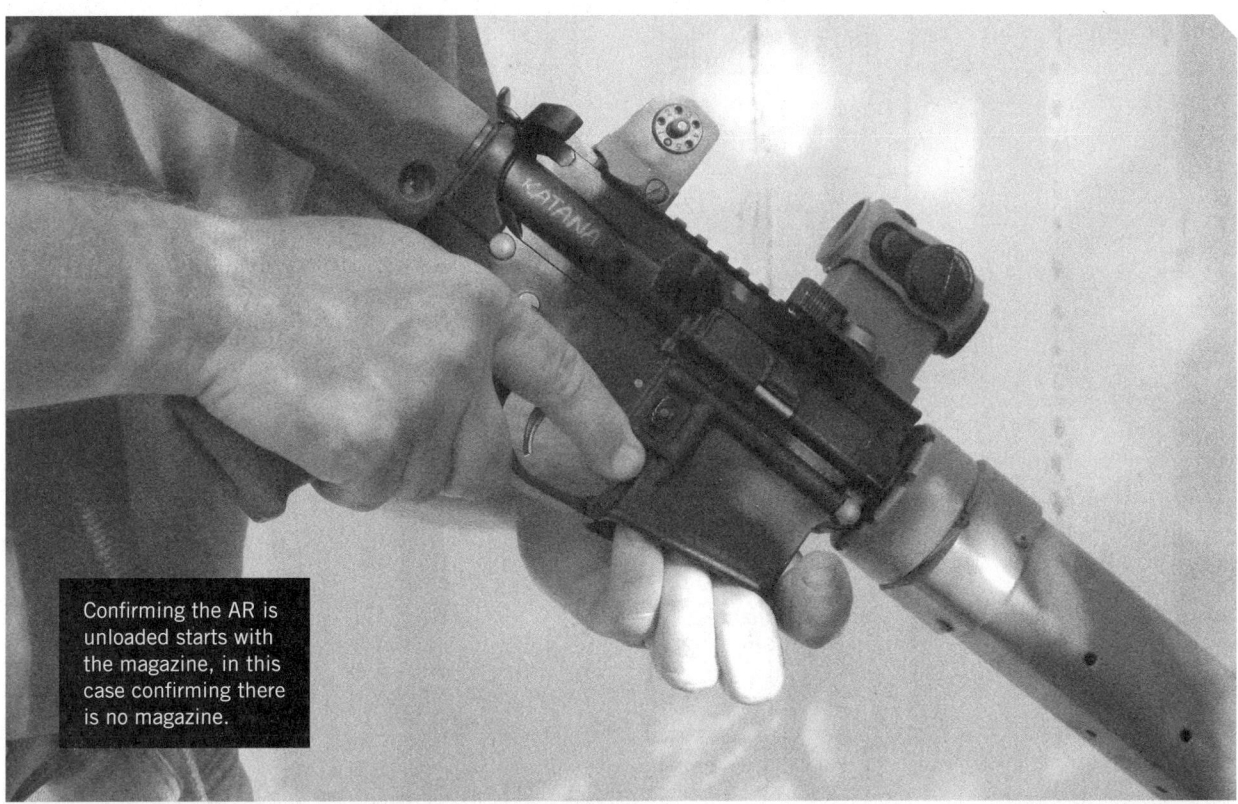

Confirming the AR is unloaded starts with the magazine, in this case confirming there is no magazine.

Cycle the charging handle three times, which is consistent with unloading.

without looking, which has to be practiced until it becomes habit. Plus, sometimes your eyes will play tricks on you. For example, you may be used to working with 30-round mags. You look, but don't see the long body of the 30-rounder sticking out. This is a "false" read though, because this AR has a 10-round mag, which is really short, and so it doesn't register in your mind's eye. By sticking fingers in the mag well, you're confirming there is no way there's a mag in there.

Cycle the charging handle three times. Again, three is the magic number and consistent with all other manipulations, except of course for loading. After cycling three times, swap hands on the charging handle and perform a visual check to make sure the chamber is clear and close the dustcover.

To sum things up, all administrative manipulations are performed in the low ready position – stock in the shoulder, muzzle down and safety on. They start with the mag – putting one in, taking it out, checking to make sure the one in the AR is loaded, or confirming there is no mag in it. The administrative actions end by checking the chamber, either physically or visually, and closing the dust cover. •

Visually check to confirm the chamber is clear, and close the dust cover.

PRACTICE

It may sound strange, but practicing these adminstrative manipulations is the best way to get familiar with operating the AR. At the beginning of every class we have students go through these actions, spending time on the proper way to load, unload or confirm the condition of the weapon. Practice these actions, using dummy rounds, so that you can perform the administrative manipulations with the AR safely and efficiently.

LOAD

1. Go to the low ready position.
2. Acquire the magazine with the support hand, unless you're using one of the alternative methods.
3. Index, align, seat the mag and tug to ensure it's seated.
4. Cycle the charging handle one time.
5. Visually or physically check the chamber to ensure it's loaded.
6. Close the dust cover.

UNLOAD

1. Go to the low ready position.
2. Remove the magazine, retaining it in the support hand.
3. Cycle the charging handle three times.
4. Visually check the chamber.
5. Close dust cover.
6. Secure magazine in pocket or pouch.

CONFIRM LOADED

1. Remove magazine to confirm it is loaded. Replace it in the AR.
2. Visually or physically check the chamber to make sure it's loaded.
3. Close dust cover.

CONFIRM UNLOADED

1. Fingers in the mag well to confirm it's empty.
2. Cycle the charging handle three times.
3. Visually check the chamber.
4. Close dust cover.

REMEMBER, these same actions will be used to reload and clear malfunctions with the AR.

CHAPTER 8
FUNCTIONAL MANIPULATIONS

THE FUNCTIONAL MANIPULATIONS are what keep the AR running. You're shooting and the mag runs empty. While firing the AR has a malfunction. The functional manipulations – reloading or clearing malfunctions – get the AR shooting again as efficiently as possible.

While these manipulations are based on the same skills used in the administrative manipulations, there are a few differences. First, the functional manipulations are performed with the muzzle on target. Efficiency or speed is the absence of excess. Dropping the rifle down to manipulate it requires you to get it up and back on target once it's running again. This is time lost in just lowering the AR and then bringing it back up. Plus, when most people lower the rifle their eyes follow it. Keeping the muzzle on target allows you to keep the eyes downrange and still be able to see the rifle if necessary. In a defensive situation keeping the muzzle on target doesn't reveal the threat that you're empty or have a stoppage. Pointing the muzzle up is not a good idea except in very special circumstances. Keep the

Ideally you should be able to press the mag release and have the mag drop free.

muzzle on target.

The other major difference is that the chamber or press check, confirming the status of the chamber, is eliminated. You're just going to have faith that when you perform the proper actions the AR is going to do what it's supposed to, and if not it will let you know, as long as you know how to "speak" AR. We are learning to communicate with the rifle.

RELOADING

You're firing the AR and it runs empty. The follower of the empty magazine engages the bolt catch, locking the bolt to the rear. The sequence to reload the AR is simple: Finger off the trigger, old mag out, new mag in, and press the bolt release.

Step one is to get your finger off the trigger and clear of the trigger guard. With right-handed shooters this isn't normally a problem, because the trigger finger is going to press the mag release. Left-handed shooters will be using the support hand thumb to press the mag release, so make sure the finger comes off the trigger and is outside the trigger guard. The muzzle stays on target. Head and eyes are on target.

Old mag out: Press the mag catch to release the magazine. Right-handed shooters use their trigger finger. Left-handed shooters will bring the support hand – the right hand – back and use the thumb to press the mag release.

The AR is designed for the mag to drop free when the release is pressed. Some receiver and mag combinations don't do this. You can either change

Left-handed shooter pressing to release mag with support hand.

mags, testing until you discover what type mags will drop free, or get into the habit of using the support hand to strip the mag free as it presses the mag release. When firing from an unconventional position you may also find it's necessary to pull the mag free. For times when you do pull the mag out, let it drop immediately, freeing up the support hand to acquire a fresh magazine.

New mag in: As soon as possible the support hand acquires a loaded mag. Bring it up to the receiver, index it as discussed previously, align the mag, seat it and tug to ensure it's locked in.

Bolt release: Press the bolt release to chamber a round. Remember, any time the bolt is locked to the rear, you want to use the bolt release as opposed to cycling the charging handle. Right-handed shooters are seating the mag with the left hand; so once the mag is seated simply slide the left hand up the mag and magwell with the thumb extended, pointing it up. This puts your thumb right where it needs to be to press the bolt release. Left-handed shooters press the bolt release with their trigger finger.

After pressing the bolt release the AR is ready to fire again. In a situation where you need to fire quickly you can leave the support hand holding on to the magazine and mag well and fire from there without taking time to reposition the hand to the handguard. For more accuracy, or when you have time, move the support hand back into position on the handguard.

Index, insert and lock the new mag into the receiver, using the same technique you do when loading.

Right-handed shooter using left thumb to press the bolt catch and release the bolt.

Left-handed shooter using trigger finger to release bolt.

After releasing the bolt you can hold on to the mag well and mag to fire if shots are needed quickly.

Key points to remember

First, always get the trigger finger off the trigger and outside the trigger guard. The muzzle stays on target. Eyes stay on the target. After locking in a fresh mag, make sure to use the bolt release to chamber the fresh round. During the reload don't worry about engaging the safety, which just means you'll have to disengage it once you're reloaded. This adds an extra step, and again we want to cut out anything that's not necessary to perform the reload.

With the AR you're using the bolt release to override the magazine follower, as opposed to using the charging handle to cycle the action. This means you can dry practice empty reloads using two empty mags. Put an empty mag into the AR, and pull the charging handle to the rear to lock the bolt back. Come up into your firing position, with safety off and finger on the trigger. Perform your empty reload, dumping the empty mag and putting a fresh mag – another empty – into the receiver. Press the bolt release and you're back on target. Now you have an empty mag in the receiver. Retrieve the other empty off the ground and put it in your pocket or pouch. Lock the bolt back and repeat.

There may be some situations where there is a round partially sticking out of the magazine you're trying to insert into the rifle. When this happens, brush the magazine against your leg, part of your gear, or any other object in order to strip that round clear so you can load the magazine into the rifle.

Sometimes, especially during Type III malfunctions, you may have a round sticking out of the mag that needs to be swiped clear by using part of your body or another object in your environment.

MALFUNCTIONS

There are five types of malfunctions that can occur with the AR. Two are common, a couple will crop up every once in a while, and the last, or Type V, you rarely see. Keep in mind this doesn't count for jams or breakage. A malfunction is something that you can apply a corrective set of actions and get the AR firing again, at least for one more shot. (If the AR is having a mechanical problem, such as a broken extractor spring, you'll have another malfunction to clear after firing the next round.) A jam or breakage is something that takes time and tools to correct.

Some malfunctions are caused by bad ammo. Make it a habit when loading to check the rounds.

Malfunctions are often caused by the shooter, for example not ensuring the mag is seated and locked into place, which means no round in the chamber. We'll discuss the malfunctions and what causes them, but for clearing them think about it along these lines: When the AR doesn't fire you're going to load it. If this doesn't work you're going to unload and then load. A problem that can't be solved by these actions is going to take time and/or tools to correct.

Basically we're using a non-diagnostic approach

Bad rounds can cause a malfunction.

to clearing malfunctions. This is why knowing how to load and unload is important. As with all other skills, consistency provides safety and predictable results from your actions. Practice and repetition is necessary to actually learn these skills, so they can be performed at a subconscious level.

Sometimes, especially with newer shooters or even experienced shooters under stress, people will forget to flip the safety off when they come up on target. Making this a habit is important, but whenever you press the trigger and it won't be pressed make sure the safety is off. This is done using the same technique as always, a physical confirmation as opposed to stopping, flipping the carbine over and looking to see if the safety is on or off.

Step one for all these manipulations is to take your finger off the trigger and get it clear of the trigger guard. You don't want to manipulate the AR, or any weapon, with the finger on the trigger or inside the trigger guard. Verbalizing this action, "finger off the trigger," will help you remember to do this.

Type I Malfunction

You press the trigger and get "click" instead of "bang." The Type I malfunction may be due to no round in the chamber; this is why we make sure to tug on the magazine to ensure it's seated and check the chamber during the loading process to be sure there's a round chambered. Or, the Type I malfunction can be due to a bad round, for example a faulty primer that doesn't ignite the powder charge. Ultimately it doesn't matter, we're going to treat it the same by loading the AR.

First, *finger off the trigger*! The muzzle stays on target, just like when reloading, and the eyes maintain visual contact with the target. Next, tap and tug on the magazine to make sure it's locked in place.

Normally you'll use the support hand to tap and tug on the magazine, maintaining your grip with the strong hand. The alternative is to take the strong hand off the grip, using it to manipulate the AR while the support hand holds the handguard. Sometimes you may be tempted to skip the process of tapping and tugging on the magazine, but trust me, I've seen more Type I malfunctions caused by the shooter not seating the mag than all other malfunctions combined.

After ensuring the mag is seated, cycle the charging handle to load, just like you always do. Tapping and tugging on the mag ensures it's seated, which may be the source of the problem. Cycling the charging handle loads the chamber. If the malfunction is due to a bad round this sequence will eject the faulty round and load a fresh one. The way the charging handle "feels" when you cycle it will tell you if this action was successful or not. You cycle the charging handle and it comes all the way to the rear and then slams forward. This action feels and sounds right. You're ready to fire. If the charging handle doesn't feel right when you attempt to cycle it then it's time to go to the next step, which is described below.

Clearing malfunctions starts by using the support hand to tap and tug on the mag to ensure it's seated.

Cycle the charging handle one time, using your preferred method, to load the chamber.

Left-handed shooter cycling to load the chamber.

Type II Malfunction

The Type II malfunction is a failure to eject an empty piece of brass. It's commonly called a "stovepipe" or "smokestack," which are terms used when this occurs with a pistol and the brass is sticking up like a stovepipe. With the AR they are sticking out to the side, partway in and out of the ejection port.

Although this is a different type malfunction from the Type I, your response is going to be the same. Again, *finger off the trigger*! Next, tap and tug on the magazine to make sure it's seated and then cycle the charging handle to load. This action clears the Type I and II malfunctions. Again, you're loading the AR; it's just that the mag is already in the receiver.

There may be some times when the case sticking out of the ejection port is wedged or jammed in there, especially after cycling the bolt. When this occurs, you'll need to lock the bolt to the rear to take pressure off the round. Then work the round clear by pulling it from the outside of the receiver. Again, once it's clear make sure to cycle the bolt to ensure the chamber is clear, and then you're ready to load.

The Type II malfunction is a failure to eject an empty piece of brass.

For consistency, make sure to tap and tug on the magazine to make sure it is seated.

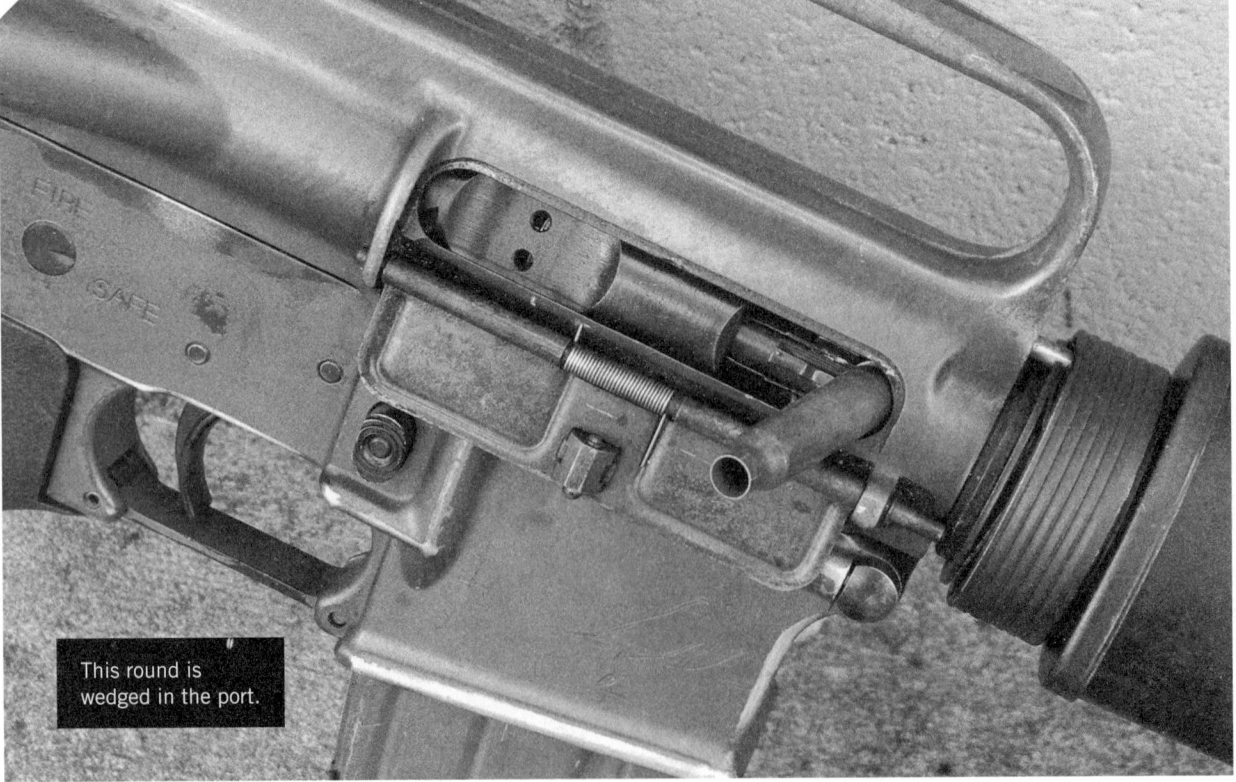

This round is wedged in the port.

116 CHAPTER 8: FUNCTIONAL MANIPULATIONS

Type III Malfunction

The third type of malfunction is what people normally call a "double feed." There can be a few different causes for this malfunction. You could have a faulty magazine that allows an extra round to slip out of the magazine and you end up with two rounds trying to occupy one chamber. The extractor or ejector and/or springs could be failing, which means the AR doesn't eject the empty case and the bolt is trying to feed a fresh round into the chamber. Sometimes it just happens, and there is no apparent reason and it doesn't occur again.

This is also where the second part of the clearing procedure will come into play. You attempt to load the AR – finger off the trigger, tap and tug on the magazine and cycle the charging handle – but you can tell by the way the charging handle feels that this action did not work, the bolt did not go into battery, so you have to unload the AR and then load.

The type problem you have will dictate what steps are required to complete the unloading process. With a Type III malfunction, or "double feed," the mag will not drop free as it normally does. The bolt is attempting to feed a round out of the magazine, but it doesn't have anywhere to go. Part of the back portion of the round, the case, will still be in the mag, which prevents the mag from falling free when you press the mag release.

Pull or strip the mag out of the receiver. Continue the unloading process as you normally do, holding the mag in your support hand and cycling

The Type III occurs when you have two objects trying to occupy one hole.

You'll have to strip the mag free, pulling it out of the receiver.

Cycle the charging handle three times, just like unloading, to clear the trash out.

the bolt three times, just like always. If cycling the charging handle clears out the trash, and you can tell this by the way it feels, then you're ready to load the AR.

You cycle the bolt three times to clear out the trash but the charging handle is telling you there are still obstructions lodged in the upper receiver. To gain access to this and clear out the stoppage you have to lock the bolt to the rear, taking the pressure off the obstructions. The support hand, still holding the mag, grasps the front of the receiver to support the rifle. For right-handed shooters this positions the left thumb to depress the bottom portion of the bolt release. Left-handed shooters are using the first finger of the right hand to engage the bolt catch. The primary hand comes off the AR's grip, and you pull the charging handle all the way to the rear and lock the bolt back.

Reacquire your grip to support the rifle and stick your support-hand fingers up inside the mag well, pushing, wiggling and shoving until you feel or see something drop free. Remember, this hand is still holding the magazine. Also be sure to keep the muzzle on target and the mag well vertical. The largest opening in the AR is the mag well, so keeping the receiver vertical allows the trash to drop out the mag well easier, using gravity to assist.

Once you feel or see something drop out of the

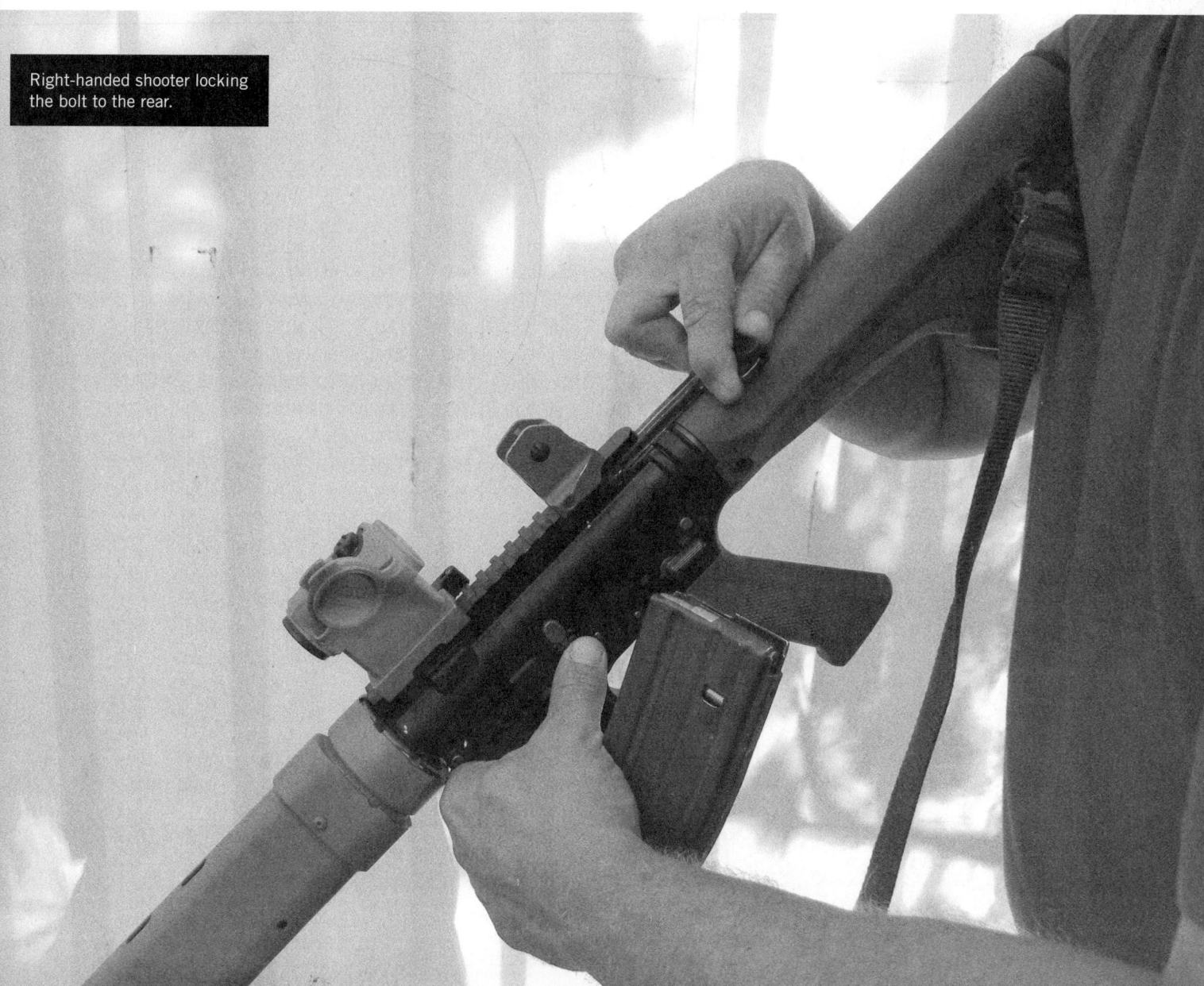

Right-handed shooter locking the bolt to the rear.

mag well, remember the AR isn't unloaded until you cycle the charging handle. There could still be a round or empty case in the chamber, and if you just immediately start to load the carbine all you'll do is create another malfunction.

After cycling the charging handle to ensure the chamber is clear you're ready to load the rifle, inserting and seating the mag and cycling the bolt manually to chamber a round. Remember, this is a functional manipulation, so you're not going to perform a press or chamber check, you're just going to have faith the AR is doing what it's supposed to. You'll be able to tell this by the way everything feels when you load.

This is why we unload the AR – an administrative action – the same way every time by removing the magazine and cycling the bolt three times. These same actions are used to clear the Type III malfunction, the only difference is that the muzzle is on target, you'll have to strip the mag free from the receiver, and you're not going to perform a press or chamber check after loading. In a situation where you have to clear a malfunction but don't have to fire again, which would tell you immediately if the AR is working or not, you might want to check the chamber, when you have the opportunity.

Left-handed shooter locking bolt to the rear.

The support hand fingers go into the magwell to dislodge the rounds wedged in there.

Once the charging handle feels "good," which means the AR is unloaded, it's time to load, using the same technique as always.

Type IV

The Type IV malfunction is a case stuck in the chamber. The cause of this could be a couple of different things. The chamber of the AR could be too tight, not honed out to the proper size. A round could be out of shape or size, causing it to stick in the chamber. The extractor or extractor spring might be failing, which means it loses it's grip on the case as the bolt moves rearward to extract, eject and feed another round.

The rifle will tell you when a Type IV malfunction occurs. Normally the charging handle will not come back at all because the extractor is locked onto the rim of the cartridge case stuck in the chamber. The AR doesn't fire. You start, as always, by making sure the mag is locked in and then cycling the charging handle. Except in this case, the charging handle will not come back. You need to unload.

The support hand removes the mag from the receiver, and then goes to the handguard to hold the carbine. To cycle the charging handle you have to get some extra momentum and force, which is achieved by slamming the rear of the stock against a hard surface. This could be the ground or any other object that is solid enough to provide the resistance needed.

For ARs with adjustable stocks there are a couple of extra steps involved. Before slamming the stock down, or back against some other object, you need to collapse the stock, moving it all the way forward. Failure to do this can cause the stock to collapse permanently, breaking parts; break or bend the extension or buffer tube, which prevents the AR from shooting; or crack/break the upper receiver where the buffer tube is threaded into it. After clearing the

To clear a case that's stuck in the chamber you'll have to get some momentum by slamming the stock while pulling the charging handle to the rear. Make sure to control the muzzle as you do this.

case from the chamber, extend the stock back out to your normal working length. With fixed stocks you don't have to worry about these extra steps.

The support hand is holding the handguard and the primary hand goes to the charging handle. Position your "snake fangs," the first two fingers of the hand, on each side of the charging handle. This helps ensure you'll pull it straight to the rear as opposed to one side or the other.

Slam or bang the back of the stock while at the same time pulling the charging handle back. If you're in a kneeling position, using the ground to slam the stock against, make sure to control the AR with the support hand, keeping the muzzle pointing in a safe direction. This action will generate enough force to pull the case out of the chamber, or it will rip the rim off the case, in which case now you have a jam which requires time and tools to correct. (When this occurs it normally requires the use of a broken case extractor to remove the case from the chamber.) Come back up to standing, get the stock back into the shoulder, cycle the charging handle to ensure the chamber is clear and load.

Type V Malfunction

Occasionally you'll see a bolt over-ride, a Type V malfunction, which is a case or live round on top of the bolt group and wedged into the receiver. The charging handle will normally come back part way, without any spring tension on it, but will come to a sudden stop before it reaches its full extension. Remove the magazine, if you haven't already. The support hand goes up the magwell so the first finger can press and hold the bolt to the rear. The primary hand goes to the charging handle. Pull the charging handle back while at the same time

The Type V malfunction is a bolt over-ride, where you end up with a round or empty case on top of the bolt.

The "bolt over-ride" is when a case or round gets wedged between the top of the bolt and the receiver.

Strip the mag out of the magwell.

CHAPTER 8: FUNCTIONAL MANIPULATIONS

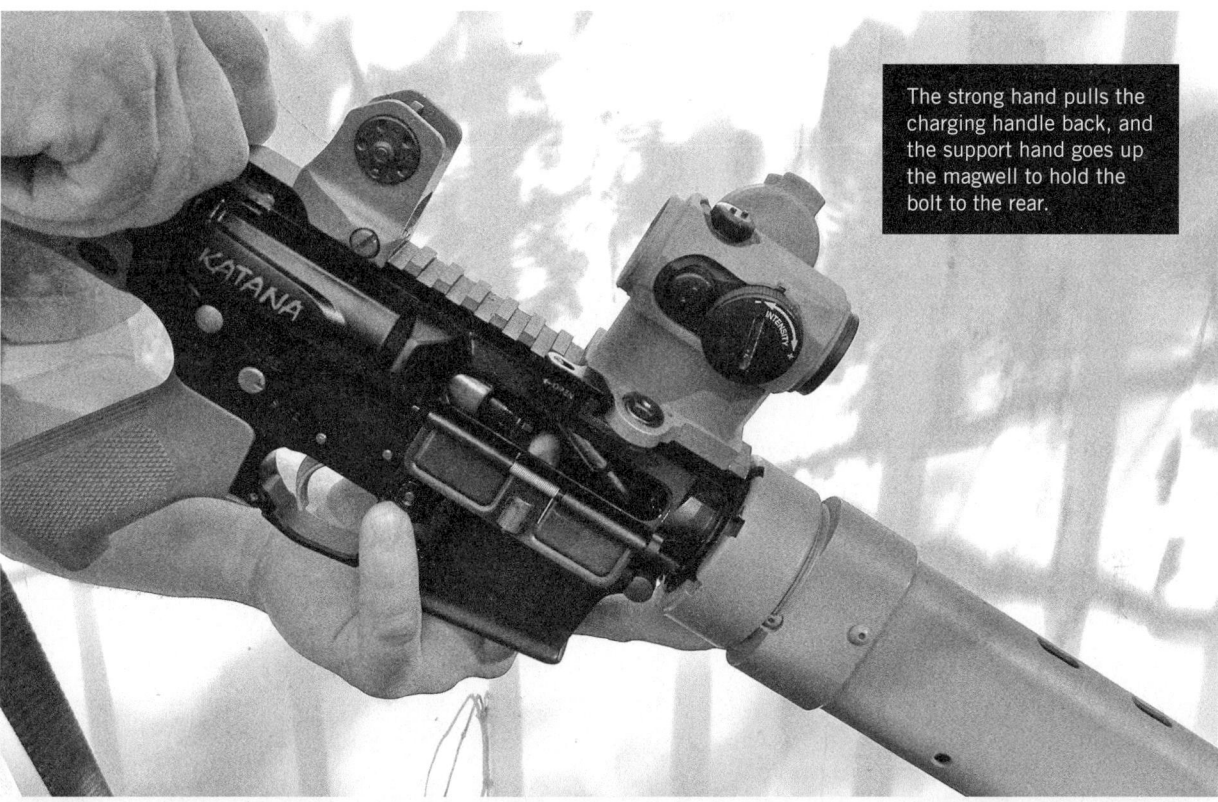

The strong hand pulls the charging handle back, and the support hand goes up the magwell to hold the bolt to the rear.

With dummy rounds you can practice malfunctions without having to go to the range.

pressing the bolt to the rear. Once the bolt is back hold it there with the finger on the support hand and work the charging handle back and forth. The charging handle will dislodge the round or brass so that it can drop out of the lower receiver through the magwell. Cycle the bolt three times to make sure the chamber is clear and load.

Safely and efficiently operating the AR is the result of consistency. For every action performed there is a correct and proper technique. Deviating from proper technique opens the door for trouble. Consistency also creates efficiency. Ultimately your goal is to be able to perform all the manipulations required at a subconscious level. The conscious mind says, "reload." The subconscious mind takes over and performs the reload. The same is true for malfunctions. This level of skill can only achieved through repetition, starting step by step and performing the same action over and over until you can perform it without needing to consciously think about the required actions.

Learning how to manipulate the AR isn't complicated, but that doesn't mean it's easy. The degree to which you need to practice these actions depends on your application. For target shooting, the ability to perform lighting fast reloads might not be necessary. The skills to reload or clear a malfunction efficiently are mandatory for armed professionals or anyone who may use the AR for self-defense. The best way to practice, getting in the repetitions necessary to learn these skills, is dry practice using dummy rounds to set up the different malfunctions. Whatever task you intend to use the AR for, you'll get more pleasure and successful results from knowing how to manipulate it properly. •

PRACTICE

With dummy ammunition you can dry practice the functional manipulations. They can also be set up on the range for live fire drills.

TYPE I MALFUNCTION

1. Load magazine with dummy rounds. (For dry practice you'll use only dummy rounds. For live-fire practice you mix in dummy rounds with live rounds.)
2. Load AR.
3. Come on target and press the trigger. When it goes "click" you know you have a malfunction.
4. Finger off the trigger.
5. Tap and tug on the mag to ensure it's seated.
6. Cycle the charging handle one time to load.

TYPE II MALFUNCTION

1. Load the AR.
2. Pull the charging handle back slightly and insert an empty case in front of the bolt.
3. Seat the charging handle.
4. Come on target and press.
5. Since the AR doesn't fire, take your finger off the trigger.
6. Tap and tug on the magazine.
7. Cycle the charging handle one time to load.
8. Fire.

TYPE III MALFUNCTION

1. Load the AR.
2. In the low ready position lock the bolt to the rear and seat the charging handle.
3. Place an empty piece of brass into the ejection port.
4. Press the bolt release.
5. Come on target and press the trigger.
6. It doesn't fire so finger off the trigger.
7. The AR doesn't fire, so you attempt to load it.
8. Loading doesn't work – you can tell from how the charging handle feels – so you unload.
9. Strip the mag and cycle the charging handle three times. If the charging handle feels right you are ready to load.
10. If the charging handle doesn't feel right you lock the bolt to the rear.
A. Fingers up the magwell to clear the trash.
B. Cycle to ensure the chamber is clear
11. Load.

TYPE IV MALFUNCTION

Setting up a Type IV is difficult to do. You can try it on the range by chambering a fired piece of brass, which may stick in the chamber. If this works you can clear it out. The problem is that if it is really stuck in there you will need to lock the bolt to the rear and then use a cleaning rod to punch it out.

TYPE V

1. Unload the AR, lock the bolt to the rear and seat the charging handle, locking it in.
2. Turn the AR upside down, and drop a dummy round or empty case into the channel of the charging handle.
3. Press the bolt release to let the bolt go forward.
4. Insert a mag.
5. Come on target and attempt to fire.
6. Finger off the trigger.
7. Tap and tug on the magazine.
8. Cycle the charging handle. It will only come back part way, and will have no spring tension on it.
9. Strip the mag and retain it.
10. Support hand finger goes up the mag well and in front of the bolt.
11. Strong hand pulls the charging handle back, and support finger holds the bolt to the rear.
12. Work the charging handle and the captured round should drop free.
13. Cycle to ensure the chamber is clear.
14. Load.

CHAPTER 9
MARKSMANSHIP

SHOOTING ACCURATELY RELIES on applying the fundamentals of marksmanship: aim, hold, press and follow through. This four-step sequence allows you to shoot accurately; when you fire a shot it's with predictable results and the hit is where you want it. In the beginning you're consciously going through these steps. Eventually, through repetition and practice, you can cycle through the sequence smoothly and efficiently. I'm not really sure how many hundreds of thousands of rounds I've fired in my life, but whenever I'm wanting to get extremely accurate shots, I go back to the fundamentals, consciously applying the fundamentals – aim, hold, press and follow through.

As always make sure you're using the proper stance, arm position and grip, starting with a good base to create stability. There are situations where you won't be able to acquire a textbook stance,

> **The speed at which you can cycle through the four fundamentals depends on the accuracy necessary for the shot you're firing.**

or you have to reposition the arms because you're bracing or resting the AR on something for stability. Any time you have to compromise in one area, you want to compensate in another area.

Keep in mind that "accuracy" is based on the situation. For example, someone shooting High Power competition has one definition of accuracy. For self-defense, accuracy has a different definition. Putting shots on a moving a threat that is 20 yards away is different from hitting a stationary target at 600 yards. The speed at which you can cycle through the four fundamentals depends on the accuracy necessary for the shot you're firing.

AIM

Aiming is the act of obtaining a sight picture. Basically this means getting the weapon on target, but it's a little more complicated than just pointing it in the right direction. This step involves the body, eyes, and of course the mind. The physical, visual and mental aspects are combined in order to shoot accurately.

The firing process starts by assuming the proper stance, as discussed earlier. I recommend starting in low ready position, facing the target with the stock in the pocket of your shoulder. Think about the stance along these lines: The body actually aims the carbine, and then we use the sights to confirm that it's right on target. With the proper stance all you need to do is bring the carbine into firing position and the sights should be very close, with little adjustment required to align the sights to the target.

Once you decide it's time to shoot, look at the target, focusing on the exact point you want the bullet to go. With the eyes focused on this point bring the weapon up so the sights intersect your line of vision. The key is to bring the sights up to your eyes, which we have a natural tendency to do, as opposed to bringing the rifle up and the head and eyes down. Raising the sights up to the eyes, while the head remains stationary, is also more efficient, consuming less time. This is much more efficient than looking at the whole target, bringing the weapon up and lowering the head down to find the sights and then having to align all that onto the target by changing your body's position. (Remember as you bring the muzzle up you disengage the safety, flipping it down to the "Fire" position.) Now we have a sight picture – the alignment of the weapon's sights between our eyes and the point on the target you want to hit.

Once the sights are on target and the safety is off, your finger goes to the trigger. This doesn't mean it's time to press the trigger yet, but the finger is in position and ready to start pressing when you decide it's time to fire the shot.

HOLD

Now you have a sight picture – Step 1, Aim – and it's time to go to Step 2, Hold. How steady do you need to hold the position? That depends on how much accuracy you need. For a close, large target, you don't have to be rock steady. For surgical accuracy, or a shot on a small target or at extended distances, you need to hold as steady as possible. One thing you need to accept is that you will never be able to hold perfectly steady. The sights will always be moving because the carbine is attached to your body at four points – the stock is in the shoulder, your cheek is on the stock, and both hands and arms are holding the carbine. Your body is always moving, even if it's just your heartbeat. This movement transfers to the rifle, which is going to move the sights. Hold as steady as you can.

Having a good, steady position is only one aspect of holding. Holding also includes controlling your breathing. As you breathe the body moves, and this movement transfers to the carbine. For surgical accuracy you need to control your breathing. This is especially important in the beginning, and you'll have to consciously think about breath control.

Under ideal conditions you want to fire the shot with your lungs empty. Empty lungs are always more consistent than trying to judge when they are half full, plus the body's position will vary according to how much physical stress you're under or how hard you're breathing. For example, half-full lungs while you're relaxed is going to be different from half full when you're under a lot of physical stress. Under some circumstances you may not be able to control your breathing to this extent. When the shot has to be fired immediately, you simply stop breathing, regardless of whether you are inhaling or exhaling, to press the shot off.

There is about a three-second window for the shot to be fired. You've exhaled, the lungs are empty, but after about three seconds things start to occur that will make it more difficult to fire an accurate shot. The first thing that happens is that the eyes start to twitch. You won't notice this immediately because the brain compensates for this, but the longer you try to hold it steady the worse it's going to get. After three seconds if the shot hasn't been fired then inhale, exhale, and start the process over again.

Holding also involves a visual aspect. With iron sights, your focus should be on the front sight. The way our eyes are designed, we can't focus on the target, the front sight and the rear sight. We focus on the middle of those three, the front sight. The target will be blurry, but you can still tell if the front sight is holding steady on target. The rear sight will be blurry, but this is the way the peep sight is designed to work. Initially your visual focus is on the target, but once you have a sight picture you shift the focus to the front sight.

The degree to which you focus on the front sight is determined by the accuracy needed. For a large target at close distance, a flash sight picture, a quick confirmation the front sight is on the area the shots need to go, will suffice. As the distance increases or target size decreases, you have to focus more intently on the front sight.

With red-dot sights or a traditional optic, your visual focus remains on target and you place the dot or reticle where it needs to be. Do not focus on the dot or crosshairs. This will lead to you "chasing the dot." You're trying to hold the dot exactly where you want it, except the dot will always be moving due to the body. Focus on the target and put the dot or crosshairs on the target.

PRESS

You have a sight picture and a steady hold. Now it's time to press the trigger. Of all the fundamentals, this is the most important one. You have to smoothly press the trigger, letting the weapon fire without anticipating the shot. Otherwise you'll end up tensing the muscles in an attempt to control the recoil. The sights are moving around on the target, but you can't jerk or slap the trigger in an attempt to time the shot with the movement of the sights. Let the sights move, smoothly press the trigger and you'll be rewarded with a good hit. Your job is to point the weapon in the right direction using the sights, hold it steady and then press the trigger, allowing the internal components of the weapon to do their work and fire the round when it's time. Jeff Cooper called this a "surprise break," in other words, the shot fires without any anticipation on your part. Trying to make the weapon fire when you're ready, thinking "now" and slapping or jerking the trigger, usually results in recoil anticipation, which is going to affect accuracy.

Where you position the finger on the trigger is also important. Ideally you want to position the finger so the trigger is in the center of the first pad of the finger. This is where most of the nerve endings are and it allows you to "feel" the trigger. This also positions the finger so you're pressing the trigger straight to the rear. With too much finger on the trigger, or not enough finger on it, you'll push or pull the trigger to one side or the other as you press it. What you want to do is press the trigger straight to the rear.

In the beginning I have shooters actually saying "pressssss" out loud, dragging the 's' out like a snake hissing. As they verbalize "presssss" they are physically applying pressure to the trigger. The shot fires without any anticipation. Eventually you're saying "presssss" in your mind, and at some point this action becomes a subconscious process. Learning how to press the trigger is a life-long study. You never master it, but with practice you'll steadily improve. In the beginning, start out slowly and methodically.

There are a variety of ways to learn how to achieve a smooth trigger press. In the beginning you have to consciously think about the press. If you're not thinking about pressing smoothly it won't happen. One technique to achieve a smooth press is to verbalize the word "press," as described above. At some point the shot is released. You can use a count method, starting at 1, slowly going through 2, 3, 4, … steadily increasing the pressure as you count up. Another technique is to see just how much pressure you can apply to the trigger without making the weapon fire. At some point the pressure will override the trigger and fire the shot. For some people imagining they are slowly pressing the bullet out of the barrel while holding the sights steady works well. We all have a different method or technique that works. Discover what works for you.

The time it takes for you to press the trigger depends on the accuracy needed. For close large tar-

> **Your job is to point the weapon in the right direction using the sights, hold it steady and then press the trigger, allowing the internal components of the weapon to do their work and fire the round when it's time.**

gets the press can occur in a short span of time. As the distance increases or the target size decreases you must be more deliberate on the trigger. The key is that it's always a smooth pressure, starting with zero pressure and steadily increasing the pressure until the weapon fires.

You have a good sight picture, hold it steady, and smoothly press the trigger and the carbine fires. Now it's time to follow through, the final step in the fundamentals.

FOLLOW THROUGH

The final step in the fundamentals is follow-through — recovering from the recoil, reacquiring the sights on the target and resetting the trigger.

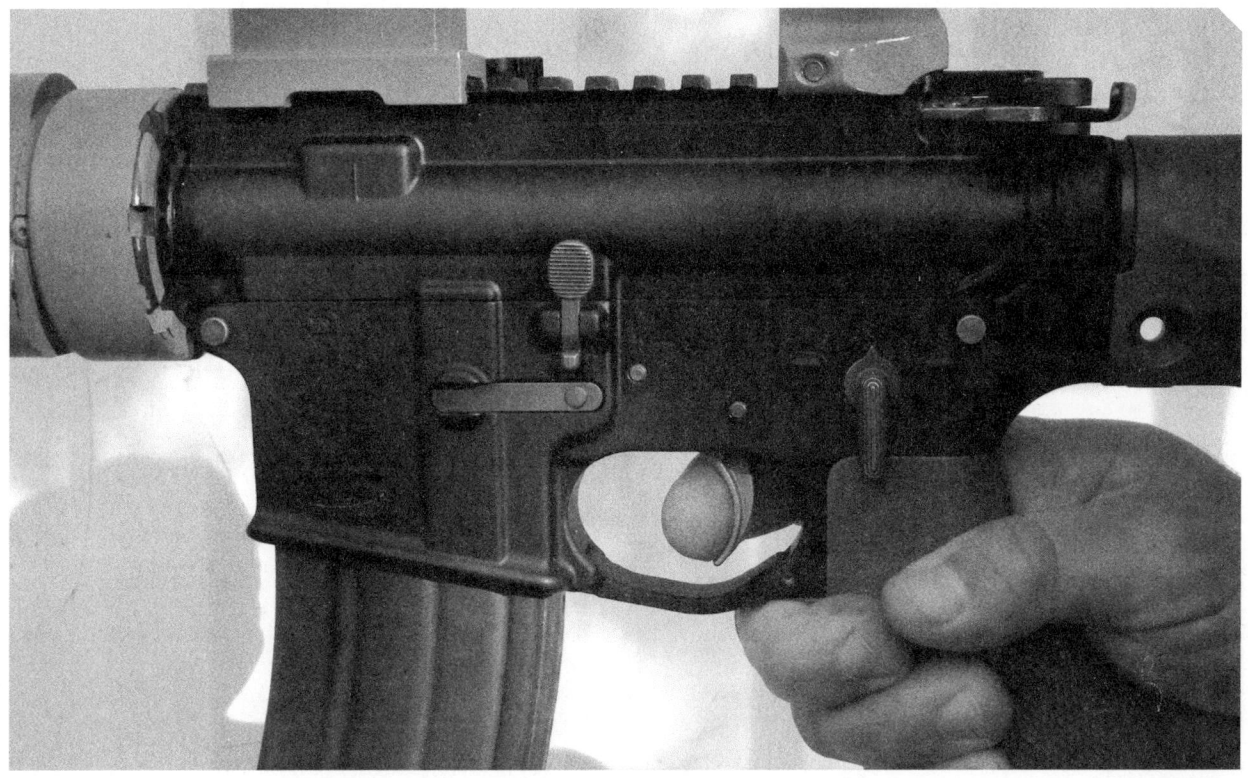

Follow-through prepares you to fire another shot, which may be necessary for hunting or self-defense. Follow-through is also a critical component to accuracy, for situations where you're shooting as accurately as possible.

This step begins by recovering from the recoil. We control the recoil as much as possible by using the proper stance, but we concentrate more on recovering from the recoil efficiently as opposed to trying to control it. When you attempt to control the recoil you tense up the muscles, which always happens before the shot occurs. The proper stance and mount allows the body to absorb the recoil and assists in recovering from it efficiently.

While pressing the trigger, your visual focus is on the front site, or with a red-dot on the target. Once the shot fires keep your eyes on the same focal point. Ideally, with iron sights you're watching the front sight travel up and back down onto target. Make sure to fight the urge to shift your focus to the target to see where you hit. This will cost you time, and without the proper follow-through you'll see accuracy degrade. When using a dot your focus is on the target and the dot drops back onto the target. One reason dots are so easy to operate is that you don't have to program the eyes to shift their focus from the target to a front sight. Regardless of the type sights you're using, acquiring another sight picture after the shot fires is essential for making additional shots without delay, often required in a confrontation, and again this is a critical part of accuracy.

The final component of the follow-through is resetting the trigger. To reset the trigger, you fire the shot then release the trigger forward only far enough so the internals reset and the AR is ready to fire again if needed. You want your finger to maintain contact with the trigger, as opposed to coming off the trigger. If the finger comes off the trigger and you need to shoot again, you'll probably rush to get back on the trigger, increasing the chances of slapping or jerking it. The speed at which you press the trigger is dictated by the accuracy required. The same thing applies to a certain degree when resetting the trigger. When surgical accuracy is called for, you want to press smoothly to fire the shot, completely recover from the recoil, and then reset the trigger. This makes sure the shot has cleared the barrel before you start changing anything in your grip or stance.

In a lethal confrontation we know it's likely multiple shots will be required to stop the threat. The proper follow-through allows you to place multiple hits accurately on the threat in the least amount of time possible. The more accuracy required, the more important follow-through becomes; for precision/surgical shooting, follow-through is a key element to success.

At this point, you're asking yourself, "Do I need to shoot again?" If yes, then you're ready to repeat the process to place another accurate hit on target. If the response is no, then you come off the trigger, off the target, engage the safety and start scanning to check your environment.

You can never practice the fundamentals of marksmanship too much. You need to improve your skills, but at the same time you're learning what you can hit, and just as importantly, the shots that you can't make. Ideally, when you press the trigger it should be with predictable results. You know it's going to be a hit. Otherwise you shouldn't be pressing the trigger. •

DRILLS

The best way to practice your marksmanship is by firing one shot at a time. The first three steps, aim, hold and press can be practiced dry. (You'll have to cycle the action after pressing the trigger to reset the internals, then safety on and start the process over again.) The only way to practice the fourth step, follow-through, is with live fire.

Even if you're firing a five-round group, you want to think about it as one shot at a time, repeated five times. Each shot is a separate action. You fire the shot, applying the follow-through. You relax, inhale and exhale and start the process over again. This can be done from bench or supported position or using the fighting stance.

1. From ready position come onto target and fire one accurate round. As you come up, disengage the safety and once you're on target place your finger on the trigger.
2. Hold steady and press the trigger to fire.
3. Follow through as though you were going to fire another shot.
4. Finger off the trigger, come off the target into your ready position and engage the safety.
5. Close the dust cover.
6. Scan.

This drill can be performed dry or live fire and in variations such as different positions or number of shots fired.

The only way to learn the fundamentals is to practice them, over and over again. It's a never-ending process, and you're always striving for improvement.

CHAPTER 10

TACTICAL USE OF YOUR EYES

USING ANY FIREARM, especially for self-defense, relies heavily on your vision. Most of these visual skills don't come naturally, and will need to be understood, practiced and developed just like all your other skills.

USE OF EYES IN AIMING

A question that often pops up when shooting the AR is whether you should shoot with both eyes open or close one eye. There is no set standard answer to this question, and it will vary from one shooter to another. Or, it can vary according to what type sights are being used and/or how much accuracy is required.

Most people have a "dominant" or "strong" hand. The same thing is true for the feet and legs. A right-leg dominant person usually steps with that leg when they start moving, regardless of the direction of movement. The dominance principle applies to your eyes as well. Normally you'll have one eye that is stronger or more dominant than the other. Some people don't have a dominant eye. And, it's not uncommon to have a right-handed shooter who is left-eye dominant, this is referred to as cross-dominance.

An easy technique to determine which eye is dominant is to point at an object with your hand at eye level and both eyes open. Close one eye. If the object you're pointing at is still lined up with your finger, the open eye is dominant. When you close an eye and the object seems to shift, and the finger isn't on "target" any longer, the open eye is your non-dominant eye. Whichever eye keeps the finger on "target" is the dominant eye.

A right-handed shooter whose right eye is dominant is good to go. The same is true for a left-handed shooter who is left-eye dominant. The real problem is when you have a cross-dominant situation, as with a right-handed shooter who is left-eye dominant.

We'll discuss several options, and then your task is to hit the range, work with the various techniques until you discover what works for you. It's not uncommon to find that you'll have to vary techniques depending on what type sights you're working with and/or how much accuracy you need.

Partially closing one eye, squinting your "strong" eye, can help make the "weak" eye take over. The other option is to shoot using the side of the body that the dominant eye is on. For example, if you're left-eye dominant, fire from the left side. But, unless you grew up doing this, it can be difficult. For most people a red-dot type sight solves this problem. With dots your focus is on the target, as opposed to the front iron sight, and you have both eyes open. It usually doesn't matter which eye is stronger, focus on the target and you'll be able to see the dot with both eyes open.

Shooting with both eyes open provides a wide field of view and good depth perception. If necessary, squint one eye slightly, shifting dominance to the other eye. Some cross-dominant people shoot pistols with their strong hand and long guns on the side of their strong eye. Ultimately, remember accuracy is about hitting the target. Each individual "sees" differently. Learn what you can get away with for close, large targets. Find out what you need to do as the distance increases or the size of the target decreases. The only way to find out how you need to shoot is to experiment, discovering what's necessary for you as an individual to ensure when you press the trigger the shot goes where you want it. Once you discover what works, practice is the path to success.

SCANNING YOUR SURROUNDINGS

We also need to talk about what to do with your eyes when you're not shooting. Scanning, looking around your environment to see what's going on around you, is a habit you need to develop. It sounds like common sense, but today most people don't have a clue about what's going on around them. For self-defense situations it's mandatory. You have to be scanning in order to spot something that's out of place and might indicate possible trouble. That way you can start planning your response before the threat attacks. After the confrontation – the threat is down or gone – you need to be scanning the environment. If we're not looking around we'll miss something important. Important in this sense could be the difference between life and death.

For purposes of this discussion we'll define "scanning" as looking around your environment, as opposed to a close examination. Being visually-oriented creatures, the majority of what we gather comes through the eyes. This is especially true under stress, when almost everyone experiences auditory exclusion; your hearing shuts down and you start relying almost totally on the eyes to determine what's going on around you. What are you looking for or trying to find? Here is a list of things to watch for, just keep in mind the details will differ according to who you are, what you do and the particulars of the situation.

There is likely to be more than one potential threat. This doesn't mean you'll need to shoot several people. You may not even have to fire your weapon. But if there are other possible threats, you need to locate them and determine what response

> **Most people don't have a clue about what's going on around them.**

from you, if any, is necessary. The act of scanning and the body language that goes with it also "tell" other possible threats you're still mentally plugged in and ready to fight if necessary. This alone may be enough to change their mind about what they were going to do (the psychological stop).

This doesn't mean you can ignore the threat that's down or gone. A downed threat may come back into the fight, attempting to fire on you from the ground. The threat that ran away around a corner may decide to come back, trying to sneak attack and catch you off guard. You need to be scanning, keeping your AR in the direction of the last known threat, and at the same time visually checking other directions.

You scan to find your family or friends. Where are they and what do you need them to do? The same applies for locating armed partners with whom you may be working. Scan to locate cover to get behind. Just because the threat is down or gone doesn't mean the fight is over. Glance around to find an exit for escape or in order to get to a safer location. For armed citizens, look to see if law enforcement officers are arriving so you can comply with their commands. Remember, at that point they don't know or care who the good guys are.

It's also not a bad idea to visually or physically check your weapon's condition. If the bolt is locked to the rear or there's an empty piece of brass sticking out of the ejection port, you need to apply the proper response to get it operational again.

A big reason to scan is to break out of the "tunnel vision" that most people experience under stress – your field of view narrows down to roughly 15 degrees to focus on the source of danger. (The level to which you experience this depends on how stressful the event is, and will vary according to the individual and their experience.) After the immediate danger is over you need to open up your field of vision. Taking your eyes off the old danger and shifting your visual focus to something farther away opens up your field of view. Your peripheral vision is working again. This allows you to look in one direction yet you can still monitor the downed threat or the corner they disappeared around in your peripheral vision in case they get back into the fight or come back around the corner.

When and where you need to scan depends on the specifics of the situation. Not every situation will call for you to scan, but it's easier to choose not to do something as opposed to trying to remember to apply a skill or technique that you haven't practiced.

You should be scanning all the time, paying attention to your environment and the people around you in order to spot possible danger in advance. You need to be scanning after the threat is down or gone, while still watching the last know threat or keeping an eye on where you last saw them. Like all other skills this takes practice and repetition, but with the proper thought process behind it. When practicing you have to make the mental connections between what you're doing on the range, plugging into how these skills apply in "real" life. Otherwise they just become motions that you perform on the range, without any real meaning attached to them. Making the mental connections during practice is necessary for your practice to be productive.

Scanning, which basically means just looking around you, should become a habit. Today most people are involved in other things and don't ever look around to see what's going on around them. This is why people will say, "He came out of nowhere." No, the threat didn't just magically appear. You just weren't paying attention. There are almost always cues prior to an attack. The best way to defeat the threat is to deny them the opportunity to attack in the first place, but in order to do this you have to be aware.

You're in the low ready position, muzzle down, finger off the trigger and safety on. Keep the muzzle pointing in the same safe direction and twist your head around so you can look to see what's surrounding you.

After a defensive encounter this is critical. The threat is down or gone. From the low ready position you start scanning. You're looking for additional threats. We know that in slightly over 50 percent of violent confrontations there is more than one threat, and they won't all be lined up in a row in front of you. Not only do we need to keep a watch on someone that we have reason to believe may be a source of trouble, but also for any partners that may be involved. During classes we constantly stress the need for maintaining visual contact with your environment, scanning with your eyes to see what the people around you are doing.

The best way to defeat the threat is to deny them the opportunity to attack in the first place, but in order to do this you have to be aware.

The visual aspects of using the AR, or any other weapon, for self-defense are incredibly important. As with all your skills, if you don't practice using the eyes then you won't be ready for a stressful event. Knowing what the eyes need to do when firing allows you to get accurate hits. Maintaining visual contact with your environment allows you to:
- **Spot potential trouble before it develops.**
- **Find your family, friends or partners.**
- **Spot other threats.**
- **Find cover or an exit.**
- **Break out of the tunnel vision we experience under stress.**

We know how to do all these things, but it takes practice for them to become habit.

EYES CLOSED DRILLS

Your ultimate goal with the AR is to get to a point where your carbine feels like an extension of your body. You know without looking where all the controls are, how to manipulate it properly, what it feels like when something goes wrong. To acquire this level of familiarity requires a lot of repetitions. Once you get the idea of how everything works, you want to learn how it feels. The best way to do this is by working on drills with your eyes closed. Taking away the visual input forces you to rely on your sense of feel, or your tactile sense.

These drills are performed only under proper and safe conditions. There must be a coach to watch the shooter. This is only something that you will do after becoming thoroughly familiar with your carbine and its operation.

From a close distance, say four yards and with an empty weapon, face your target in the low ready position. Close your eyes and bring the carbine up on target, just as if you were going to fire a shot, safety off and finger on the trigger. Open your eyes and see where the sights are aiming. If they are off, change your stance, and repeat. Eventually you get to where you know what it feels like to be on target.

For dry practice you can use two empty magazines to practice empty reloads. (Since we're using the bolt catch to release the bolt, overriding the follower in the mag, we can practice empty reloads without having to use dummy ammunition.) Put an empty mag in the receiver and cycle the charging handle to lock the bolt to the rear. Seat the charging handle, locking it in place. Come onto your "target." Close your eyes and perform an empty reload. Running the empty reload with your eyes closed teaches you to operate the AR without needing to see it, and your efficiency will improve as well. The same technique can be used with dummy ammunition and malfunctions.

On the range, again under controlled conditions, you can work on live fire with your eyes closed. You're working at a close distance, four or five yards. Come up on target with everything ready to fire a shot. Close your eyes, press off the shot, follow through and then open your eyes. The first thing you're looking for is where the sights are. With a good stance the sights should be very close to the center of your target. If not, this tells you that you probably need to adjust your stance. This drill also really forces you to pay attention to pressing and resetting the trigger. Again, once you take the visual input away you're relying on what you feel. Manipulation of the trigger, pressing and resetting it, is all based on your sense of feel. There are a lot of times when students don't understand what they should be feeling until after firing shots with their eyes closed.

Proprioception is the term for our body's ability to know where all of it's parts are in relationship to each other. This is what we want to create with the AR. We know where all the parts are, how they work, and how to use them together efficiently. •

CHAPTER 11
FIRST SHOTS

IF YOU ARE new to the AR I highly recommend plenty of dry practice before ever firing a shot. It's important to get a good idea of how the AR works before going to the range.

In the beginning don't worry about zeroing the AR or adjusting the sights for a precise alignment for you and the carbine. (See the Zero section for details when you're ready for that step.) Start with a close large target, such as 25 yards or even closer. Your shots may not go into the center of the target until it's zeroed. What you're looking for is a tight group size, all the shots in the same area. Then, later, you can adjust the sights to move that group so the bullets are impacting on the center of the target.

DRY PRACTICE AND ESTABLISHING YOUR NATURAL POINT OF AIM

Start by confirming the AR is empty and clear. Make sure you're in the proper stance, and run a mental checklist from the feet up through the body and out the muzzle to confirm that everything is correct.

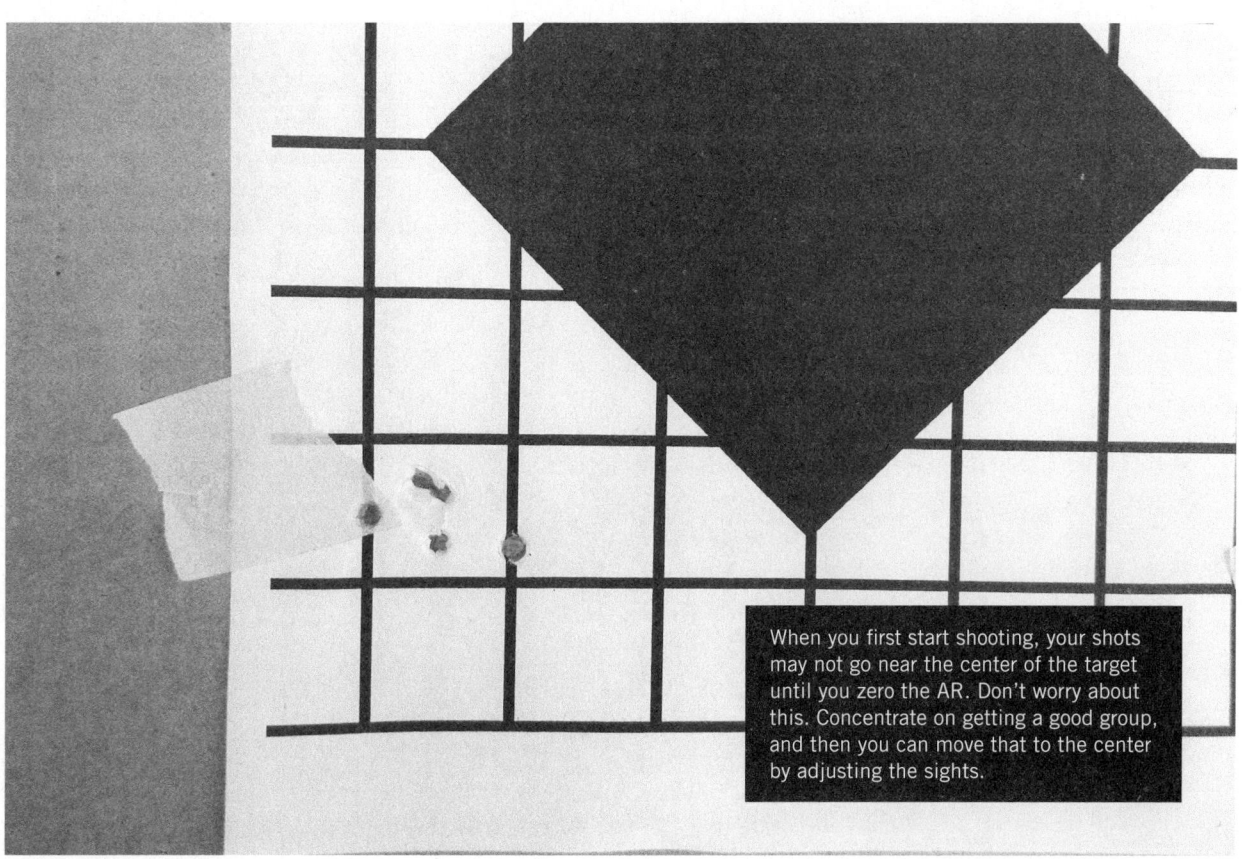

When you first start shooting, your shots may not go near the center of the target until you zero the AR. Don't worry about this. Concentrate on getting a good group, and then you can move that to the center by adjusting the sights.

Once you have everything squared away, come up from the low ready and on target. As you come on target the safety is disengaged, and once you're on target your finger goes to the trigger. At this point, if you have a good base or platform you should have a sight picture, the alignment of the sights between your eyes and the target.

Hold this position, close your eyes, and inhale/exhale about three times. Open your eyes, and see where the sights are aiming. If the sight picture has drifted left or right, then you need to adjust your stance by repositioning the feet so the sights are back on target. Everything from the feet up should remain the same. (Don't worry about the elevation, or up and down. The focus here is on the lateral positioning, left and right.) Repeat the process. Once you have a good stance the sights should be on target when you open your eyes. You are establishing your natural point of aim, which means your body is in a relaxed, consistent position, relying on bone support as much as possible as opposed to muscle tension. (The same technique applies to all other firing positions.) Eventually you'll be able to acquire a good point of aim without having to go through this process, but in the beginning it's important to take your time and get a good position before ever firing a shot.

LIVE FIRE

For your first shots, start at a close distance of about 15 yards or so. After establishing your stance, keep everything in the same position, and from the low ready load the AR. Remember to use the proper technique, and focus on loading, as opposed to thinking about shooting while you're trying to

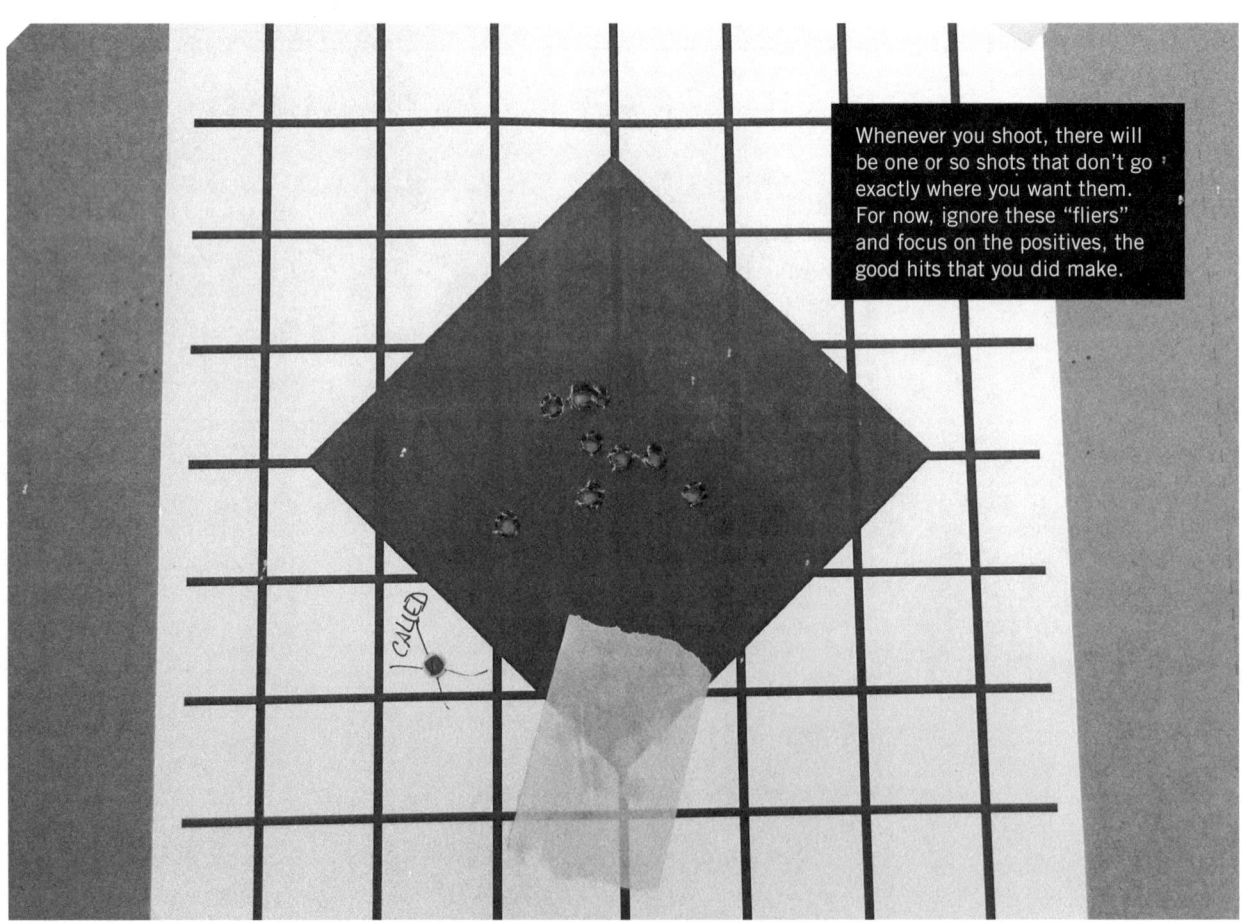

Whenever you shoot, there will be one or so shots that don't go exactly where you want them. For now, ignore these "fliers" and focus on the positives, the good hits that you did make.

load. Think about one thing at a time.

From the low ready, come up, disengaging the safety as the muzzle rises. Once you're on target place your finger on the trigger. Perform any adjustments that may be necessary to fine-tune your sight picture. Focus on the front sight, or with a red-dot your focus in on the target, and smoothly start applying pressure to the trigger. Eventually the AR decides it's time to fire.

Follow through, which means recover from the recoil, reacquiring a sight picture and resetting the trigger. "Do I need to shoot again," you ask yourself. The answer is no, you're only firing one round. Come off the trigger, off the target, into the low ready position, and engage the safety. Now, finally, you can look to see where the round hit. But, don't worry about where the hit is. I know this sounds confusing. The purpose of shooting is to hit the target, right? Actually, right now the main point is to focus on the fundamentals and make sure to follow through completely, as opposed to immediately coming off the trigger and target to locate where the shot went. You've got to establish good habits from the beginning. Plus, remember you haven't zeroed the AR yet, so the hit may not be exactly where you're aiming on the target.

Repeat the process, performing the same sequence and firing another shot. Do it again, consciously thinking about each step, one step at a time. Eventually you start to see a group forming. All the shots are clustering in one location on the target.

When you're working on these fundamentals you may have a round or two that isn't grouped with the others. For right now ignore these. I know, they stick out and cry out for attention. If you start thinking about what went wrong you're not thinking about what to do right. As long as you're shooting you're always going to have a "flyer" here and there. Ignore the fliers, focus on the group you've shot and think about what you did right for all of those instead of thinking about the anomalies. It's all about reinforcing the positives and creating confidence in your abilities.

Once you've got the hang of firing one shot at a time, start working on firing two-shot groups. After that's looking good work on shooting three-round groups. Although you're firing multiple-round groups, think about each shot as a separate entity all it's own. Slow down, make one good shot, and then repeat as needed. Regardless of how many rounds you fire, after the last one always follow through, preparing to fire another shot. Ask yourself if you need to shoot again, and then you're off the trigger, off the target and safety on.

Once you're getting good groups, then you can start adjusting the sights to zero the AR, and working from extended distances and/or with smaller targets. Don't worry about shooting or firing fast, especially in the beginning. Concentrate on applying the fundamentals and making good hits. •

CHAPTER 12
ZEROING THE AR

"ZEROING" THE AR means adjusting the sights so your point of impact – where the bullet strikes the target – is the same as your point of aim – where you are holding the sights. There is a variety of methods or formulas for zeroing the AR. Instead of trying to use different size targets at various distances and flipping back and forth between one aperture and the other on the rear sight – as required by some methods – I prefer to use the simple technique described below. In my opinion, to get a "hard" zero with the AR you have to actually shoot it at the distance you've chosen for your zero, rather than simulate distance by using smaller targets.

Once you've zeroed the AR, it's time to fire it various distances to discover what the difference will be between your point of aim (POA) and the point of impact (POI). This will vary according to barrel length and twist rate, and the type ammo, such as bullet weight and the design or shape of the round. Changing ammo, switching between one type ammo and another – even when they are the same weight or design but different brands – will usually change the trajectory of the round, sometimes dramatically.

When it comes to choosing the distance for your zero there are several factors to consider. First is the offset between the sights and the barrel; the sights are higher than the barrel. This offset comes into play especially at close distances, where the POI will be lower than the POA. You have to aim or hold high for your round to hit where you need it to go. You also have to consider the trajectory of the round. For example, with a 55-grain bullet firing with a one hundred yard zero the POI will be approximately two inches low at 200 yards.

Before beginning the zero process you need to pick the distance for your zero. I use a 100-yard zero. The sights are adjusted so that at 100 yards the bullet strikes the exact point the sights are holding. A 75-yard zero gives you the least deviation between your POA and POI between 25 and 100 yards. At 25 yards the POI will be roughly one and one half inches lower than your POA. The POI at 100 yards will be and one half inches higher than your POA, which will give you a POI of about an inch or so low at 200 yards.

For zeroing it's important to use the ammunition that you anticipate shooting when using your AR. If you're trying to zero using different types of ammo, it's going to be a frustrating process because each one will have a different POI.

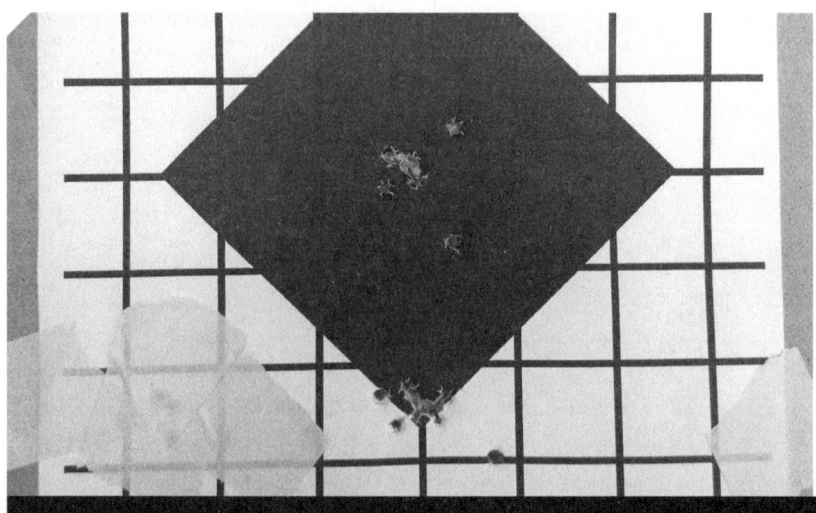
These groups were fired from 15 yards, with a 100-yard zero. The low shots were fired aiming at the center of the diamond. This shows how low your offset is. The group of shots in the center were fired aiming at the top of the diamond.

POINT OF AIM VS. POINT OF IMPACT

	RANGE			
	25	50	75	100
25 ZERO	0	2 ½" H	4 ½" H	5 ½" H
50 ZERO	1" L	0	1 ½" H	2" H
75 ZERO	1 ½" L	¼" L	0	1 ½" H
100 ZERO	2 ½" L	1" L	½" L	0

At distances less than 25 yds, regardless of zero the point of impact will be approx. 2.5" low

Actual figures will vary according to barrel length, twist rate and bullet weight and design.

ABOVE: Different ammo will change your point of impact according to the weight of the bullet and its velocity. Plus, your barrel length and twist will affect accuracy. BELOW: This chart gives you a rough idea of what the difference will be between point of aim and point of impact according to te distance at which the AR is zeroed.

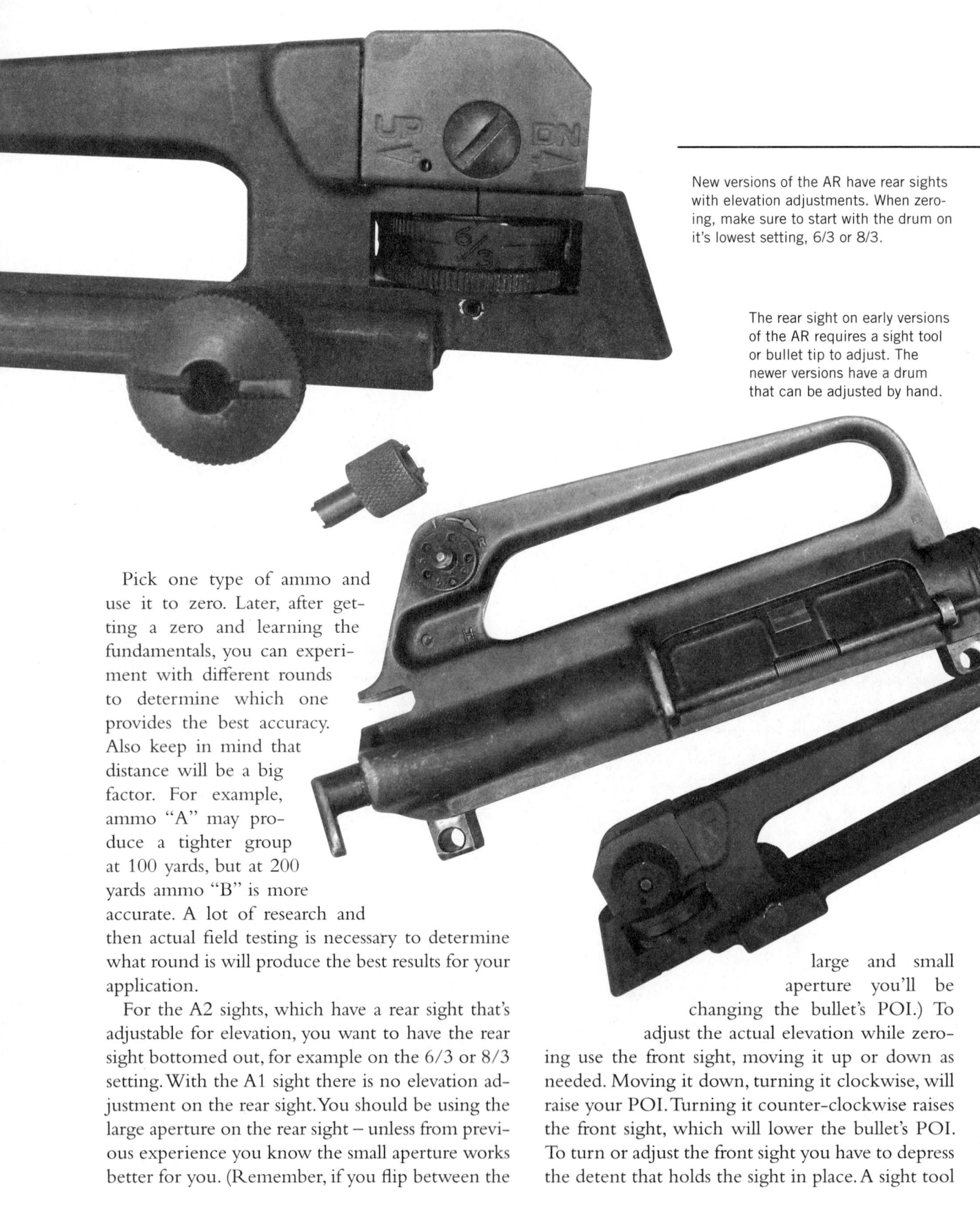

New versions of the AR have rear sights with elevation adjustments. When zeroing, make sure to start with the drum on it's lowest setting, 6/3 or 8/3.

The rear sight on early versions of the AR requires a sight tool or bullet tip to adjust. The newer versions have a drum that can be adjusted by hand.

Pick one type of ammo and use it to zero. Later, after getting a zero and learning the fundamentals, you can experiment with different rounds to determine which one provides the best accuracy. Also keep in mind that distance will be a big factor. For example, ammo "A" may produce a tighter group at 100 yards, but at 200 yards ammo "B" is more accurate. A lot of research and then actual field testing is necessary to determine what round is will produce the best results for your application.

For the A2 sights, which have a rear sight that's adjustable for elevation, you want to have the rear sight bottomed out, for example on the 6/3 or 8/3 setting. With the A1 sight there is no elevation adjustment on the rear sight. You should be using the large aperture on the rear sight – unless from previous experience you know the small aperture works better for you. (Remember, if you flip between the large and small aperture you'll be changing the bullet's POI.) To adjust the actual elevation while zeroing use the front sight, moving it up or down as needed. Moving it down, turning it clockwise, will raise your POI. Turning it counter-clockwise raises the front sight, which will lower the bullet's POI. To turn or adjust the front sight you have to depress the detent that holds the sight in place. A sight tool

When zeroing, work in the most stabile position you can, using rests or support to create stability.

will make adjustments easy, or you can use the tip of a bullet. The front sight will have either four or five slots for the detent; the sight tool must have the same number of prongs to match the front sight.

Windage, moving the bullet right or left, is adjusted with the rear sight. The A1 rear sight requires the use of a sight tool or the tip of a bullet for adjustment. The A2 rear sight has a drum that you turn with your fingers; no tool required.

Take your time during the zeroing process. This isn't something you can do quickly. For the best results, work from a bench, with rests or bags for support. Make sure the handguard is supported, as opposed to the actual barrel touching or resting on the bags. If the barrel is making contact with your rest, it will throw the shots off. For example, when the bottom of the barrel is touching the rest it will throw the shots high. Your goal is to create a solid, stable position – consistency – and apply the fundamentals of marksmanship for every shot.

Start the zeroing process at 25 yards. Make sure you have a steady position, using a rest in order to take out as much of the human element as possible. Normally I'll fire five or six shots, enough to satisfy myself that I've got a good group established. By firing several rounds, even if you have one or two shots that weren't good, you're still going to have a solid group to work with.

After establishing a good group you're ready to adjust the sights, but first unload the AR. Do not get into the habit of adjusting or doing any work on your firearm while it's loaded. Unload, check and check again to confirm it's clear, and then remember the safety rules are still in effect. After making adjustments you load and start again. The additional benefit of all this is that you're getting in

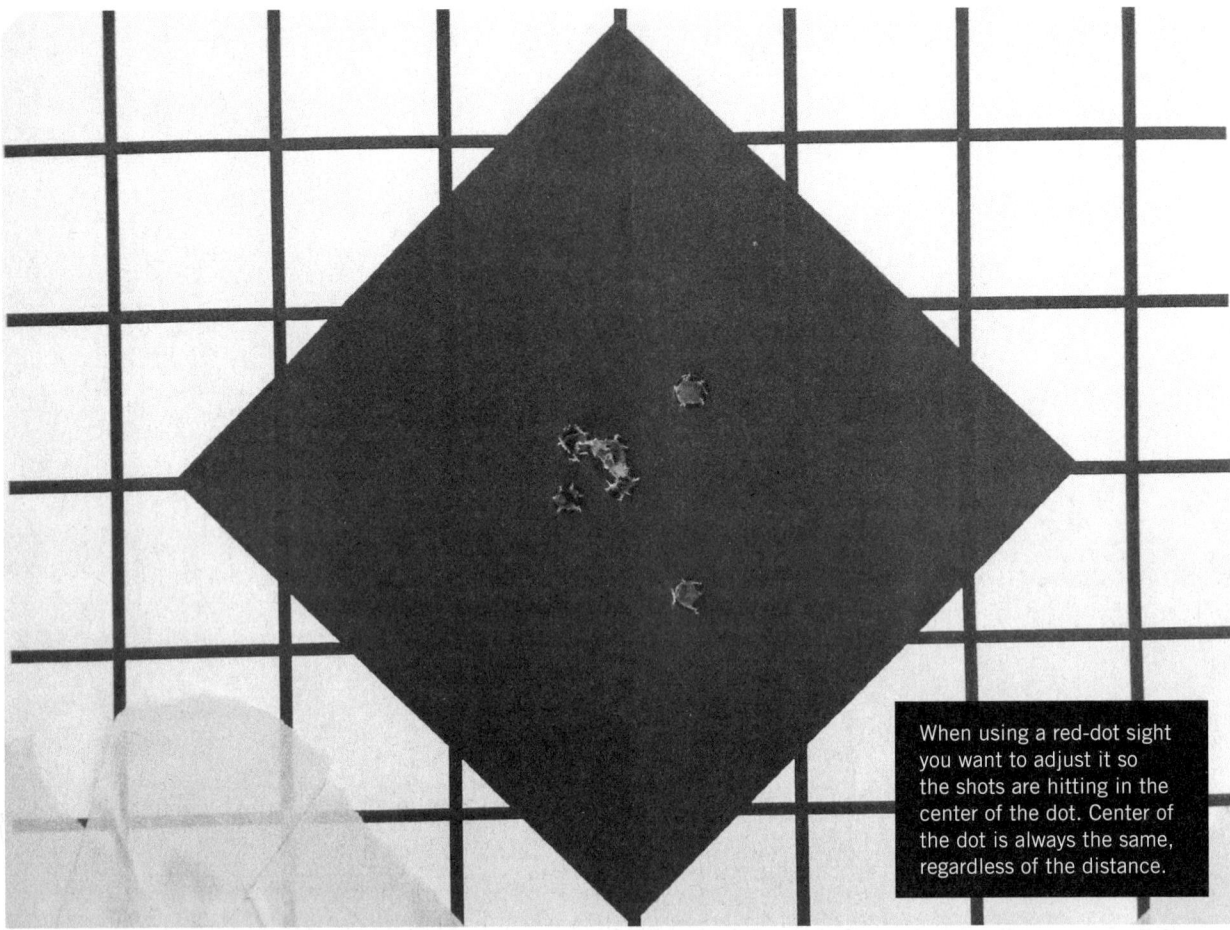

When using a red-dot sight you want to adjust it so the shots are hitting in the center of the dot. Center of the dot is always the same, regardless of the distance.

practice on your manipulations.

As mentioned earlier, at 25 yards your bullets should be hitting lower than where you are aiming. This low POI is necessary because of the offset between the sights and barrel. (Don't get too worried about exact measurements here; you're just looking to get it close, and will fine tune the sights as you move back, creating more distance.)

Once you have a rough zero at 25, again with the bullets striking about two inches below your point of aim, move back to 50 yards. Fire a good group, and adjust as necessary. At this distance your point of impact will be closer to the center of the target where you're aiming. As you increase the distance the POI will move upward towards your POA. For example, if you've decided to work with a 100-yard zero, at 50 yards the bullets should be hitting about an inch below where you are aiming.

Fire a good group, and then adjust the sights as needed. Normally I will only adjust one direction at a time. For example, I'll adjust the elevation with the front sight until getting that right, then adjust windage to get it in the right spot. Trying to adjust both the elevation and windage at the same time can sometimes get a little complicated, for example as you adjust the windage it can change the elevation slightly. You may find that after adjusting the front sight and then the rear sight for windage that you have to go back to the front sight for final adjustments.

After getting close at 50 yards, move back to 75 and repeat the process. If you want a 75-yard zero your bullets should be hitting where you're aiming. Point of aim and point of impact are the same. For a 100-yard zero you'll need to move back to that distance and repeat the process one last time, adjusting

You need to zero your iron sights and the red-dot.

until your POI is spot on for where you are aiming.

When you have the opportunity, shoot your AR at longer distances to find out how much the bullet will drop. (This will vary, sometimes greatly, according to barrel length, twist and bullet design and weight.) For general-purpose use, you're holding high, aiming above the point you want the shot to go so when the bullet drops it's hitting the target. The other end of the spectrum is High Power competition, where you're adjusting the rear sight to compensate for extended distances so you're always aiming at the center of the target.

You'll also need to shoot it at distances closer than your zero, again to find out the difference between your point of aim and the point of impact. Remember, the sights are offset, higher than the barrel, so as you move closer than your zero the point of impact will begin to drop. At distances closer than 25 yards you'll be aiming about two and one half inches high to compensate for this offset. (XS Sights have a modified rear sight that has a notch on top of the peep sight that you use for aiming at close distances that compensates for the offset.)

For zeroing a red-dot sight or a more traditional optic with magnification I use the same process. I start at 25, get a rough zero with the point of impact two to two and one half inches lower than the point of aim. Don't' worry about an exact measurement, you'll have to be making more adjustments as you increase the distance.

With red-dot sights, work on getting the shots where they are hitting in the center of the dot, as opposed to somewhere in the dot.

Remember the dot's "size" will vary according to distance. A two minute dot covers up two inches at 100 yards. At 200 yards the two minute dot covers up four inches of target, and at 300 the dot is covering six inches of the target. If you zero with the shots hitting at the top of the dot, this means your point of impact is going to vary according the distance you're shooting. Regardless of distance and the "size" of the dot, center is always center. Adjust until your hits are in the center of the dot for the distance you've chosen to zero.

There are a lot of optics available that have graduated reticles, varied points for aiming that compensate for distance and trajectory. These are good, but the only way to confirm these "holds" is to actually fire the AR at the distances indicated. As mentioned previously, barrel length and twist and the type round you're firing will all affect the bullet's trajectory. The only way to know where your AR is going to shoot is by firing it at those distances.

Another factor to deal with is the actual adjustment of the optic. One click on the elevation knob is supposed to adjust the POI one quarter of an inch, or one-quarter minute of angle, at 100 yards. But, again, the length of the barrel and its rate of twist and type ammunition you're shooting may mean that one click is greater or less than a quarter inch of movement in the bullet's point of impact.

Any time you change anything on your AR it will be necessary to recheck your zero. The AR is a surgical instrument and modifying anything is going to change what happens when the shot is fired. Something like changing the stock can affect where the bullet hits. Changing ammo is definitely a reason to check your zero. There might not be much difference, and then again there may be a drastic shift in the bullet's point of impact.

Zeroing the AR requires application of the fundamentals of marksmanship. Your goal is to be as machine-like as possible, trying to repeat the process the same way for every shot. If your eyes get tired then stop, take a rest and start again. The same thing goes for your body. Anytime the body gets tired or stressed it's going to affect your ability to hold steady. Remember to control your breathing. You need to shoot accurately, produce consistent results – a good tight group – then you can move that group wherever it needs to be by adjusting the sights. •

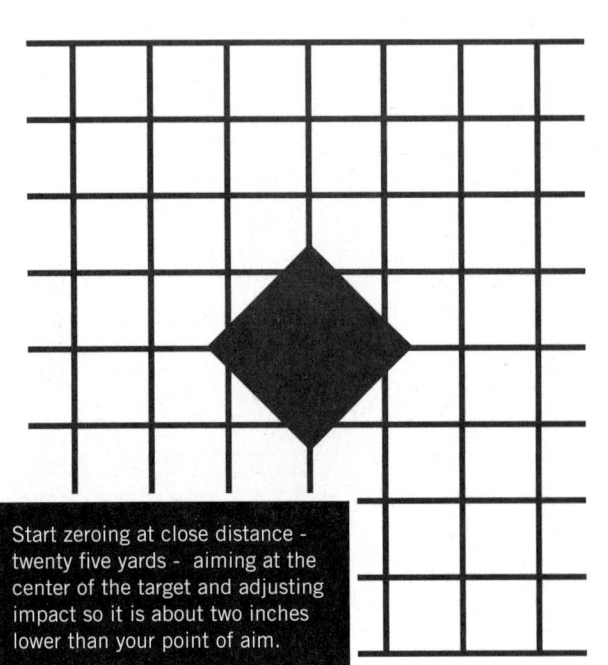

Start zeroing at close distance - twenty five yards - aiming at the center of the target and adjusting impact so it is about two inches lower than your point of aim.

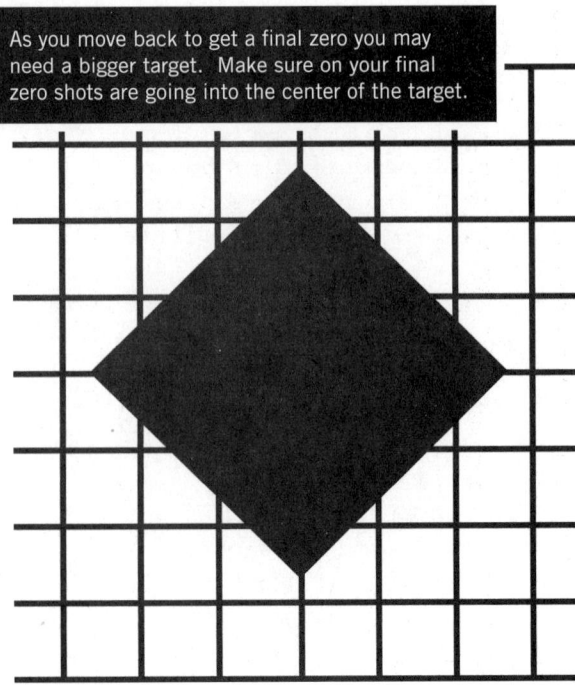

As you move back to get a final zero you may need a bigger target. Make sure on your final zero shots are going into the center of the target.

CHAPTER 13
TRAINING, PRACTICE & LEARNING

TRAINING IS THE introduction of new techniques, skills or principles. You attend a training class to get exposure to new or different techniques. Practice is what you do after the class, working on these techniques in order to learn them. You perform the skills over and over so that you're able to apply them under various conditions. Most people think of training and practice as the same thing, but they are not. Understanding the difference is an important part of the learning process.

You attend training to get exposure or an introduction to new or different skills and techniques. Having an instructor explain, demonstrate and then watch as you perform drills is the best way to train. There are books, videos and DVDs that you can read and watch, but these sources should be thought of as reference only. A video can show you how to perform a task, but it can't point out all the minute details that are involved, specific problems you may have or alternative methods to use if one way doesn't work for you.

Practice is when you take what you've been exposed to during training and actually learn it through repetition. Most experts agree it takes thousands of repetitions to ingrain something into your thought process and for the body to perform those actions efficiently. Practice is also where you learn your personal abilities and limitations.

Once you have learned something it takes additional practice to retain those skills, and even more practice to improve them. The problem for most of us is that time is a precious commodity, and there are the costs of driving to the range and the expense of ammo to consider.

The best way to learn and improve the majority

Having an instructor watch you and supply corrections is the best way to learn the skills you need.

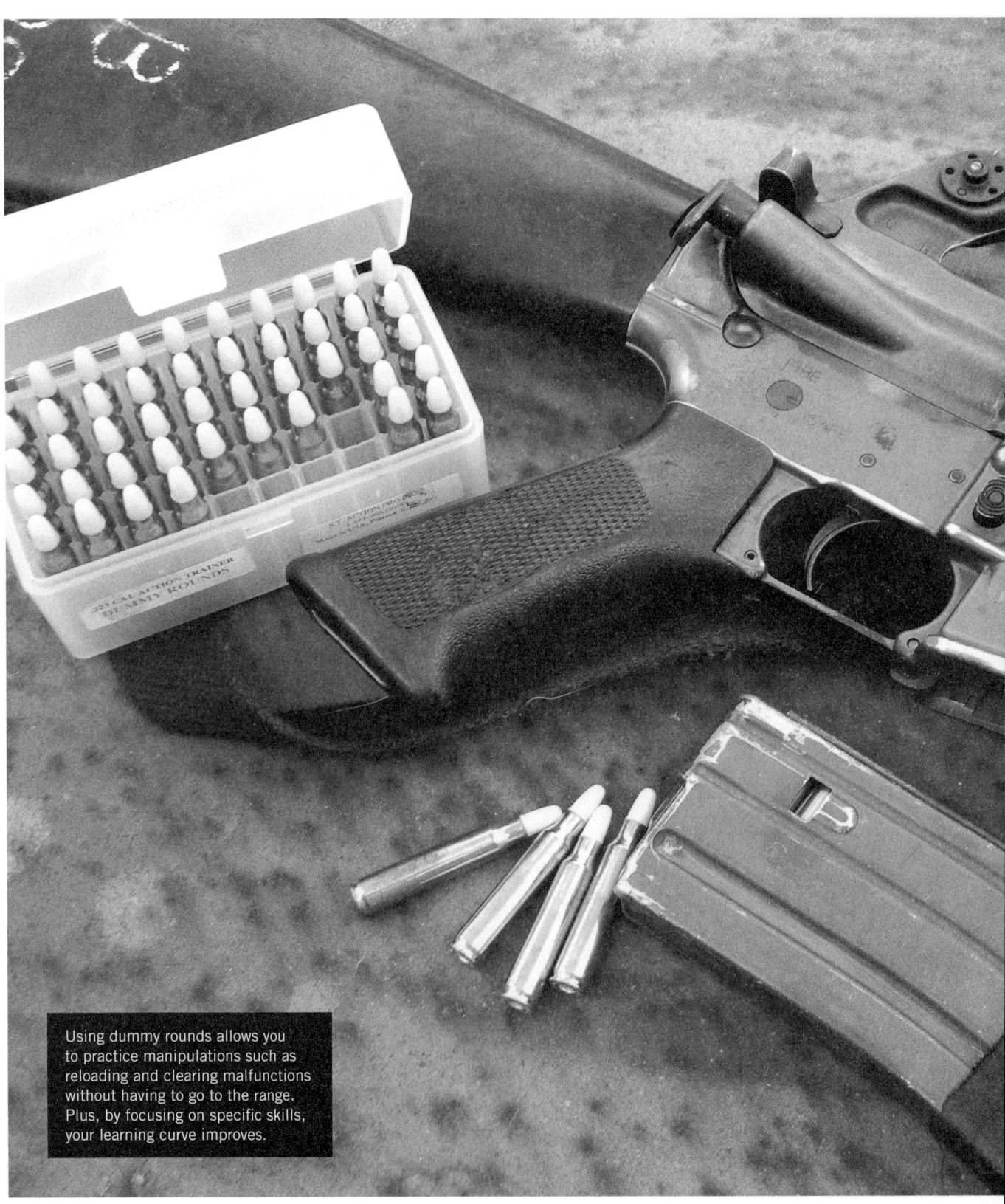

Using dummy rounds allows you to practice manipulations such as reloading and clearing malfunctions without having to go to the range. Plus, by focusing on specific skills, your learning curve improves.

of your skills is with dry practice. Dry practice applies to any skill or technique, and experts agree that this is the best way to improve your skills. A lot of people consider dry practice boring. After all, you're not getting any bang, recoil or noise. But, those who do dry practice immediately recognize its value.

You can use dummy ammunition or snap caps to set up and practice weapon manipulations such as empty reloads and malfunction clearances. With a dummy weapon you can practice various techniques in your home without the dangers associated with using an actual AR. You can even do the pretend thing, imagining you're holding the AR while working on a variety of different skills. The main thing is getting in the repetitions necessary to actually learn the skills you need.

Your dry practice sessions should be short, about ten to fifteen minutes. Every day you should work on some dry practice, focusing on one or two particular skills each session. This short time investment will greatly increase your abilities without having or to go to the range or spending money on ammo. At this point in my life I actually do more dry practice than live fire.

Dry practice will work for other skills, such as moving and using cover. Using your dummy or "pretend" AR you're move tactically down the hallway to the couch, which is your cover. Pick out an aiming point, concentrating on maintaining a sight picture on target as you move. These repetitions are important for becoming familiar with the skills, both mentally and physically.

Each day contains opportunities to practice your skills. For example, get in the habit of scanning your environment as you work up from a position such as prone or kneeling into standing. Every time you change your position you get a new view of the world around you. So, you work at a desk all day. Before standing you scan, then once standing you're scanning again. This is practice, and also eventually scanning will become a habit, a skill you perform without having to think about it.

Even when I do get to the range to live fire I'll work dry runs of drills before performing them live-fire. I run several repetitions of a drill without shooting, and then finally run it live-fire to insure

My dummy rifle is made from an old SKS stock, which has an opening that an AR mag fits perfectly, with a section of web for a sling. Having dummy pistols is good too, especially for practicing transitions.

that when pressing the trigger the shots are going where I want them.

MENTAL ASPECTS OF LEARNING

Working with the AR safely and efficiently is 90 percent mental. The physical part is not that difficult, the mental aspects make the difference. In order to get the best return from your training and practice you need to think about the mental aspects, and there are several things that will help you develop and cultivate the mental aspects required.

First, always approach learning from a positive viewpoint. Consider this statement: Do not think about a football. Your brain ignores the "do not" part of the statement and you're mind is thinking about the football. Thinking about what you *don't* want to do increases the probability you will do exactly what you're trying to avoid. Instead of thinking about the negative aspects of a task or skill (what you don't want to do), think about the positive aspects, focusing on what you want to accomplish. In order to press the trigger smoothly, I think about pressing the trigger as opposed to thinking about not jerking or slapping the trigger.

Performing properly requires thought at both the conscious and subconscious level. But, during the action you can't be thinking about how well you're performing or the outcome of your actions. Thinking about the outcome will prevent you from performing well. You can't be using "outcome based thoughts" because this will distract you from thinking about what you need to be focused on.

"I can't do that." Whenever I hear this or anything similar it lets me know the student is in the wrong frame of mind. It's also a "self-fulfilling prophecy" and practically guarantees you won't perform correctly. Your performance is always equal to your self-image, or how well you think you'll do. You must maintain a positive mindset. This doesn't mean you create a big ego, an "I can do anything" attitude. You do have to have confidence that if you go slowly, work step-by-step, then you'll get predictable results from your actions.

Learning an action begins at the conscious level, until enough repetitions have been performed that the sequence becomes a subconscious process. In the beginning it's important that you go slow, performing the actions step-by-step at a speed that allows you to consciously think about each step of the sequence. Speed should not even be a consideration, and is detrimental to the learning process. Doing it once correctly means you can do it again. Three successful performances and you can do it right 30 times. After about 3,000 repetitions you've developed the confidence necessary to perform efficiently and at a subconscious level.

Mistakes will occur, which means you have to learn to correct and compensate as necessary, continuing with your primary task. Our natural instinct when we make a mistake is to stop, pause, or start to self criticize. During practice, when you make a mistake you fix it, focusing on the corrections necessary.

The conscious mind can only focus on one thing at a time. The subconscious, according to experts, can process millions of bits of information all at the same time and is responsible for the majority of your actions. You just don't realize it because your conscious mind isn't thinking about them. The subconscious performs simple tasks. Imagine how many times you've tied your shoes. You're thinking about getting to work on time while your hands are tying the knots. The subconscious also processes complex tasks. Think about the multitude of actions involved in driving a car. You see a car roll through a stop sign, pulling into your lane. Automatically your hands are repositioning on the steering wheel, you're placing your foot on the brake pedal while you're checking the mirrors to see if you can switch lanes safely. All this happens without you consciously thinking about it because you've been doing it for years.

Now let's apply this to fighting with firearms. You're in a fight and your weapon malfunctions. The conscious mind says "malfunction," then the subconscious takes control to clear the stoppage. You don't have time to stop to think how to clear the malfunction; the subconscious just does it. Your conscious mind is then free to evaluate the situation, making decisions on how to end the fight, which may be avoidance and evasion, physically fighting, or a combination of several strategies.

Fighting is a mental process, and you have to be thinking both at the conscious and subconscious levels. The various 'parts' of your mind must function as one. With the mind 'thinking' properly, the body follows. The physical part is easy, once you've performed enough repetitions to truly learn the skills. Your weapon, barring a stoppage, will do its job. Your task is to create a seamless package consisting of the mind, body and weapon. Then, when the attack occurs, you're prepared to apply your skills without delay to win the fight.

THREE MODES OF LEARNING

All of us learn in basically three ways: visually, by watching an action being performed; kinesthetically, physically performing the action; and by reading, listening, thinking and talking about the subject matter or specific skills. Each individual will have one of these modes that works best for them, but all of us use these three methods.

When training or practicing, watch other shooters, observing the physical actions as they perform different drills. Ideally you want to watch someone who is better than you so that you're getting a good example to go by. As humans we have a gift when it comes to imitation. In order to imitate you have to use your powers of observation.

We also learn through repetition, physically and mentally performing the same sequence of actions over and over. Repetition is a mandatory requirement for learning any skill, maintaining your existing abilities and improving. The more you correctly perform an action the better the results. At some point you reach a place where the majority of these skills become a subconscious process, it simply takes practice.

Finally, listening, reading and thinking or talking about something – always in a positive light – will improve your skills. Whenever you get the chance, talk with someone who knows more than you do. Take advantage of the opportunity to ask them questions. During your day there are a lot of opportunities for you to think about your skills. You have a few extra minutes so you block out any outside interference, close your eyes, and mentally imagine performing empty reloads. Reading and research help you learn more about a particular subject. Make sure to read the classics like Jeff Cooper's works, Bill Jordan, Ed McGivern, and all the others that were laying the groundwork for the skills that we're still using today. By reading the "old" works you'll discover that, although the gear and equipment have changed, the fundamentals are still the same.

You also need to discover whether you're a "global" or "analytical" learner. Global learners see the "forest" first, the big complete picture, and then start focusing on the individual aspects. Analytical learners will do best by focusing on the "trees" first, then assembling them together into one package. Again, we all learn using both approaches, but there will be one that works better for you than the other.

Ultimately we all end up at the same place, with the skills and knowledge to work with the AR safely and efficiently. The key is that each of us will take a slightly different approach to get there. Also, keep in mind that the learning never ends. There is always something new to learn, a different way to test out and opportunities to improve your skills.

TAKE NOTES

Taking notes during training, practice and studies should be considered mandatory. During a training class you take notes. Keep a training diary to record your progress and things that need more attention. When reading a book or other reference material take notes. Note-taking is important, and should be part of your training and practice.

Make notes during training or instruction. Taking notes forces you to pay attention, and helps keep your mind focused on the material being presented. It's not important to record every thing, just make bullet points of the main topics and later you can fill in with additional notes as needed.

Recording the material in your own words often makes it more relevant, providing you with a better understanding of the subject. The instructor may say or present something in one way, but it makes more sense for you to think about it from a different perspective. It's the same material, just revised or paraphrased to create a stronger connection between you and the subject matter.

The act of writing something down implants it into the brain. There have been numerous studies concerning this, and all of them say that writing something down helps immensely with the learning process. One study by psychologist Michael J. Howe in 1970 concluded that students who took notes during classes were seven times more likely to remember the material a week after their exposure than those who didn't make notes. Howe stated "the activity of note writing *per se* makes a contribution to later retention..." (Journal of Educational Research, 64 (2), October 1970)

Studies have also shown that during a class, especially firearms courses that are both physically and mentally demanding, you'll only retain about 10 to 20 percent of the material presented. Notes provide an accurate reference source of what was covered in the class instead of trying to rely solely on your memory. Relying on your memory means there is a chance you could get it wrong. You'll discover that, as you review your notes over time, there will be different things that stick out, or you've developed a better understanding of that topic. Learning is a constant process. The things that are important or significant will change according to your experiences or the way you filter the material.

You should also take notes during your practice sessions. Each trip to the range is a learning experience. Keeping a training log shows you where you're improving, areas that need more attention and additional practice or possibly an equipment issue that needs to be addressed. Again, if you rely on the memory a good idea is likely to slip past, forgotten.

Keep your notebook close when you're reading a book or other materials. With notes it's easy to find a point of interest or something that you need to research. This way you're not trying to shuffle through a stack of books to find what you need. Your reading will spark various thoughts or point you in the direction of something else that needs research. Write it down so you don't forget.

Taking notes ensures a better learning curve. The more notes, the better your grade when it comes test time.

SPEED

Speed, in this context, is the pace at which you are performing. Most people try to do everything, regardless of what it is, at the same speed. And normally this speed is way too fast. The speed at which you function should constantly vary according to the actions you're performing. This is just like driving a car. You slowly accelerate. In order to merge with traffic you accelerate, rapidly gaining speed. As road conditions change or traffic builds you adjust your speed accordingly. The same applies to operating the AR. There are some things that can be done quickly, especially once you've learned them well enough that they can be performed at a subconscious level. Other actions must be performed slower, ensuring application of the fundamentals and ensuring a proper repetition.

You may be performing different actions at the same time, except the rhythm or tempo of one part of the body is different from another. Moving and shooting is a good example of this. The feet and legs are moving at one speed while the upper part of the body is applying the fundamentals of marksmanship. The speed of the feet and legs is different from what's occurring from the waist up.

There are times when the pace will vary for the same skill or technique. You're moving at a smooth speed so you can shoot accurately. The AR runs empty. Since you can't shoot, you pick up the pace of your movement. At the same time the reload is taking place. If you need to fire after reloading then you have to slow the movement back down to create the stability necessary for the accuracy required.

Don't try to do everything at one speed. Slow down, and learn how the different parts of the body function together. This requires repetition, and plenty of it.

SLOW DOWN

Once you have an idea of the skills you're working on it's time to slow down, so that during training or practice you're getting the best possible repetitions.

Slowing down goes against our natural tendencies. After performing an action a few times our inclination is to start speeding up. Fast is detrimental to the learning process. I like to think more about becoming efficient. The more efficient I become, the better.

By slowing down your speed, the mind has time to think about and focus on each individual step of the sequence you're performing. When it comes to using the AR efficiently the small things, such as how you hold a magazine, make a big difference, for example being able to index, align and seat the mag into the AR efficiently.

Also remember that the conscious mind can only think about one thing at a time. When you're working on new skills or trying to modify an existing skill, you're functioning at a conscious level. Eventually, through repetition, these skills are moved over to the subconscious mind, which can literally process millions of things at the same time.

LIVE FIRE PRACTICE

For most of us time and ammunition are precious commodities, so when you do get the opportunity to go to the range you need to maximize the return on the time and ammunition invested. This means having a plan for your practice. Otherwise it normally turns into a shooting session, and while "plinking" is fun it isn't really conducive to the learning process.

Before heading to the range to practice, make a list of the specific skills you want to focus on. The list does two things. First, it mentally prepares you for the drills you're going to practice. Remember, learning occurs in the brain, so the more you think about your skills the better. Second, the list ensures that you don't get sidetracked. Your practice list helps you stay on track.

I normally choose three or four skills to concentrate on. I put these skills on paper and then list the various drills that include these skills or techniques. You may need to practice one specific technique, such as empty reloads, or you can work drills that incorporate several different skills, such as moving, shooting and reloading while moving. All three of these skills can be combined into one drill.

So the drill is "Move, Reload and take Cover." I load two or three rounds into a mag, which is the one I'll use at the start of the drill. At the beginning of the drill I'm moving towards cover or creating distance and then moving to my cover, focusing on smooth stable movement. I'm shooting while moving, concentrating on making good accurate hits. The AR runs empty. I continue to move and at the same time perform an empty reload. At some point I'm behind cover, finishing out the drill by scanning, creating more distance or getting to better cover. All of this is done slowly, so I can focus on the small details that make a big difference.

The number of shots you fire has nothing to do with the quality of your practice. You can shoot a lot of rounds and not learn anything. In fact, unless you're applying the proper techniques, chances are that your practice is actually doing more harm than good.

When planning your live-fire sessions, make it a point to work on the things that you don't like. This will normally be the skills that you don't do well. You want to constantly strive to strengthen your weak areas. Take notes. While practicing, make notes on how you performed and skills you discovered that need fine-tuning. This reference can help determine the direction of your next practice session and document your progress.

CONFIDENCE

Confidence is essential to using the AR efficiently, unless you just happen to get lucky. If you don't have confidence in your abilities you won't perform well under stress, no matter how much you train and practice. Without this belief in yourself, you'll probably go into the "Ohmygosh I can't believe this is happening" mode. All you'll do is react, instead of correctly and properly responding.

You must have confidence in your weapons and the skills to operate them properly. This includes marksmanship, manipulations – when your weapon runs empty or malfunctions, you have to know how to reload or clear the weapon at a subconscious level – and the tactics to employ your weapons to their full potential. Having confidence allows your conscious mind to focus on what's important. With confidence you take control of the situation, and your skills determine the outcome.

This belief should be present regardless of your skill level. No matter where you are in your ability level, focus on what you *can* do, not what you don't know or can't do. At the same time, it's important to know your limitations. By recognizing your limits you don't make mistakes, which creates an efficient, safe performance.

MAKING MISTAKES

Part of learning a new skill, regardless of what it is, is making mistakes. Making mistakes allows you to identify weakness, which can be corrected. Finding just the right piece of gear involves making mistakes. If you're not making mistakes then you're probably not learning as much as you could be.

Acquiring new skills, especially complex sequences of actions, is a difficult process. Nobody expects to sit down at a piano and start playing classical music. Time and practice are involved. The same is true with firearms. People attend training so they can learn. Yet, for some reason during this training, when they do make mistakes you see them mentally beating themselves up. Their mind gets wrapped up in the mistake instead of correcting the problem and continuing with the drill.

We have to learn how to deal with mistakes on the range so we know how to cope when they occur in real life. On the range you're going to jerk a shot, fumble a reload or move in the wrong direction. When a mistake occurs on the range you immediately correct or compensate as necessary and continue with the drill. Very few people perform flawlessly; there is always something that could have been done differently. Part of learning how to fight is knowing how to deal with mistakes or miscalculations.

Dealing with mistakes and taking the steps to correct them is a mental process. You discover a weakness you can correct. Slow down, identify the specific source of problem and correct it through slow repetition, practicing over and over until it's right. Under stress you miss an "easy" shot. Instead of getting flustered, speeding up and missing more shots, slow down, ensuring the next one is accurate. On the range you discover that you can't do "rollover prone" – a position where you roll over on your side to fire underneath something such as an automobile. Perfect, you've figured out in advance that this position doesn't work for you. Now find an alternative that does.

You decide to test out a new piece of gear. Not everything you try is going to work for your particular situation, but you won't know until you check it out. When you find out the "new" doesn't work like you thought, go back to the "old" until you discover something better. Unless you experiment – and make mistakes – you're not going to get "there," which is where we all want to be.

Make mistakes. (This doesn't mean be careless or unsafe.) Learn to accept and handle mistakes on the range so when something similar happens you know how to deal with it. Take joy in discovering a weakness, because this means you can correct it. Test and experiment with gear until discovering what works best. Learning or growing involves making mistakes.

There are a variety of ways to learn and countless opportunities to practice. Take advantage of all these modes, so that you're learning every day. Learning to use the AR properly, regardless of the application, is a life-long process. You won't ever get it perfect, but as long as you're constantly improving then you're heading in the right direction.

COACH AND SHOOTER TECHNIQUE

The "coach and shooter" technique, which means one person is shooting and the other is watching and coaching, is an excellent technique to use when practicing. Normally when you go to the range everyone is shooting. Having one person shoot while the other acts as the coach is beneficial to both parties, and helps with learning.

We learn by doing, but we also learn by observation and instructing. The coach watches the shooter, ensuring they are being safe, which is always the primary concern. Watching the shooter also allows the coach to apply constructive criticisms. Your goal is to perform as well as possible so that every repetition is a good one. You will make mistakes, skipping a part of the process or failing to perform efficiently. The problem is that, often, people aren't even aware of the mistakes they are making until someone points them out. Having a coach to watch you can help you avoid developing bad habits.

The coach learns by watching and observing. And when you start instructing someone else is when you really start learning about all the small details that must come into play in order to perform properly. When your "shooter" doesn't have the proper stance, you have to be able to identify it and then apply suggestions on how to correct the stance. Coaching applies to the mental aspects as well. Applying the fundamentals of marksmanship is a mental process. The shooter fires the shot, but they are slapping or jerking the trigger instead of pressing it smoothly. You see the problem, and then remind them of the different methods to help mentally focus on getting a smooth trigger press.

This technique applies to both dry fire and live fire practice. There's nothing wrong with practicing by yourself, but whenever you have to opportunity work in teams, use the shooter and coach technique to increase the learning curve for both parties. •

CHAPTER 14
DEFENSE FUNDAMENTALS

MOST VIOLENT CONFRONTATIONS are sudden, dynamic and unpredictable. After all, if you knew there was going to be a fight you would apply our number one tactic, which is avoid and escape. There are times however when this isn't an option, and an immediate defensive response is required. The fundamentals of responding to a threat or attack are move, communicate, use cover, shoot if necessary, and think.

The problem with these fundamentals is that none of them are natural; almost everything you need to do in response to a threat goes completely against our natural instincts. Our natural response to a threat is to freeze until we figure out what's going on. Once we decide to fight, our instinct is to root to the ground. What we need to do is move. Communication consumes a large part of our brain's resources. Under stress it's extremely difficult, and it requires practice to overcome the lockjaw you'll experience. The same thing is true when using cover. Almost everything you must do to take advantage of the protection cover offers goes against our natural inclinations. Shooting isn't instinctual to begin with, and it's even more difficult under stressful conditions. We aren't built to have explosions going off in our hands, even the controlled explosion of shooting a firearm. Finally, thinking is mandatory. Defending against a violent attacker is a mental process – problem solving at high speed. If you're not thinking and acting, then all you're doing is reacting, which is a bad place to be when someone is trying to harm you or your family.

MOVE

There are a lot of reasons to move. Creating distance from the threat (or threats) greatly reduces the chance of being injured, regardless of the type weapon being used against you. There are bystanders in the environment, so you're moving in order to get a clear angle of attack on the threat, reducing the possibility of injuring someone if you have errant rounds. You move to get to cover and the protection it provides. You move to the exit, toward your family or to get to better cover.

A moving target – you – is more difficult for the threat to engage. Moving is one of the best ways to put the threat into a reactive mode. The threat charges at you. You move a few steps to the side. Now he has to react to your actions, assessing, creating a response, and redirecting the attack.

COMMUNICATE

Communication is a key tactical skill that's often overlooked during training and practice. You communicate with threats. "Leave my home now!" "Stop, drop the weapon!" Millions of times every year, strong verbal commands accompanied by a firearm defuse violent confrontations, and this is only the number times that this is documented. You communicate with friends and family, telling them what you need them to do or where to go. Communication is mandatory when working with an armed partner in order to coordinate your tactics and actions. As discussed previously, sometimes it's good idea to talk to yourself, verbalizing your actions in order to help maintain mental focus.

In most situations, moving should be your first response to a threat. You move to put the threat in a reactive mode, move to cover, or move to get a clear angle on the threat. Moving in response to danger must be programmed.

You communicate with the threat, issuing verbal commands, or with a partner to co-ordinate your actions as a team.

Communication is an exchange of information. I talk to my dog but I communicate with my wife. Keep your communications short and sweet. Under stress, simple works best. Using names, in order to get someone's attention, makes communicating more efficient. The act of communicating consumes a large part of our brain's resources, or "random access memory." In order to communicate effectively under stress you need to practice it in advance.

COVER

Get to cover as quickly as possible, preferably as soon as you spot potential trouble, before the confrontation gets physical. Cover provides protection against the threat's weapon. Cover is relative to what type weapon the threat is armed with. If they are trying to physically assault you, or they are armed with a knife or impact weapon (which means they have to be close in order to attack) something like a large table provides cover, as long as you can position it between you and the threat. When it comes to protection against firearms, everything is relative to what type weapon the threat is using. Cover stops or redirects incoming rounds. Something that protects you from a handgun round may not hold up against a high-velocity rifle round.

Concealment hides you, but doesn't offer any protection, but that doesn't mean it won't work in response to an attack. If the threat can't see you, they don't know where you are, it greatly reduces the chance of them attacking. Then, if you decide it's necessary, you can let them know where you are when you decide it's time.

STOP THE THREAT

There are two ways to stop a threat – the psychological stop and the physical stop. Moving, issuing verbal commands and using cover may force the attacker to change his mind about what he was going to do – the psychological stop. The other way is to

Cover provides you with protection. As soon as possible you move to cover, and when you have the chance move to better cover.

If necessary, you put accurate hits on the attacker in order to stop the threat. Remember, accuracy is defined by distance and size of the target; when you press the trigger it should be because you know the hit is going to be a good one.

The fundamentals of responding to a threat are move, communicate, use cover, shoot if necessary, and think. Practice is necessary to learn and apply these skills.

physically stop the threat by shooting, placing accurate hits on the threat and inflicting the physical damage necessary to stop the attacker.

When it's necessary to shoot, you have to apply the fundamentals of marksmanship — aim, hold, press, and follow through — in order to get accurate hits. The speed at which you can shoot depends on the accuracy you need. With a large, close target you can fire fairly quickly, putting the hits where they need to go. As the distance increases and/or the size of the target decreases you need more precision, ensuring that when you do press the trigger you get accurate hits.

THINK

Defeating a lethal threat is problem-solving at high speed. You have to constantly be thinking, forcing threat to react to you. Normally you have a very short amount of time to come up with a solution to the problem and then implement the action. Once you gain the upper hand, you keep pressing the advantage, which means thinking about what you're going to do next and what you'll do if that doesn't work; and mentally plugged in and ready for the unexpected, which occurs in fights with regularity.

In order to focus on the problem-solving aspects of the conflict, the majority of your skills must be applied at a subconscious level. The AR runs empty. The conscious mind says "reload" and then the subconscious mind takes over to perform the actual reload. There's no time to think about how to reload, it just has to happen. Ditto for clearing malfunctions if they occur, using cover or transitioning to the handgun. The ability to perform these actions at the subconscious level frees up the conscious mind to think about your problem.

Self-defense is more art than science. Your 'artwork' will be different from everyone else's. Train, practice, learn, and remember that your ultimate weapon is your mind. If you're not thinking and acting, then all you're doing is reacting, which means the threat is in control. The only thing you can control in a fight is what you do, so make sure to practice so that you can apply your skills efficiently, safely and under all types of conditions. •

CHAPTER 15
TARGET ZONES

WHEN SHOOTING, WE'RE putting hits on the threat in order to stop the threat. Placing the shots in the proper location will help stop the threat as efficiently as possible. There are three zones to put your shots; the situation and/or how the threat responds to the hits will dictate where you place the hits.

One thing to remember is to apply the term "center mass" to any part of the body. People are three-dimensional, as opposed to the usually flat targets we shoot during training and practice. Your point of aim will be dictated by the angle of the attacker's the body. You want to picture where the shots would need to go so they end up in the center of the area, whether it is the chest, pelvis or head. Practicing with a target that is shaped more like an actual person will help you with shot placement.

Also, even thought we're talking about using a high-velocity rifle round, it may still take several shots, sometimes in multiple areas of the body, to stop the threat. The human body can take an enormous amount of punishment and still function. A lot of it has to do with the level of dedication of the threat. Someone who has decided that no matter what happens they will never stop fighting is a problem. Plus, approximately ten percent of the population doesn't "feel" pain like everyone else. When you add in mental instability, drugs and alcohol, that percentage starts to increase. The key is to

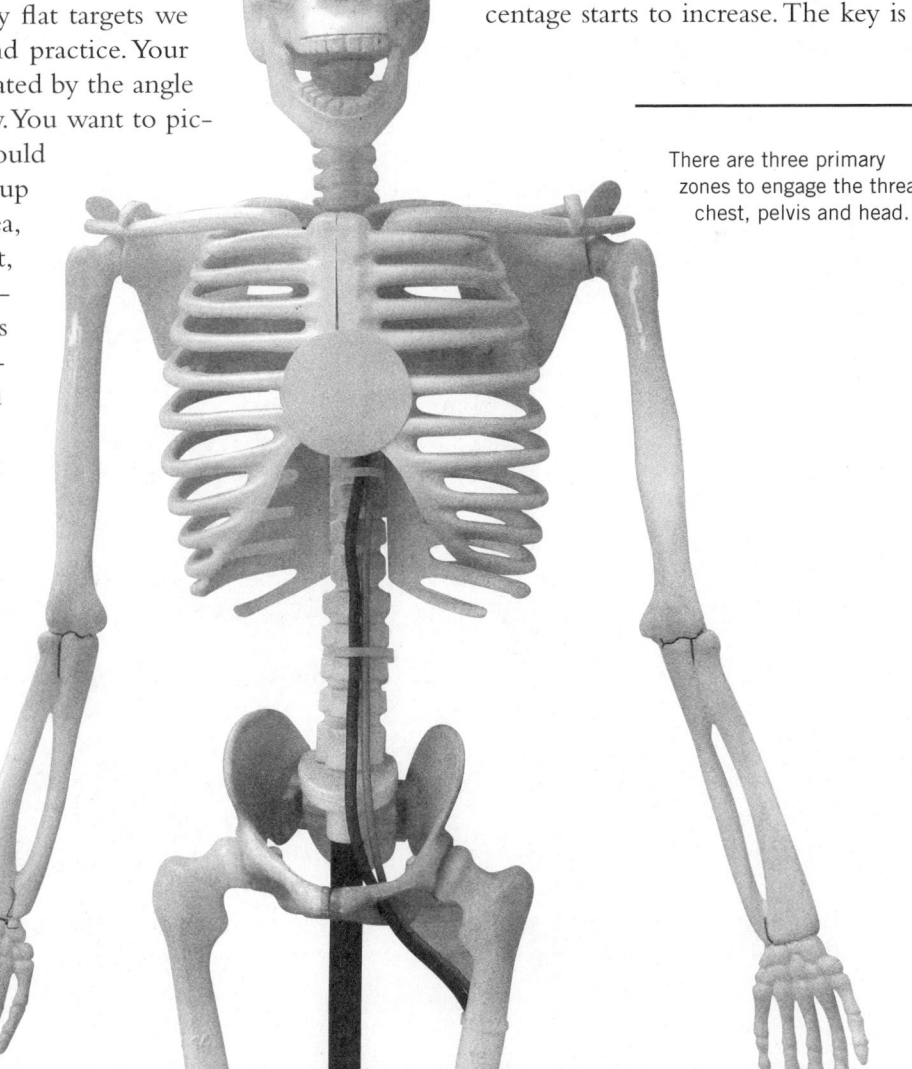

There are three primary zones to engage the threat: chest, pelvis and head.

put accurate hits on the threat until you get the response needed, which is they either run away or won't/can't fight any more.

For example, you put two or three accurate hits into the chest, but the threat is still active. Maybe they don't feel the pain. They could be wearing body armor, which is happening more and more on the street. Ultimately it doesn't matter why, all we know is these shots didn't stop the threat. You've probably done all the damage you can to that area, so it's time to put hits in another area of the body. If that doesn't work, change to a different area, and if necessary shift again. Keep putting hits on the threat, shifting from one zone to another, until you get results.

The threat is down, or they ran away around a corner. Stay mentally plugged in. Just because the threat is down or gone doesn't mean the fight is over. They may be on the ground but still able to fire at you. It's possible they may get up off the ground, ready to fight some more. The threat could come back around the corner, possibly with more help. Always expect the unexpected, and be ready for the fight to continue.

Where do you put your hits? This is determined by the situation. There is no standard order that you should engage.

CHEST

The chest area is a fairly large part of the body, and offers a good chance of inflicting the damage necessary to stop the threat, especially with rifle rounds. The chest may be your first choice to put hits. Remember to think about where the actual center of the chest area is to determine your point of aim.

If you start with the chest, and after several hits you realize the shots are not having any effect, it's time to shift zones and put hits into another area.

PELVIS

The pelvis is actually a good place to put your hits. Pelvic shots can be very effective, again especially with rifle rounds. This is a large target area and it moves less than the upper body or head. The higher you go, the more movement occurs in the body.

In the front of the pelvis is the pubic symphysis, where the two halves of the pelvis meet. They are joined by fibrocartilage, which can be split apart by bullets. Once this area of the pelvis is shattered, the two halves are split apart, the pelvic girdle can no longer support the body and the threat will go to the ground. Taking away mobility is a good thing.

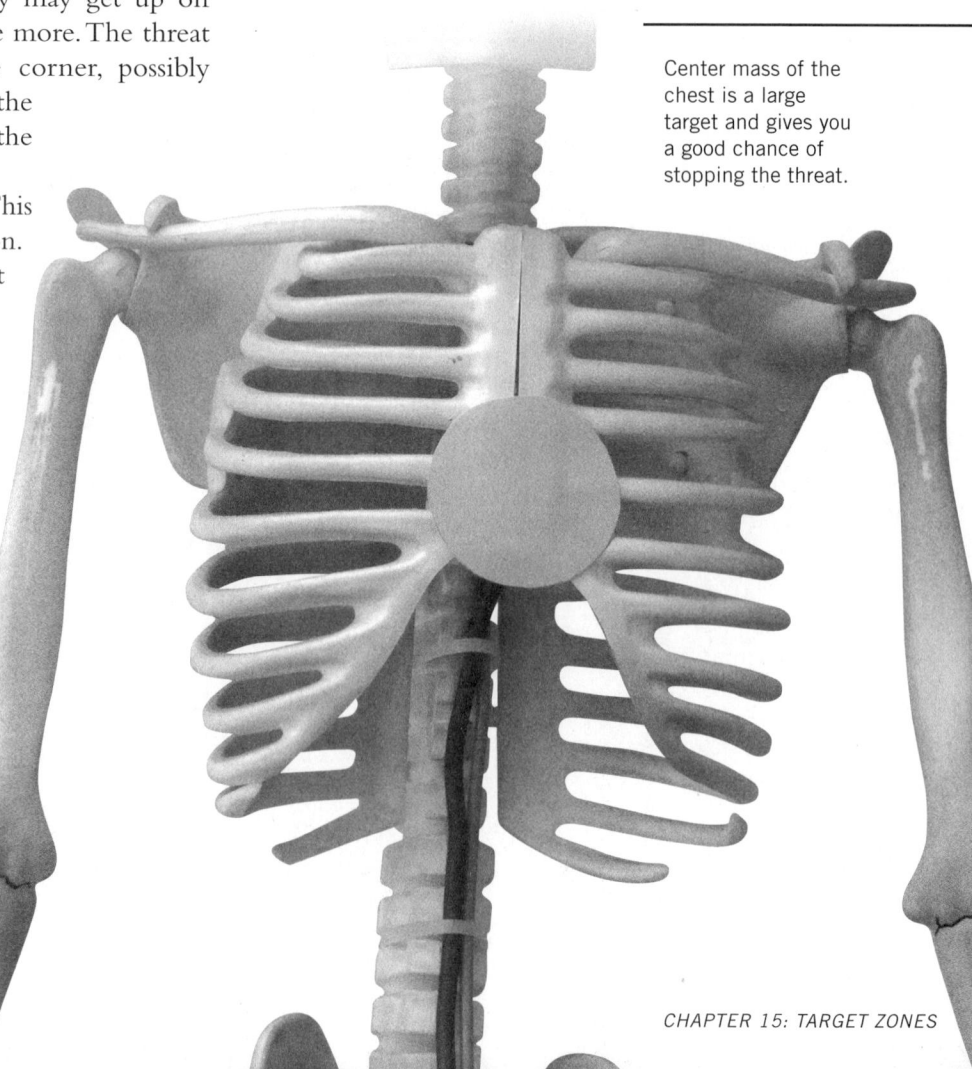

Center mass of the chest is a large target and gives you a good chance of stopping the threat.

Major veins and arteries run through the center of this area before splitting and extending down the inner part of the legs. Blood loss is another way to stop the threat. At the bottom of the spine is the *cauda equina*, or "horse's tail" nerves. When this nerve center receives a sharp, violent shock, the legs will generally fail.

The pelvis also offers a chance to shoot at a downward angle. This might be important when there are bystanders or homes behind the threat, and you need to change the trajectory of the bullets. Also useful when you can see that the threat is wearing body armor. It may or may not be rifle-rated armor, but you can't take the chance. So you start by putting hits into the pelvis. Your partner, who starting firing first, is already placing hits to the chest, so you go for the pelvis. Putting hits into two locations at the same time is more efficient than everyone shooting the same area. Depending on the situation, the pelvis may be the first place you put hits.

HEAD

The headshot shuts down the "computer" that operates the body. It's a very effective shot, but it is also the most difficult shot to make. The skull does a great job of protecting the brain – even against high velocity rifle rounds – and the target zone for a headshot that will guarantee the bullet enters the skull cavity is a small area. The head normally

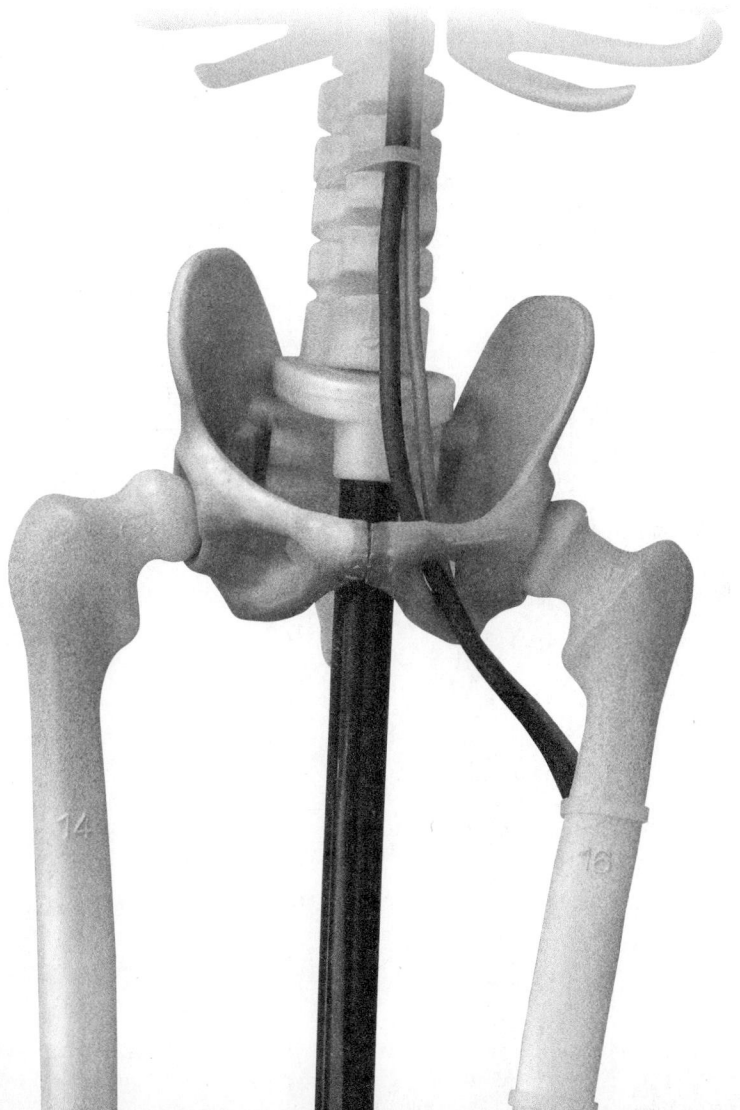

Although it's often overlooked, the pelvis is a great place to put hits.

The headshot is effective, but the head is a difficult target, especially if you and the threat are moving.

moves more than any other part of the body, plus people will instinctually move their head when something is pointed at it. Add in the fact that you and the threat are probably going to be moving, and the head becomes a difficult target to hit.

From a frontal view, the shot needs to be place into what I call the "ocular cavity," which is the area between the eyes and nose. Above this area the skull is thick and curved; it deflects bullets all the time. This doesn't mean they won't be hurting later, but it may not provide you the immediate results you're looking for. Cheekbones, teeth and the jawbone can also deflect rounds, preventing them from entering the skull. When engaging from different angles, you want to think about a band that runs around the skull from ear to ear.

In situations where the threat may be elevated, on higher ground, or lower than you, it will be necessary to think about changing your point of aim. Again, remember to think about the shape of the head and where you will need to aim in order to hit the center mass of that area.

The head may be where you have to start putting hits because the threat is behind cover or they have a hostage. Also remember that just because you shot at the head doesn't mean it was a good hit. Always be ready to put additional shots on the threat, possibly in different areas, until you get the desired results.

AMMO

When it comes to choosing ammunition for self-defense work you need to do a lot of research to see what works best. There are all kind of tests out there using ballistic gelatin and other substances, but the only true test is when it's used on flesh and bone. Deer hunters can provide you with a lot of information on the effectiveness of particular rounds. The deer's body is shaped a lot like a person's, so hunting provides you

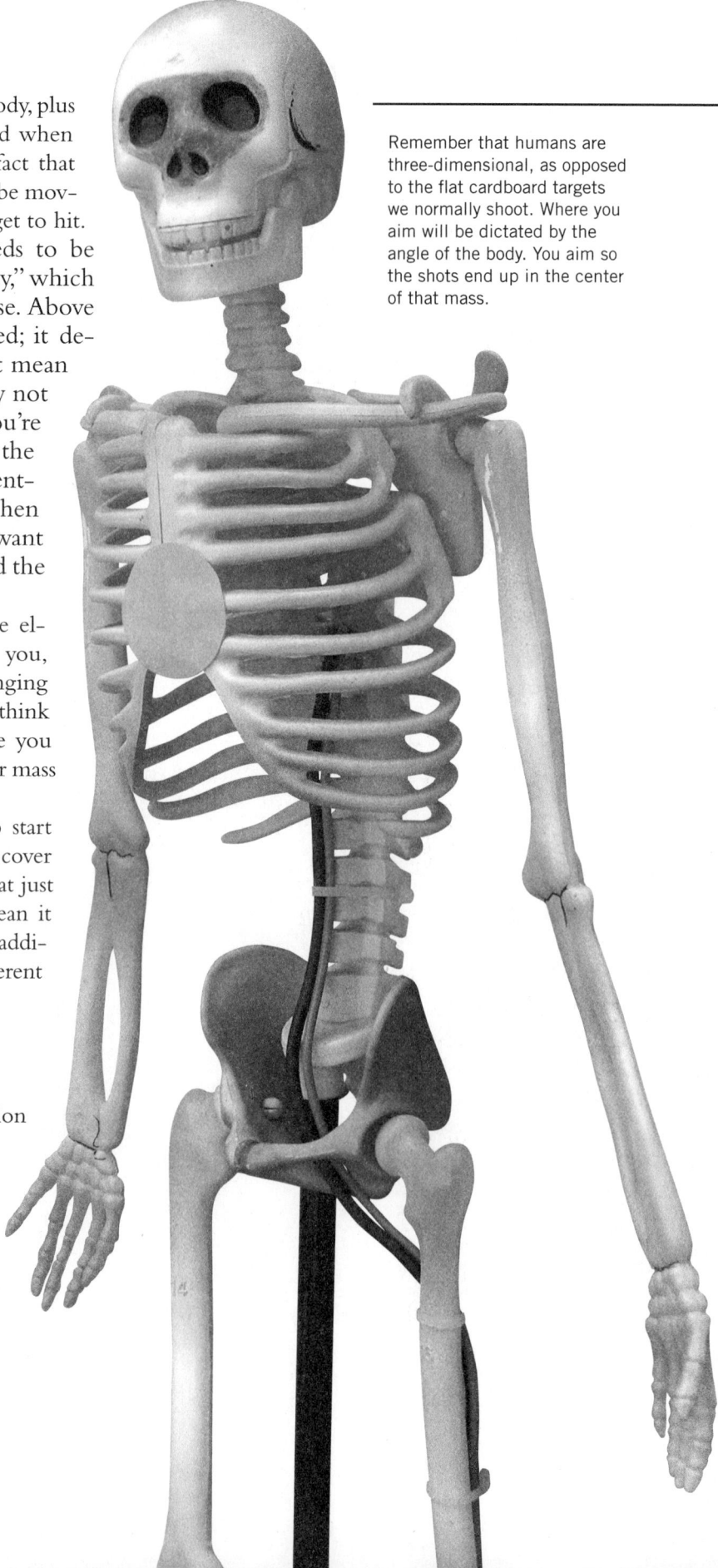

Remember that humans are three-dimensional, as opposed to the flat cardboard targets we normally shoot. Where you aim will be dictated by the angle of the body. You aim so the shots end up in the center of that mass.

with good information on how bullets perform. Researching law enforcement shootings will also give you good data on how certain bullets perform. Plus, law enforcement agencies have already done a lot of research on what bullet they are going to use, so picking a round that they use will sometimes save you a lot of time.

The one round you don't want to use, unless the situation specifically calls for it, is anything that is specifically designed to penetrate through objects, such as the steel core NATO round. This bullet is made to punch through solid objects, and on flesh and bone it zips right through without creating a large wound channel or transferring its energy into the target.

The AR was never designed to use steel case rounds.

You want a round that is designed to expand, which creates a larger wound channel and at the same time expends it's energy, minimizing the chances of the bullet punching through the body and ending up somewhere else. Or, choose a bullet designed to tumble and fragment, which creates multiple wound channels and the body absorbs all the energy. The original 55-grain full metal jacket round is made to perform this way.

Accuracy and reliability are other factors to consider. The beauty of the AR is that you can put that one round exactly where you need it, so you want a round that is accurate enough to allow you to take advantage of this capability. Reliability is mandatory. The round you choose has to function flawlessly in your mags and carbine every time, all the time, and under a variety of conditions. You'll want to zero the AR using your "defensive" rounds.

For training and practice you can use pretty much everything, other than steel case ammo. The AR was never designed to use steel case rounds; steel expands and contracts at a different rate than brass. Us-

ing steel case ammunition can case problems, such as a Type IV malfunction – a case stuck in the chamber. It will also lead to premature wear on the AR's parts, and can cause breakage, like the extractor.

PRACTICE

During practice you want to work on all different types of responses, placing shots into the different areas of the body and in various combinations, between the chest, pelvis and head. You never know where or how many times you'll have the hit 'em to stop the fight.

For example you start by putting shots into the chest. Imagine this isn't working, so you go to the pelvis. The threat is behind cover, so you put a hit to the head. Then, imagine the threat stumbles out from behind cover so you place hits into the chest. You're worried about the trajectory of the bullet, so you begin by placing hits to the pelvis. Making the mental connections between what you're doing on the range and how this applies in real life is critical

Using a 3-D target with a cardboard backer allows you to work on engaging "center mass" of the body. After firing from various angles the cardboard target should have a good group in the center of the chest, pelvis or head.

You can make a "primitive" 3-D target by adding a paper target with its center bowing out over a cardboard target. The goal is to fire from various angles, adjusting your point of aim so you get good groups on the cardboard backer.

for preparing you for actual combat.

You can create a simple three-dimensional target by attaching a paper target over a cardboard backer target. Attach the paper target to the backer so that it creates a convex shape with it bulging away from the cardboard target. This gives you a shape that is closer to the human body, as opposed to a flat two-dimensional target.

There are also three-dimensional targets like Action Target's "3-D Torso Shell Target." By positioning a cardboard target behind the 3-D target you can shoot from various angles and then inspect the cardboard target to see if your shots are going into the center mass of the body. (This won't be exact, but will provide you with a good way to practice engaging three-dimensional targets.)

Anoter good target to work with is Action Target's "PT TURN SWING Target, AT-114." (I provided the basic design for this target system, and Action Targets improved on the concept.) This target, which is portable and rope operated, can work as a stationary target stand. By pulling one rope the target will rotate, so you can have the target present facing the shooter, then after they've put hits into the proper location you pull the rope to have the target blade away from the shooter. Using this target, or something similar, will teach shooters to put hits into different zones, engaging until the threat goes "down." Pulling another rope will cause the target to "wobble" leaning to the left and right as though the threat was bobbing and moving. This is a good way to work on engaging a moving target that isn't predictable – the person pulling the ropes dictates what direction the target is moving.

You can also attach Action Target's 3-D target to the stand, getting closer to a realistic three-dimensional human target. As the target moves and rotates, you're presented with different angles of the body, which requires you to shift your point of aim in order to get hits into the center mass of the threat.

In order to respond to the threat, you have to practice under as realistic conditions as possible. Using a variety of different shaped targets and reactive and moving targets is mandatory. •

Action Target's PT TURN SWING Target is a rope-operated target system that moves, mimicking the motion of a human target.

CHAPTER 16
DATA BOOK

EVERYONE WHO OWNS a precision rifle keeps a dope or data book on that weapon – at least they do if they are serious shooters. Typical information includes details on cold bore shots. Normally the point of impact on the first shot fired from a clean, cold barrel will be slightly different from shots fired after that. You record each cold shot, building up enough data to know exactly where that first shot is heading. By gathering and recording data, you know the difference between a shot fired when the air temp is a chilly 15 degrees and the humidity is low vs. a hot day of 95 degrees with humidity to match. You have a record of the changes that will occur if you switch from a 55 grain bullet to one weighing 75 grains. I recommend doing the same thing for every firearm you own.

Most of the people I know who get into firearms, no matter the reason, eventually end up with a small collection of weapons. After all, you need a few pistols for carry, a variety of rifles and car-

Special-purpose rifles are made to shoot as accurately as possible.

bines, and of course probably a dose of shotguns. At some point it becomes difficult to keep track of everything, especially like when you changed out a buffer spring, how many rounds have been fired through a specific barrel, or what make bolt group is in a particular AR. The solution is to develop a log or data book for each firearm you own.

In my spec sheets I include detailed information about what parts were used to assemble that weapon. There is a record of when it's been cleaned, how many rounds it's fired, or when the recoil spring was last changed. I keep track of when the battery was changed in the red-dot sight. When a part breaks I know what brand it was, how long it lasted and what to replace it with. There are targets in the file so I know what group to expect from that particular weapon with specific type or brand ammo.

Keeping targets gives me a reference to look back at. If all the sudden AR #3 is shooting three-inch groups at 100 yards instead of one-inch groups, I know there's a problem I need to look at. Keeping this information is also good if you need to take your AR to a gunsmith for repairs or modifications. This way they don't have to try guess about anything; it's all written down and recorded for reference.

I'm an old school guy and keep written records. Plus, if I have a clean sheet of paper I can draw out illustrations for documenting a certain point, or attach pictures to the file. Yes, you could keep your notes on a computer, but remember that the act of writing something down helps implant it in the mind. Typing or entering data on a computer spreadsheet provides you with a record, but it doesn't make the same mental connections.

For the average AR, you probably don't need to record every shot or the weather conditions and the amount of info you would with a precision rifle. Unless of course your precision rifle is an AR, a Special Purpose Rifle, or SPR. But you do need to keep a record of all the different modifications made, bullet trajectory for different distances — including wind shifts — and other major details of that weapon.

Owning and using a firearm is serious business, especially if we're talking about possibly using it for self-defense. Approach all the different aspects of this accordingly. Document everything about your weapons, just as you do with your training and practice. •

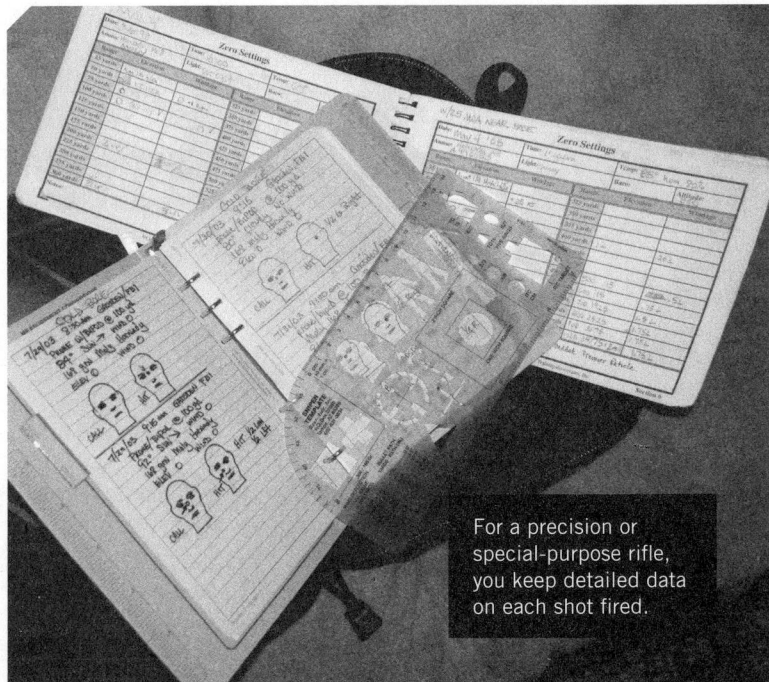

For a precision or special-purpose rifle, you keep detailed data on each shot fired.

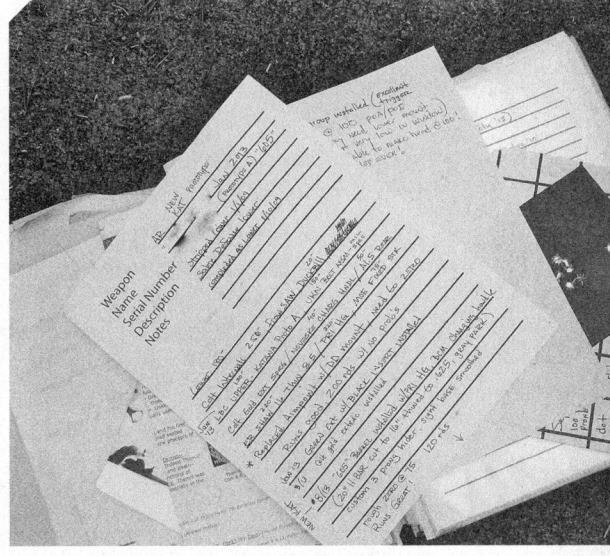

Keeping a log book or sheet for each firearm you own helps keep track of what's been done to that AR and when. Keeping targets lets you know what accuracy should be expected with each type of round.

CHAPTER 17
MOVING

AS DISCUSSED PREVIOUSLY, one of the fundamental responses to a threat should be movement. There are several reasons to move when faced with a threat. Creating distance between you and the threat(s) greatly reduces your chance of being injured. Regardless of the weapon the threat is armed with, moving makes you a difficult target. You move to get to cover and the protection it provides you. There are bystanders in the environment, so you move to obtain a clear angle of attack on the threat. You move to your family or friends or move to get them to a safe area. Initially you're reacting because the threat started the confrontation. Movement puts the threat into a reactive mode. There are a lot of reasons to move.

In a fight it may be necessary to move, for the reasons mentioned above, and at the same time place accurate hits on the target. This isn't as difficult as it may seem, but it does take a lot of practice. Applying the fundamentals of marksmanship – aim, hold, press and follow through – becomes even more important when you start moving. Generally, the more complicated things become the more critical the fundamentals.

Incorporating movement into your response is difficult; it goes against our natural instincts. When faced with sudden, unexpected danger we instinctually want to freeze. When large predators like cats and bears roamed about, if you were downwind and froze in place maybe they didn't see and eat you. Once we decide to fight, the tendency is to root to the ground. This natural desire to freeze, remaining stationary, must be overcome through repetitive practice.

The situation may call for quick movement, for example to get behind cover and then shoot if necessary. You may need to move smoothly in a manner that allows you to shoot accurately. Regardless of the speed at which you're moving, it needs to be stable and balanced.

Most "shooting" ranges won't allow you to move and fire. The good thing is you don't have to actually shoot in order to practice moving. With a "blue" gun or dummy weapon you can practice moving, concentrating on maintaining a sight picture. Or, just practice footwork using your make-believe AR. When and where you can practice moving and shooting, live-fire drills, concentrate on slow smooth movement, focusing on accurate hits instead of trying to be fast. Speed – efficiency – comes with repetition.

Taking one step always means moving both feet. Moving only one foot or leg, except when necessary to adjust your stance, puts you in an unstable stance. For example, if you only move one foot the feet are too far apart. You're not going to have any stability, and it makes moving again more difficult. After taking one step, again moving both feet, you should be in a stable, balanced stance with the feet shoulder-width apart.

The general rule is to keep your hips and upper body indexed towards the target. The hips should be slightly angled to the target, for example a right hand shooter will have the left leg and hip forward. The upper body is in alignment with the hips. When the hips twist the upper body tends to follow, and even though you do have some flexibility with the arms, this makes it more difficult to keep your sights on target. Remember, the AR is connected to your body at four points – the stock is in the shoulder, cheekweld on the stock, strong hand on the grip and support hand on the handguard. Crossing your legs twists the upper body, making it difficult to keep the weapon on target, puts you in an unbalanced position and there is always a danger of tripping over your own feet.

To move left you step with the left foot first. You step with the right foot first in order to move right. To move to the rear a right-handed shooter steps with the right foot, which is slightly to the rear. Forward movement starts by stepping with the left foot. Moving in this manner allows you to keep the hips, the upper body and the carbine indexed on the target.

After initiating the movement with the foot in the direction of your movement you reset the other foot, stepping just the right amount so that you end up in a stable, balanced stance. As you reset the other foot make sure to maintain the shoulder width distance between your feet. Think of it as taking a full step with one leg and then and then a half step with the other.

Most ranges are smooth and sterile. Real life contains many things to trip you up, like doorjambs, curbs, holes and slippery surfaces. Bend the knees a little more so that the legs can act like shock absorbers for the body. Bending the knees also lowers your center of gravity, which allows you to step and test your footing before shifting the weight to that leg. To avoid losing your balance, feel with the toes of the foot as you step to ensure there is something to hold your weight. After the toes confirm good ground, shift your weight, redistributing it from one leg to the other, and reset the other foot. Normally it's better to take two short stable steps rather than one long or wide one. Avoid crossing the legs and feet. Don't shift the weight until you know you've got good footing, and the weight shift should occur in the hips. This "shuffle" type movement requires practice in order to apply efficiently.

If you do lose your balance then it's better to go down on your terms with a certain amount of control as opposed to completely losing it. Falling is an art. Seek out instruction on how to do a controlled drop, reducing the chance of injury and ensuring a quick followup after regaining balance. Practice it using a dummy weapon, making sure you're getting your finger off the trigger and learning how to control the muzzle. Learning how to get off the ground and on your feet again efficiently is just as important as learning how to fall.

Apply the fundamentals of marksmanship while moving in order to get accurate hits. If you come on target slapping the trigger and tensing your muscles in anticipation of the recoil, you won't get good hits. Shoot when you have the sight picture you need, but don't create that opportunity by slowing down or stopping your movement. You're moving for a reason, so keep moving until you get where you need to be. You can either move smoothly and shoot accurately, or move quickly and not shoot. The situation will determine which is best. If you have cover two steps to the side, it may be better to move quickly, get to cover, then worry about shooting.

Start out with lateral movement, taking one step to the right. This means you're going to step with the right foot first, the foot in the direction you're moving. Once the right foot has solid ground then shift your weight to that foot and reposition the left foot, ending up in your fighting stance.

After practicing the lateral step you can start working on live-fire drills. As you step, come on target and make one hit. The key is once the first foot moves you're bringing the muzzle up, safety off and finger on the trigger to fire one accurate shot. Once that's working well, move two steps, taking one shot. Then move three steps, again taking one shot while moving. In order for this all to work well you have to start slowly, moving at about one-quarter speed. Moving at this speed creates time for you to apply your marksmanship and get a good hit. If you're moving too fast you'll want to shoot too fast, and the results will be less than satisfying. Ultimately your goal is to move smoothly, whether it's one or six steps, and at the same time place accurate hits on target.

This takes practice, and lots of it. In the beginning don't get frustrated if your group size is larger than you're used to. Remember, you're moving. The hits are not going to be as accurate as they are when standing still. But with practice and repetition you can get to the point that you're moving smoothly and putting accurate hits on target. You gotta crawl, walk and then eventually you're walking and shooting. There are very few situations where you would be running and shooting at the same time. Remember, you are responsible for every round that

1 To move to the right, step with the right foot first.

2 After placing the right foot, reposition the left foot, so that after taking one step you end up in your fighting stance.

1 While moving to the rear, keep the hips and upper body indexed on the target. Step with the strong-side leg first.

2 After positioning the strong-side leg, step with the support leg to end up in a fighting stance.

3 After taking one step to the rear, you wind up in your normal stance.

exits the barrel. Knowing when to not shoot is just as important as knowing when to shoot.

MOVING REAR

To move to the rear we initiate the movement with the strong-side leg – the right leg for right-handed shooters, left for lefties.

The knees are bent so the legs act as shock absorbers. Step back with the strong-side leg first, and then with the support-side foot so that, again, after taking one step to the rear you're in a fighting stance.

Think about it as taking a full step with the dominant leg, and then a half step with the support-side leg.

Start off in the low ready, taking one step to the rear. As you step, come up on target, firing one accurate round. Once this is looking good, work on taking two steps, again firing one round. Eventually you're taking multiple steps to the rear and shooting at the same time. Keep in mind that your movement should be smooth, and although you're shooting while moving you cannot try to time your shots with the footwork. Trying to time your shooting with the movement will only cause you to anticipate the shots, which will have a negative effect on your accuracy.

FORWARD MOVEMENT

To move forward, the same technique applies: step first with the foot that's in the direction you're moving. The first step you take is with the support-side leg.

Normally when moving forward you'll be in the low ready position. It would be unusual to want to move toward something that you need to shoot.

As you move forward you should be scanning. Remember, every step gives you a new view of the world, so you're looking, scanning and visually checking out all the "corners" you see while moving. Moving steadily in this form allows you to change directions as needed, efficiently moving in a different direction if something appears and you need to start backing up to create distance, move laterally to get behind cover or any of the other reasons for moving.

You also need to learn how to manipulate the AR while moving. Our natural instinct when the weapon runs empty is to stop to reload. Remember, you're moving for a reason, and you don't let an empty AR or a malfunction cause you to stop moving. To set this up for practice, load the AR with a magazine with only one round. After the first shot you'll run empty. Keep moving, old mag out, new mag in and hit the bolt release, firing at least one more round while moving. The objective is to keep moving while shooting, reloading or clearing a malfunction. Again, this doesn't come naturally, so practice is mandatory. The best way to acquire the necessary repetitions is dry practice.

COMBAT TURNS

Normally when practicing you start out with the target in front of you. In real life the threat can come from any direction, so we need to learn how to index on the threat in a safe and efficient manner. Start out working this dry, and once you've got a good feel for it then you can work it live fire.

Go to the cross-body ready position, as described in the section on ready positions. Face to the right of the target. Now you have "threat left." Step one is to look left, visually acquiring the target. The target is to the left, so you'll step forward with the right foot.

After placing the foot, raise your heels up off the ground and twist the hips towards the target by rotating them counter-clockwise, rotating on the balls of the feet.

The upper body follows the hips, and once you're indexed or facing the target you should be in your firing stance, with the left leg slightly ahead of the right foot. At this point the muzzle comes up on target and you're ready to fire. (For a left hand shooter this same movement would be applied to threat right, and you're stepping with the left or strong foot, pivoting clockwise.)

This technique allows you to get on target safely (without sweeping or covering anyone with the muzzle as you twist), efficiently and with stability.

1 To move forward, step with the support-side leg first.

2 Plant the leg to ensure solid footing.

3 Reset the strong-side leg, which completes one step.

The first step to responding to threat-left is to **LOOK**, visually acquiring the target.

STEP forward with the strong-side foot.

PIVOT on the feet, with the movement coming from the hips. The muzzle is down, pointing in a safe direction.

Once you're indexed onto the **TARGET**, bring the muzzle up to fire.

With a threat to the right, you'll step across with the left foot, basically pointing it towards the target. Pivot in a clockwise direction, which should index you onto the target and position your feet and legs in the proper stance.

At this point you bring the muzzle up into a firing position.

With the threat to the rear you'll look over the left shoulder. Step across with the strong-side foot and then pivot, turning counter clockwise. After pivoting, you're on target in your fighting stance and ready to bring the muzzle on target.

For a left-handed shooter, with "threat left" you step across with the right leg, again pointing it towards the target, and pivot counter clockwise to index onto target. With "threat rear" you'll look over the right shoulder, step with the left foot and turn clockwise.

You could perform these same actions in reverse, for example stepping backwards with the opposite feet than discussed, but I think it's much better to step forward to index as opposed to stepping backward, especially when necessary to step across. Practice this action.

1. Threat is to the right, so you look first.

2. Step forward and across with the left leg.

3 Pivot, and once on target bring the muzzle up to fire.

With threat to the rear, **LOOK** over the strong-side shoulder.

STEP across with the strong-side foot.

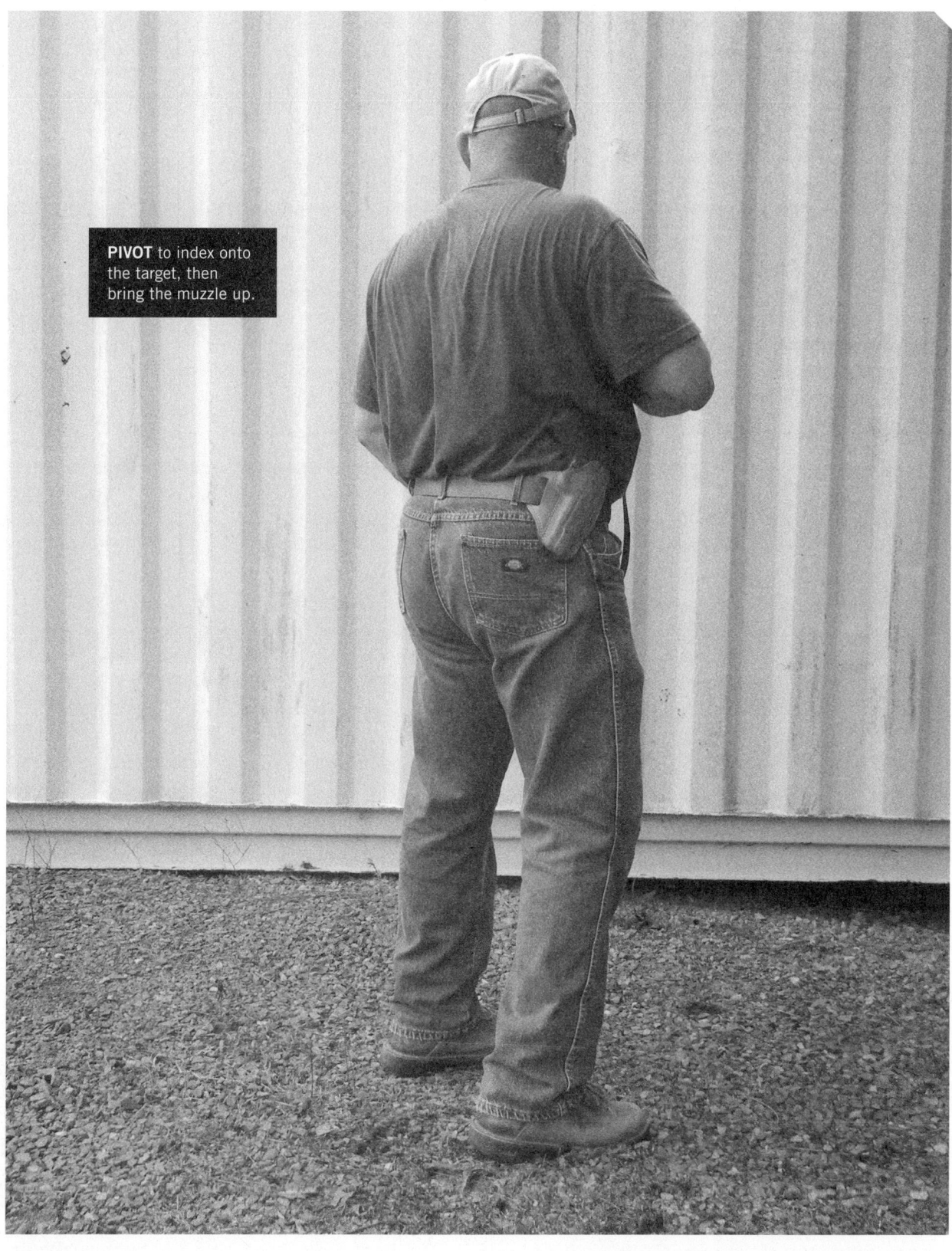

PIVOT to index onto the target, then bring the muzzle up.

Using this index technique to turn into the target also sets you up to move in any direction, using the same techniques as described for moving laterally, to the rear or forward. Practice indexing on target and immediately flowing into movement to the right, left, rearward and forward until the transition and movement is smooth. The key element is safety, keeping the muzzle down until your body is on target.

The best way to practice this is dry, and again you can use your pretend AR so that you can practice almost anywhere. A few minutes a day of this work will greatly improve the learning curve.

When moving over rough terrain you want to always concentrate on keeping the muzzle pointing in a safe direction. For help and stability use the support hand, maintaining your firing grip on the weapon as much as possible.

When working in cramped or tight areas, you generally want to lead with the muzzle, working it through the opening first. This way you can control it, keeping it pointing in a safe direction as you move the rest of the body through the opening.

Ultimately the environment and the situation will determine what direction you need to move or how many steps you need to take. You may start out moving in one direction, and then need to change up, stepping in another direction. For example, my pre-programmed response is to take one lateral step. This buys me time to assess the situation

Whenever possible, use the support hand for stability, maintaining your firing grip on the weapon as much as possible.

and puts the threat into a reactive mode. Then I may move back to create distance. While moving back I see cover, so I move a couple of steps left to position the cover between the threat and me. At that point I'm moving back again, to put distance between me and the object that's being used for cover.

Use your dummy weapon to practice moving and changing directions. On the range you can work live fire, for example taking one step left then three steps back. Or taking several steps back, then moving laterally. •

In tight quarters you normally want to lead with the muzzle, keeping in pointing in a safe direction.

PRACTICE

Movement and the footwork that goes with it is extremely important. Practice doesn't mean having to go to the range. You can use your dummy weapon to practice. You can even practice just using your "pretend" AR, acting as if you're holding the AR and going through all the same motions of flipping the safety and getting your finger on and off the trigger. As with all your skills it's the repetition that is important, and the brain doesn't know whether it's a real AR your holding or a pretend one, as long as you perform all the proper actions. The shooting part isn't that difficult; apply the fundamentals and you'll get a good hit. It's all the other skills, such as moving smoothly so you can shoot or indexing onto a target from different directions, that take a lot of practice to become proficient. Every day has opportunities to practice moving.

On the range it's simply moving and shooting. You step right, moving several steps while engaging. You can move left one step, moving out of the line of attack, and then move to the rear, creating distance while engaging the threat. As you're working live fire drills remember to engage the different areas of the target, putting hits to the chest and pelvis. Headshots should only be attempted while stationary.

During live fire drills think beyond what you're doing on the range to how these actions fit into the "real" world. You've moving towards cover. Set up "bystander" targets, so you're moving to acquire a clear angle of fire on the threat. Remember to control the muzzle so you're not sweeping or covering the bystanders, who could be family members, with your muzzle. As always, you're operating the safety, controlling the trigger finger and concentrating on shooting accurately.

CHAPTER 18
FIRING POSITIONS

THE MOST COMMON firing position is standing or "offhand." But there are times when you need more stability, for accuracy, or you need to lower your profile, for example to take advantage of cover and the protection it provides. In situations like these you need to be familiar with the various firing positions.

Standing or offhand sounds simple, but even with that there are a few different variations. There is a normal stance, as discussed previously. Another option is Olympic offhand, which creates a little more stability and allows you to get a little "taller" in order to shoot over the top of something. For the Olympic offhand you blade your body more than normal and bring the support arm in close to the body, positioning so it's underneath the AR and bracing it against the upper torso.

The support hand can be positioned in a variety of ways, for example on the handguard except with the hand twisted or reversed from what would be normal. You can rest the support hand against on the bottom of the magazine, this works really well with 20-round mags.

For most people, having the feet closer together works better than the more aggressive stance. This offhand position is more of a shooting position as opposed to a fighting stance.

For longer distance shots or shooting a small target, you need more accuracy than a standing position provides. You increase accuracy by creating more stability. To increase stability, lower your body's center of

In "Olympic" offhand the body is bladed and the support hand rests against the upper torso.

gravity and/or create more contact points between your body and a solid object, in other words rest or brace against something more stable than your body. Or, it may be necessary to lower your profile in order to take advantage of cover and the protection it offers.

I separate positions other than standing into two categories: reactive and premeditated. Reactive positions are quick to get into, and equally important quick to get out of, sort of general-purpose positions.

Most positions used for self-defense and law enforcement engagements fall into this category. Reactive positions are also used when you need to change your angle of fire. In close quarters with the threat surrounded by non-hostiles, it may be necessary to get low, changing the angle of the muzzle and the trajectory of the bullet in order to get a clear angle of fire or guard against over-penetration of your round. The variations of kneeling are a good example of reactive positions.

Premeditated positions take longer to get into, more time to get out of and back into standing, and are more for specific applications.

These positions require more deliberate thought and action to execute and to recover from than the reactive positions, but they create extremely stable firing platforms or radically change the profile of your body in order to take advantage of cover. The variations of prone are good examples of premeditated positions.

As you're working from one position to another, for example from standing to prone, remember to keep the muzzle pointing in a safe direction and remove your finger from the trigger guard, keeping it off the trigger.

Once you've finished shooting, finger off the trigger and safety on. In our example you're in prone, so you'll scan from there. You want to look around and make sure it's safe to come up to a standing position. After scanning, come up kneeling, scan from there, and then up again, repeating the process until you're standing, where you'll scan again. The entire

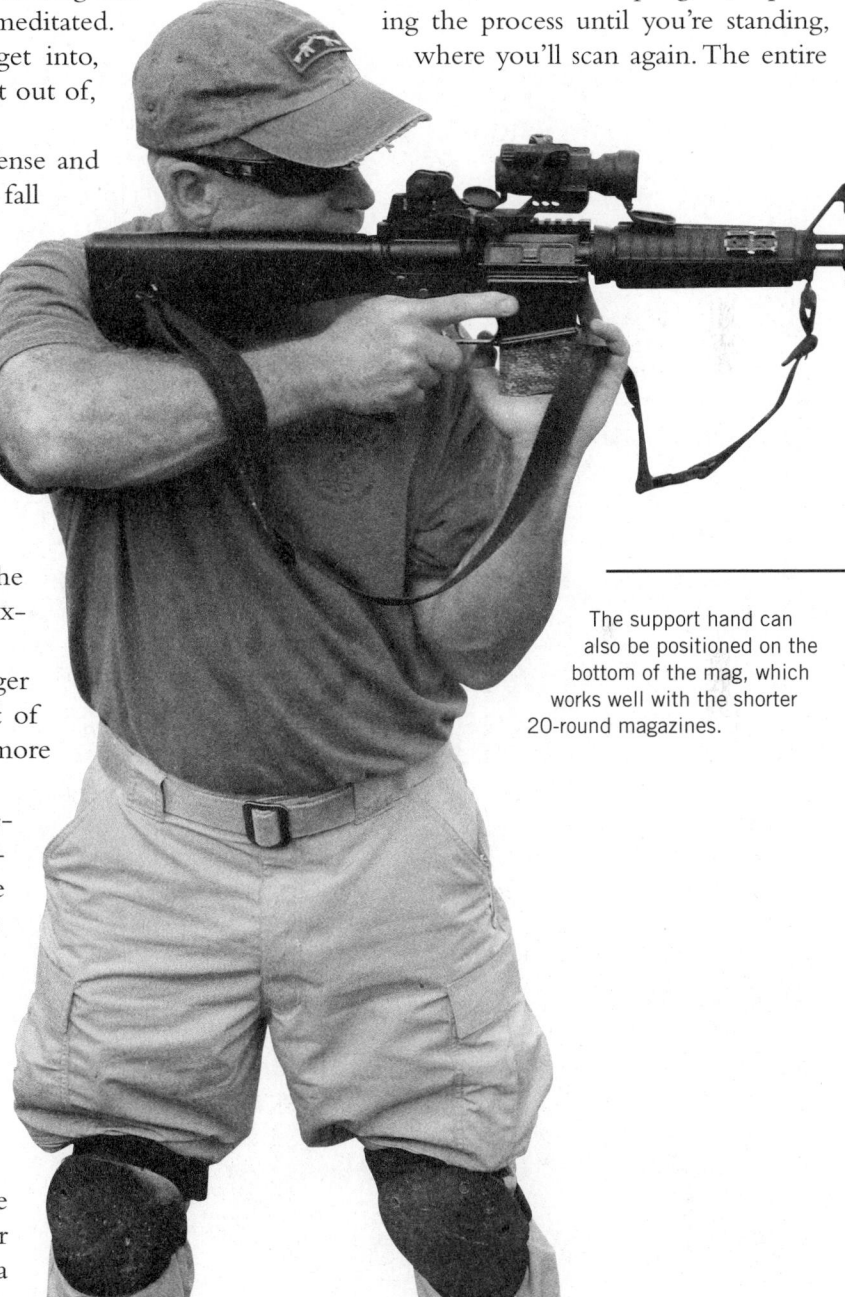

The support hand can also be positioned on the bottom of the mag, which works well with the shorter 20-round magazines.

Reactive positions, usually variations of kneeling, are quick to get into, and easy to get out of.

Premeditated positions, such as prone, take longer to get into and out of and are usually for specific applications.

time, stock is in the shoulder and the muzzle is pointing downward – the low ready – your finger is off the trigger and clear of the trigger guard and the safety is on.

KNEELING

"Speed kneeling" is simply dropping down onto the strong knee. This position is quick to assume, and it's easy to get up and into a standing position.

Dropping onto the strong-side knee keeps the hips indexed on the target so that everything from the waist and up is the same as if you were standing.

"Braced kneeling" starts out the same as the speed kneel, except then you want to lower the upper body more so you can brace the support elbow on the support knee. You want to create a tripod between the strong foot and knee and the support-side foot. If the strong foot and knee are too close in line to the support foot, there's more chance of wobbling from one side to the other.

The support-side elbow is resting on the support knee, and this should be underneath the carbine so you're relying on bone support as opposed to muscle tension. Ideally you want to rest your

"Speed kneeling" is simply dropping down onto the strong-side knee. Quick to get into, and easy to come back up to standing.

rear-end on the strong-side heel, which again increases stability.

"Reverse kneeling" is used when you have an object to rest or support the front of the weapon. In a traditional kneel the primary knee is on the ground, however in reverse kneeling the support knee is placed on the ground and the strong-side knee is up. The support hand braces the front of the weapon against a solid object and the strong elbow rests on the strong knee for support. With both the front of the weapon and the primary elbow supported the weapon is locked into an extremely stable platform.

"Double kneeling," firing with both knees on the ground, is one of my favorites. It allows you to lean out to both right and left sides or cover or the object you're bracing against, and you can raise or lower your profile slightly if necessary.

Although technically not a kneeling position the "squat" or "rice-paddy prone" is an extremely quick position to assume, and quick to come back up to standing, if it works for you. The squat position is a "love it or hate it" kind of thing. To get into squatting all you do is bend at the knees until you're squatting. The key is that you need to have both feet flat on the ground. If the heels are

"Braced kneeling" is the same as the speed kneeling, except you lower the body so the support-side elbow is resting on the support knee.

"Reverse kneeling" is used when you have a support to rest the front of the carbine. The strong-side knee is up, and the strong-side arm is braced against the knee.

"Double kneeling," with both knees down, is good for leaning out to the left or right of cover.

off the ground you won't have stability. If you don't' have the flexibility to do this then it's definitely not for you.

The key with firing positions is to learn what works for you, and understand how the various positions are suitable for different situations. Equally important is learning what doesn't work for you. Once you discover something doesn't work, you can figure out what will work by modifying or, if necessary, using a completely different position.

Equally important is how quickly you can recover from reactive positions, getting to your feet and reacting to the fight as it unfolds. Fights are fluid and dynamic. Getting into position quickly is critical, but the ability to get back on your feet and moving to a new location is just as important.

PREMEDITATED POSITIONS

Prone is the most stable of premeditated positions and allows extremely precise shots. The problem is that normally it's too low. Drop down into prone in the woods or an urban environment and you'll discover a limited field of view due to scrub, brush, and the countless obstructions found in urban settings. However, there are situations where prone is the best choice, and usually in a modified configuration.

There are several variations of prone. They all start out by going to a kneeling position, as always controlling the muzzle, and then using the support arm to help lower the body down onto the ground.

From there you can flow into the specific prone position that you need. Again your task is to work with these variations so you know how they work and apply to different environments or situations.

The squat, or "rice paddy prone" is a great position, if it works for you. The key is to have both feet flat on the ground for stability.

Under ideal conditions you want the body and spine straight in alignment behind the carbine. In this position the recoil runs straight back from the carbine into the center of the body, and recovering from the recoil is more natural and efficient.

Another option, especially if you're trying to get your body behind cover, is to have the spine at an angle behind the carbine. For example, a right-handed shooter thinks about the hands on the clock when it's seven o'clock. The carbine is the long hand of the clock, on twelve, and the body is the short hand of the clock, roughly on the seven.

When working in the prone positions there are several ways you can adjust the elevation on the muzzle to acquire a sight picture. You can shift the location of the support hand, moving it closer or farther away on the handguard. The support elbow can be repositioned; the more underneath the handguard the higher the elevation. You can also change the position of the stock in the strong-side shoulder, raising or lowering it. You may need to do a combination of these in order to find just the right position. When working on pure accuracy, you want to make sure to check your natural point of aim as described earlier before you ever start shooting.

"Roll over prone" is used for shooting underneath an object, such as a vehicle.

The shooter rolls over onto the strong-side shoulder, which puts the head parallel and carbine parallel with the ground. The support arm is forward, and the support hand is underneath the handguard touching the ground and supporting the carbine. (Make sure your hand isn't blocking the ejection

To get into prone, start by getting on both knees, then use the support hand to help get onto the ground. Make sure the control the muzzle.

port, which would create a stoppage when you fire.) Bend the knee of the support leg and bring it toward the torso. This may seem strange at first, but after working with it most shooters find that it's actually a comfortable and stable position.

I originally learned this position from Clint Smith, director of Thunder Ranch. "I would not say I came up with it," Clint told me when I asked him about it, but he also admits not "remembering being taught it by anyone." "I started doing it to compensate for scope offsets and in my eye it was an adaptation of (Ray) Chapman's rollover prone for the handgun," he explained. "With the rifle it was more about lowering the upper body, shoulders, and head."

There are a lot of other variations of prone, and the best thing to do is go to the range, experiment and have some fun, and in the process you'll learn what works for you, and just as importantly, what doesn't work.

SITTING

Sitting is definitely a position reserved for specific applications. Normally it takes some time to get into the sitting position, and it's very slow to work your way back up to standing from a seated firing position.

There are three variations of the sitting position: crossed leg, crossed ankle and open leg. Your body's build or shape, flexibility, old injuries, the environment and particulars of the situation all affect which variation works best for you.

To get into the sitting position, start by kneel-

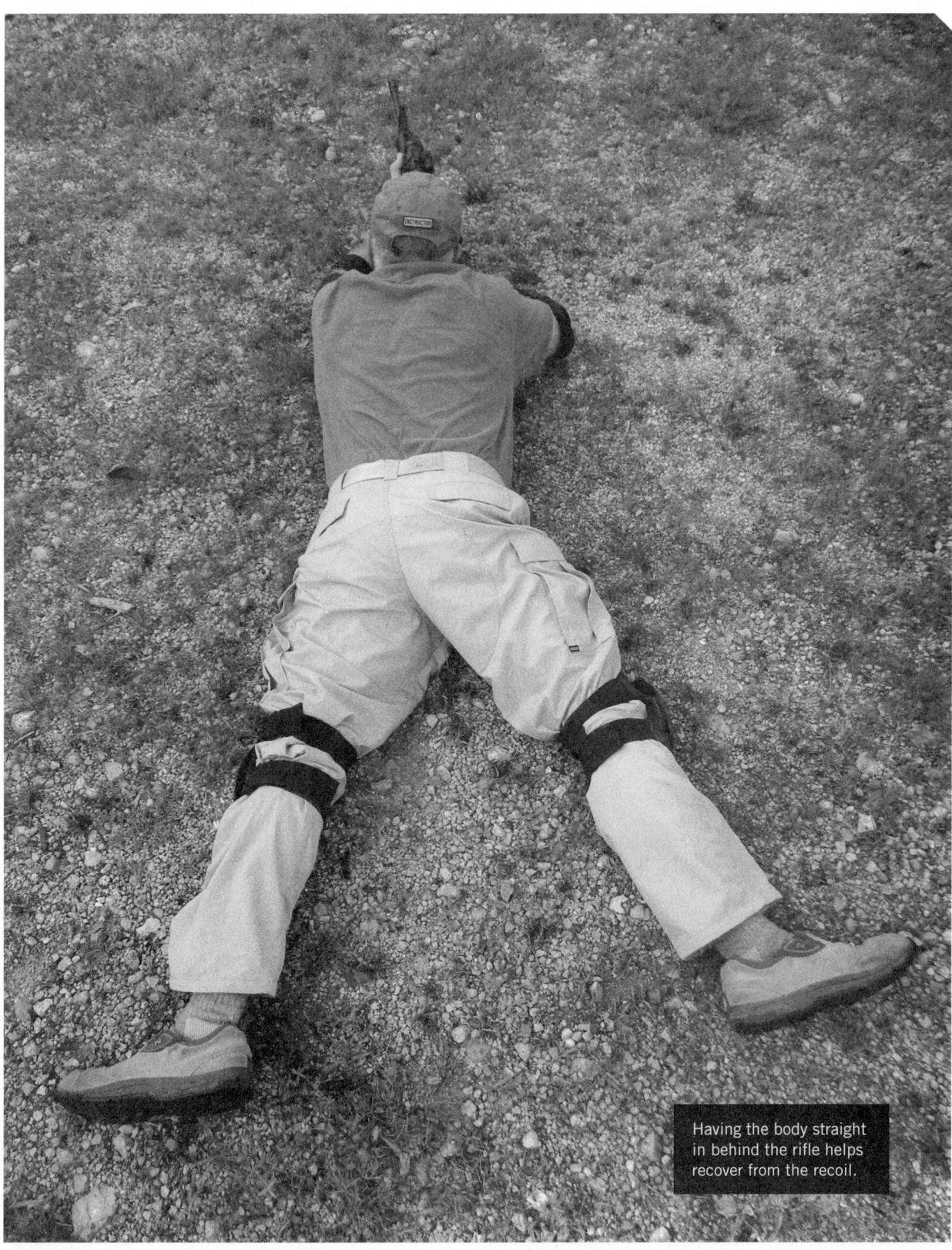

Having the body straight in behind the rifle helps recover from the recoil.

The body can be at an angle behind the carbine, for example when shooting from behind cover.

Bending the support-side knee toward the body rotates the torso slightly, which may make prone more comfortable.

"Roll over prone" is used to shoot underneath an object, such as a vehicle.

Having the support hand on the ground and supporting the handguard creates stability, but be sure not to block the ejection port.

There are a lot of variations of prone. The environment will dictate what you need for stability, so practice all different types of prone positions.

ing, then slowly work into a sitting position. The crossed leg position means just that, the legs are crossed, one over the other.

You can change the elevation of the muzzle by swapping which leg is on top and bottom. Both elbows should be braced against the knees for stability. The crossed leg position works really well for shooting downhill.

Crossed ankle position is with the legs extended out in front of you, and with the ankles crossed, one over the other.

Again, you can change the elevation of the muzzle by swapping which ankle is on top. The elbows are braced more on the inside of the knees, and it usually helps if you apply a little pressure against the elbows with the knees.

In the open leg position the legs are extended out farther, with the feet separated. Your elbows are inside the knees a little, and you definitely want to apply pressure against them with the knees, applying a slight amount of tension inboard.

To work up to standing, first move to kneeling, usually strong-side knee down, keeping the muzzle in a safe direction. Use the support hand and arm to maintain balance while going to the kneeling position. From kneeling you go to standing, as always scanning as you work you way up from one position to another.

These same positions work when resting or bracing against something solid to add extra stability for accuracy. Just be careful of sticking the muzzle past anything, you don't want to stick it out there where someone could grab hold of it.

Be sure the barrel isn't touching anything, which will change your point of impact, sometimes dramatically. For example, if the barrel is touching something on the bottom it throws the shot high, or opposite from where the pressure on the barrel is coming from.

Obviously there are too many different firing positions to discuss in this book. Start with the basic positions, and after you've mastered them then you

Crossing the legs completely and resting the elbows on the knees is a stabile position, and great for shooting downhill.

In the crossed ankle version of sitting, the feet are extended out farther away from the body.

In the open leg position, the elbows are braced against the inside of the knees.

For combat purposes, be careful of sticking the muzzle out past your cover. Someone may grab it, and it's also a great way for someone to spot your position.

Make sure the barrel isn't touching or pressed against anything or it will change the bullet's point of impact, sometimes by many inches.

can move into unconventional or more complicated positions.

Initially, every time you drop into a position you should confirm your form and location in relationship to the target by checking your natural point of aim. This is accomplished by getting into your firing position, sights on target and ready to fire. Close your eyes, inhale and exhale a few times, and then open your eyes to see where the sights are aiming. Breathing, with your eyes closed, helps your body settle into its natural position, which relies on bone structure as opposed to muscle tension. If the sights have drifted to the left or right during the settling then you need to reposition your entire body, instead of using the muscles to bring them back onto target. Reposition, close your eyes, breath a few times, and open the eyes. Adjust if necessary, repeating the process until once you open the eyes the sights are on target. Now you're ready to start actually firing. If your shot groups are spread out laterally, a left and right dispersion, that's tells you that you didn't have a good firing position to start with. After doing this enough you'll get to where you can automatically drop into position and have a good sight picture on target, but in the beginning you have to start slowly, going through the actions

Firing from unusual positions will require you to focus on the fundamentals of marksmanship in order to get good hits.

step by step and establishing a good, stable position prior to firing.

No matter what position is being used, remember to apply the fundamentals of marksmanship, properly using the sights and trigger to make good hits. Also, keep in mind that accuracy at longer distances and/or small targets requires you to control your breathing. Whenever you have to give up something in one area, for example you can't get as stable as you would like to, then you need to compensate for it in another area, like controlling your breathing, getting a good smooth press on the trigger and then following through.

Everyone has seen shootera who can just drop into position and fire off a nice, tight group, seemingly without effort. This isn't magic, or some secret ninja technique. They cultivated these skills through plenty of practice, and dry practice is the best way to improve your abilities. Practice getting into position, working back up into standing, and applying all the fundamentals. Do it one hundred times, and then start working on doing it ten times one hundred. •

PRACTICE

Again, practicing doesn't mean having to go to the range to fire. Dummy weapons allow you to work on your different positions until you can drop into them smoothly. Furniture in your home can be used for "cover" or as a rest or brace for stability. A little practice each day will greatly improve your skills and the stability of your positions.

Make sure your live fire practice is focused, concentrating on doing everything safely, your number one concern, and efficiently. Speed will come naturally, but if you try to focus on being fast you'll never become efficient.

Set up different stations so you can move from one to another, using a different position to fire. Or you can start from standing, fire five shots, go to kneeling, fire five more, then into prone for five more shots. Load your mags with five rounds so you can practice reloading while going from one position to another. Once the basics are working well you can start combining various skills into one drill.

Your position has to fit the environment, which usually means modifying in order to use cover or to brace and rest for stability.

Working in different positions is the best way to practice. Once you get the basics down you want to practice in all different types of environments, varying to conditions as much as possible.

There's a lot of chainlink fence in the world. The key to shooting through it is to work the muzzle through the links, then grab the fence and push against it for stability so you're not bouncing as you fire.

Your position has to fit the environment, which usually means modifying in order to use cover or to brace and rest for stability and accuracy. In the "real" world it's rare that you can use a perfect textbook position.

There's no golden rule that says you'll be in a great position. You need to practice "ground" fighting, which is firing from unusual positions. As you work up to standing, finger is off the trigger and you must concentrate on keeping the muzzle pointing in a safe direction.

Regardless of your position, always make sure the muzzle is clear. Remember the offset between the sights and muzzle? You can have a good, clear sight picture but the muzzle be blocked by an object in your environment.

CHAPTER 19
USING COVER

FOR DEFENSIVE USE of the AR you need to think about using cover and taking advantage of the protection it provides. Cover creates a physical barrier between you, the threat and their weapon. The attacker is armed with a knife. To use the knife he has to be within arms reach, so positioning something like a car between him and you denies him the ability to use the knife. That's a pretty simple concept to grasp. Using cover for protection against a threat armed with a firearm is more subjective. The degree of protection cover provides depends on what type rounds are coming your way, for instance. An object that protects you from handgun rounds might not hold up against high velocity rifle rounds. Even among rifle calibers there is a significant difference in penetration capabilities. A round of 5.56mm ball ammunition penetrates about 1.5 inches of concrete. A round of .30-06 armor-piercing ammunition can punch through five times that much. Most objects in our environment are probably better thought of as bullet resistant rather than bullet proof. With enough rounds, usually three to four, even a handgun round can punch a hole through a concrete block.

Regardless of the caliber, when rounds hit a hardened surface, skip off something or pass through and exit out the other side, the bullet fragments and debris created from the concrete, glass, plastic, and metal of those objects is dangerous. Now, in addition to the bullet, you've got 20 sharp projectiles flying at you.

With this in mind, one of the first principles to apply when using cover is creating distance between you and the object you're using for pro-

If at all possible, keep distance between you and the object you're using for cover.

One round of 9mm hitting a section of concrete block will crack it. Several rounds will punch a hole through it.

The block is cracked from one round.

tection. Having at least six feet of distance from cover greatly reduces the danger of being injured by fragmentation and debris. Creating this distance is difficult because it goes completely against our natural instincts. Our instincts tell use that the closer we get to cover the safer we are. This overpowering desire to crowd cover is a excellent example of where our natural instincts are counterproductive to fighting with firearms. This takes a lot of practice to overcome.

To illustrate this point I set up a test. I positioned a target 18 inches behind a concrete block – about the distance you would be if you had the AR in hand and were close to the block using it for cover. I skipped bullets off the side of the block using .45acp, .223/5.56 and 7.62x39, the Russian "short" used in AK-47s and SKS rifles. The first target has lots of holes in it. The holes marked in the square are from the .45acp. The holes that are circled are from the AR. All the other damage is from the 7.62x39, which is a very violent round.

The second target was positioned six feet from the block, with the same angles, just extending the distance. This target wasn't hit by any of the debris or bullet fragments. Distance is a good thing.

Another advantage of distancing yourself from cover is that it widens your field of view, allowing you to see more of the environment around you.

You're driving down the interstate and there's a semi-truck in front of you. When you get right on the tail end of the truck, all you can see is truck. Backing off the truck, creating some space, allows you to see what's going on in the next lane and ahead of the truck. The same thing applies when using cover.

When you get too close to cover it blocks of you from seeing, and you need to see what's happening in order to act appropriately.

In order to use cover properly you have to apply geometry. Creating distance from cover puts more ground between you and the threat. Distance also creates a larger area of protection. You have more space to work in; you can move laterally, forward or to the rear and still have cover. The more dis-

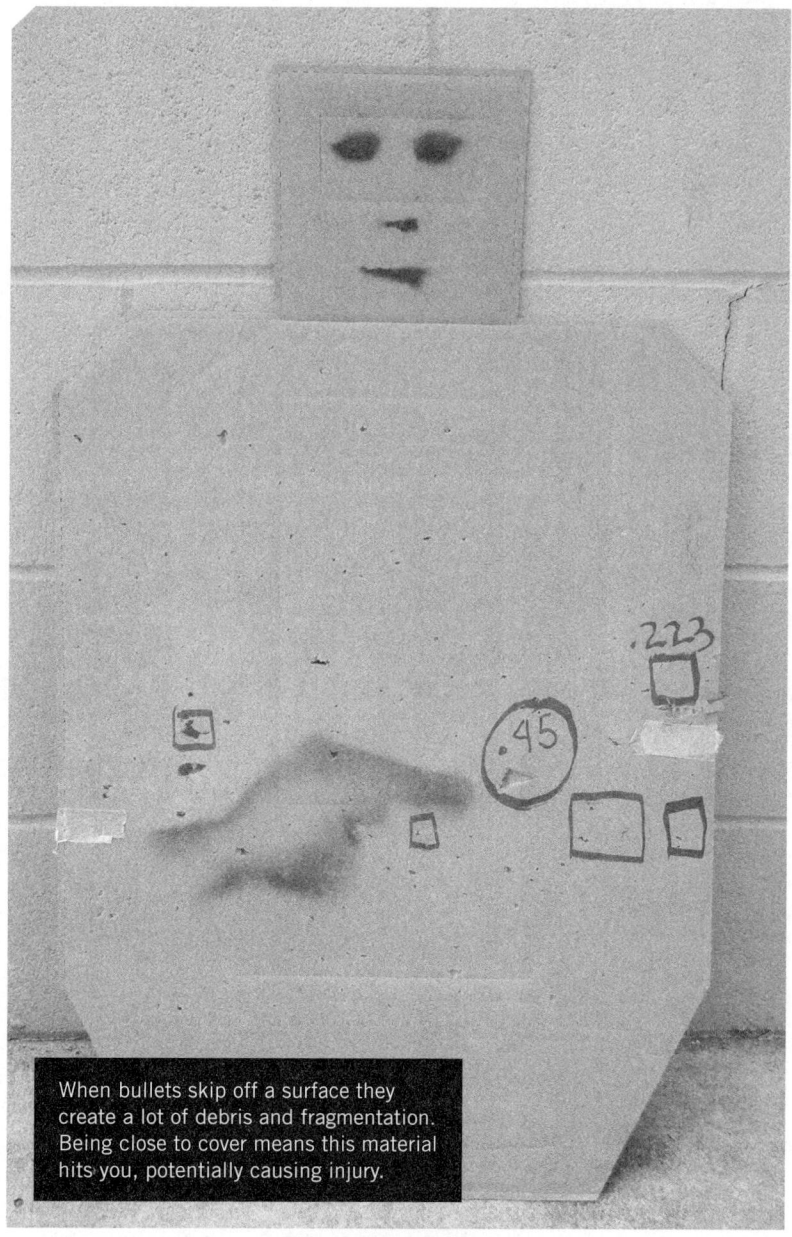

When bullets skip off a surface they create a lot of debris and fragmentation. Being close to cover means this material hits you, potentially causing injury.

The back of the target shows all the holes created by the different rounds.

CHAPTER 19: USING COVER

Moving the target away from cover, in this case six feet, greatly reduces the chances of being injured by debris and fragments.

Getting close to cover will restrict your field of view, blocking you from seeing what's going on around you.

Creating distance from cover opens up your field of view so you can see more of the environment around you. Being visually-oriented creatures, it's important to be able to see the area surrounding you.

tance the better. Your cover can be 50 feet away, but position it between you and the threat and it provides protection.

There are some situations where the geometry won't allow you to have this distance. If you are fighting more than one threat the geometry of the situation completely changes. The farther away you get from cover, the less area of protection you have, and if you move too far back you're exposed to multiple threats at the same time. You have to get closer to your cover, but no more so than necessary. Or, if the threat is on higher ground, you have to get closer to cover because of the angles involved. You need to visualize the geometry to determine where you want to be positioned.

Most fights are fluid and dynamic, normally everyone is moving. The geometry changes in the time required for someone to take one step. You can have a good position behind cover, and all the threat has to do is step right or left and your geometry completely changes. Either your whole body is now exposed to the threat, or you can't see the bad guys and they are using "your" cover to advance or flank you. Remember Newton's law: For every action there is an equal and opposite re-action. This applies to physics and fighting. If the threats are moving, chances are you need to be moving as well, which means maintaining visual contact so you can act accordingly. Always keep in mind that cover is a two-sided coin. You may be facing someone who knows just as much as you do, or more, about fighting and using cover. Don't underestimate the threat's abilities or overestimate your skills.

Once you're behind cover, as soon as possible, start looking for better cover. When you get the opportunity, move to more substantial cover, a location that puts you in a better location or nearer an exit, your family or partners. Before leaving a known safe place, scan to be sure it's safe — as safe as you can determine — and locate your next position. Under ideal conditions, you know where you're going before you start moving.

There are other principles we need to apply to maximize the protection of cover. Whenever pos-

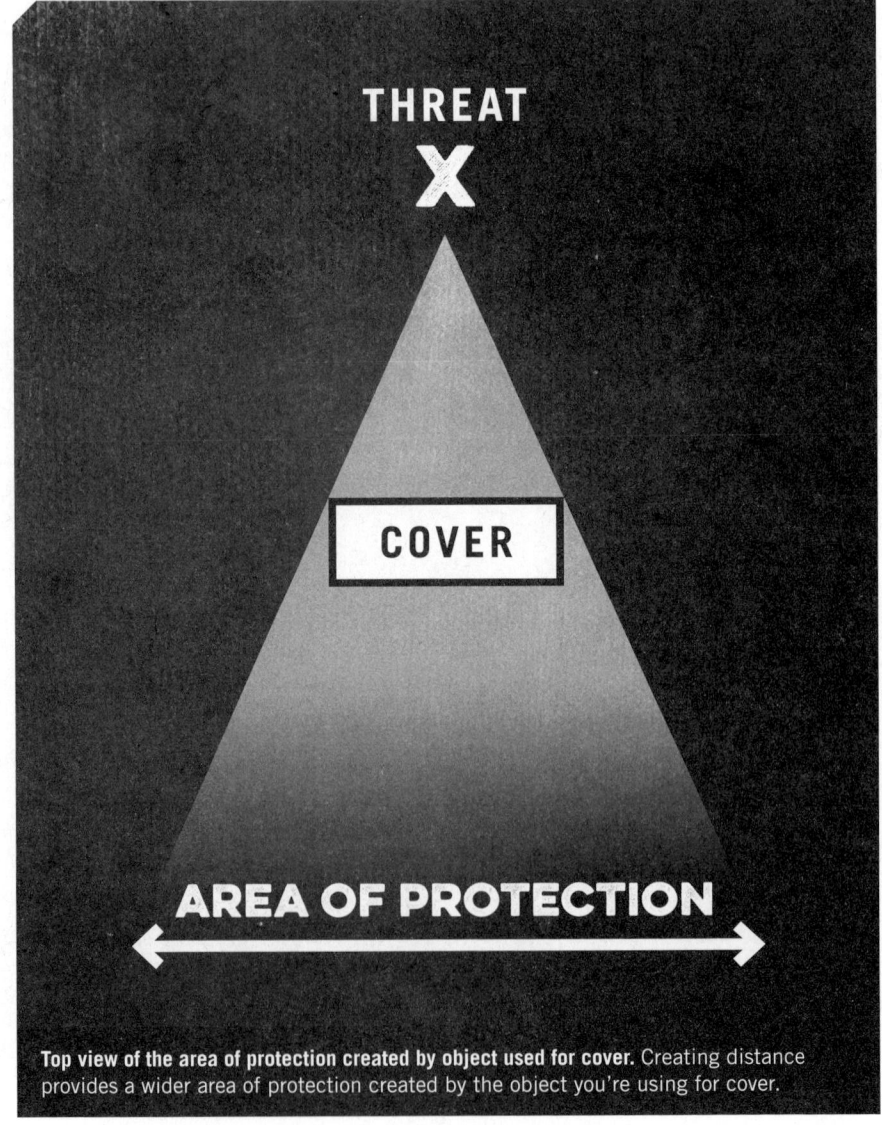

Top view of the area of protection created by object used for cover. Creating distance provides a wider area of protection created by the object you're using for cover.

sible, remain standing, staying on your feet you so can move. However, there may be times when your cover requires you to get lower. When a lower position is necessary, we want to use positions that are quick to get into, and quick to get up and mobile as necessary. "Reactive positions," such as variations of the kneeling positions, are quick to assume and, equally importantly, quick to get up and on your feet ready to move. Remember, you want to move to a better location as soon as possible.

"Premeditated positions," like rollover prone used to shoot underneath an object such as a car, may be required. Just remember these positions take longer to get into, restrict your ability to move, and require more time to come up to standing. Every position has advantages and disadvantages. Your job is to train and practice enough to understand the application of various positions and when to use them for cover.

You may be able to use cover to create a more stable platform for accuracy. Keep in mind the dangers of getting too close to your cover, and if you're sticking your muzzle past something make sure there's nobody there than may try to grab the barrel in an attempt to disarm you. Also take care to keep your hands and fingers away from where they could be injured by debris and fragmentation from incoming rounds.

Another important factor to remember is the offset between the sights and barrel. You can have a great sight picture, but the barrel may be blocked by something in front of it. Each situation will be unique, and the conditions determine your best option.

When using cover, expose the least amount of your body necessary to locate, identify and if necessary engage the threat. You should use as close to a normal stance as possible, leaning out the left or right as needed. Using a mirror will help you fine-tune your position so you're not sticking elbows out too far or extending a leg past cover. The edge of the mirror is the edge of your cover. As you work to the side, the mirror's reflection allows you to see the view from the bad guy's perspective. Use your dummy weapons and a partner to work cover so they can tell you what parts of your body are exposed.

A good reference to use when practicing is to line up the edge of your cover with the edge of the target. If you see open ground between the two that

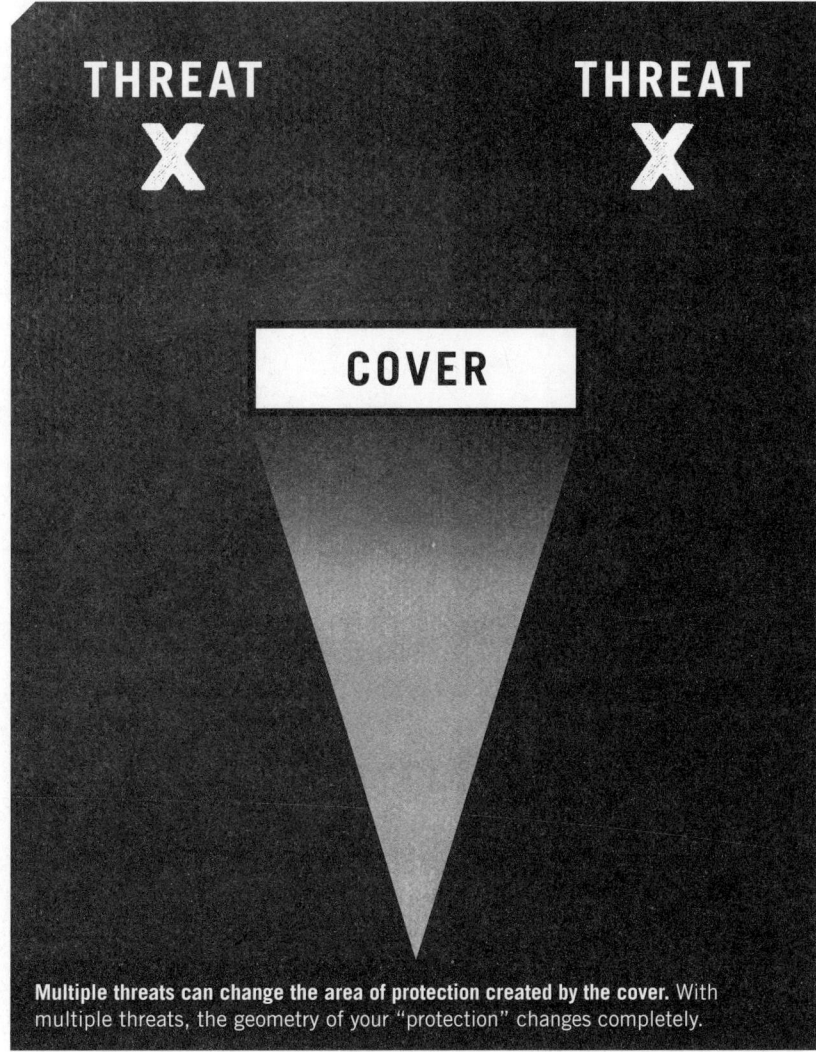

Multiple threats can change the area of protection created by the cover. With multiple threats, the geometry of your "protection" changes completely.

With multiple threats you may have to get closer to cover than you would like, but if you don't you'll be exposed to both threats at one time.

When using cover you have to think in three dimensions. If the threat is elevated, you have to get closer to cover. On the other hand, if you can control the high ground that's always good.

CHAPTER 19: USING COVER

All the threat has to do is move one step and the geometry is completely changed. If the threat is moving, you need to be moving.

Reactive positions are quick to get into and quick to get out of.

Premeditated positions, such as rollover prone, are used for specific applications.

You may be able to brace against cover for stability and better accuracy.

Be careful any time you're sticking the barrel past your cover or concealment. This could allow someone to grab it, or give away your position.

You may have a good sight picture, but the barrel be blocked by something. Make sure the barrel is clear prior to firing.

Visually you want the edge of your cover bumping up against the edge of the target. This alignment indicates you have as much of your body as possible behind cover.

If you see open ground between the edge of your cover and the target, you're exposing too much of your body. You need to move more to the side, getting more protection.

When ever possible, work around the side of cover as opposed to working over the top.

CHAPTER 19: USING COVER

Working over the opt of cover, using horizontal angles, exposes all of your head.

Working in low-light environments means learning how to use handheld lights, even if you have a weapon-mounted light.

means you're exposing too much of your body, and you need to reposition. The ideal position is to have the majority of your body behind cover, and only exposing what's necessary to locate, identify, and if necessary engage the threat. Normally this means using your normal stance, and leaning out to the left or right of your cover.

Whenever possible work around the side of cover, using vertical angles as opposed to going over the top. Shooting over the top of an object exposes everything from your shoulders up. Working around the side of an object, using vertical angles, you expose less of your head to the threat as opposed to using horizontal angles, shooting over the top of something.

The golden rule for cover is to use it. When there is incoming fire, get behind your protection. Avoid exposing parts of your body where they can be injured. Then, at the right time, you can start working around your cover.

Most violent confrontations occur in low-light environments, so your training and practice with cover should include learning how to work with flashlights.

Even if you have a light mounted on the carbine, you still need to know how to use handheld lights. The light on the AR may stop working. A handheld light provides more options and versatility. You may have to use someone else's carbine that doesn't have a light, so you use the light that you normally carry. There are a lot of different techniques for using a handheld light with a carbine, but try to keep it to a minimum. Having too many techniques is just as bad as not having enough.

When using a handheld light and working around the right side of cover, the light should be positioned on the right side of the AR. For using the left side of cover the light is on the left side of the weapon.

Positioning the light this way provides maximum penetration of light into the threat area, and less chance of your light reflecting back off that sur-

LEFT: For using the right side of cover, or a left-hand corner, the light needs to be on the right side of the weapon. RIGHT: For working around the left of cover, or a right turn, you need the light on the left side of the AR.

face, illuminating you and affecting your night vision. The more distance you have from cover the wider your light beam is, so it may be necessary to get closer, for example if you're working through a window, or aim the light a little more to the left or right of cover. The cone or center of the beam won't be positioned exactly on the threat but there's still have plenty of light to work with.

Many people will switch the weapon from one side to the other, depending on which direction they're working around cover, but in my opinion this is not a good idea. Think about time, efficiency and accuracy. Transitioning the AR from one side to another consumes time, and increases the possibility of fumbling or dropping your weapon. Unless you are truly ambidextrous – physically and mentally – you won't manipulate the weapon as efficiently using the support hand. Add in the use of a handheld light and all of this is more complicated. As for accuracy, you probably won't shoot as quickly or as accurately from the support side. With practice you should be able to modify your stance and positions so you can keep the AR on your strong side and work around either side of cover without exposing much more of your body.

CONCEALMENT

Although concealment hides you from view, it doesn't offer you any protection. That doesn't mean it won't work in some situations. If the threat doesn't know where you are, that provides you safety. Then, when the time is right and you are ready, you can escape, get to a better location with cover, or engage the threat if necessary. Also remember that anything you can put between you and the threat is better than nothing. A sheetrock wall may not appear to offer much protection, but one thing about small arms fire is that it's unpredictable. Once the rounds strike an object it's hard to predict how they will react. Regardless of what you're behind, remember to create distance, as much as possible according to the situation.

Vehicles should be thought of more as concealment than cover. With the lightweight materials that go into their construction, vehicles today don't offer much protection against bullets, especially high-velocity rifle rounds. I've seen a 9mm handgun round go through the trunk, back seat and front seat, and then lodge itself in the windshield.

When using a vehicle as concealment, make sure to create distance. If rounds are coming out of it on your side, there will be a storm of debris and fragmentation. Creating distance reduces the odds of being injured by this material.

Whenever using cover, make sure to prevent the barrel from touching against an object. If the barrel is touching it will throw off your shot placement.

Pay attention to your environment. Always be on the lookout for cover so that if something does happen you have an idea of where to go. At the same time, watch for suspicious actions, so if you

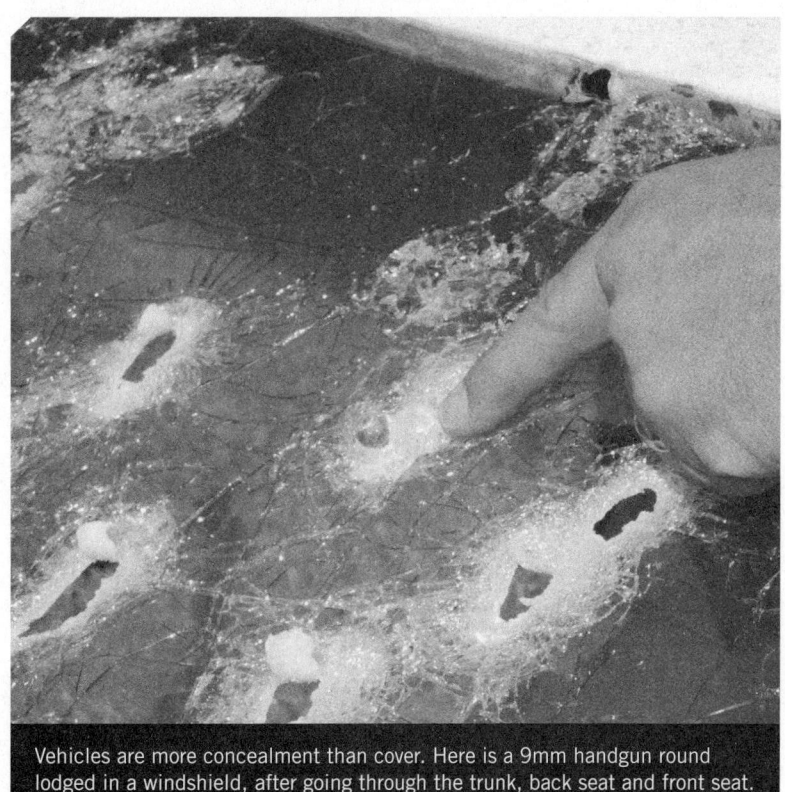

Vehicles are more concealment than cover. Here is a 9mm handgun round lodged in a windshield, after going through the trunk, back seat and front seat.

If you ever get the chance to shoot through a vehicle, take to opportunity to find out what bullets do after going through the various parts of the car.

If the barrel is touching at the bottom, that will throw your shots high, sometimes high enough to make the difference between a hit and a miss.

Through practice, you learn to adapt any of the traditional positions to unusual objects or terrain.

see something that could lead to trouble you're moving to cover before the fight starts. So, while watching the people around you and what they are doing, make it a habit to also study the objects in that environment. "If trouble developed," you ask yourself, "where is my cover?" This way, if something does happen you already know where to go. Also remember that your position doesn't have to be pretty, it just has to offer protection and provide you with the ability to make accurate hits. •

PRACTICE

Properly using cover requires plenty of practice. This doesn't mean you have to go to the range. Use a dummy weapon or your pretend AR, practicing at home with walls and furniture for your cover. Get into position behind cover, with some distance and making sure you have a good sight picture and that the muzzle is clear. On the range try to work around a lot of different objects, getting familiar with all the different positions that may be required, again making sure the muzzle is clear of your cover.

CHAPTER 20
LOW-LIGHT CONDITIONS

OVER 70 PERCENT of violent confrontations occur in low-light environments. This is especially true for security and law enforcement personnel. The big thing is to remember that low-light environments exist 24 hours a day. If it's a bright sunny day and you go into a parking garage, it will take time for your eyes to adjust. The power goes out, and with it the lights. A major part of being ready to use the AR is learning how to work in the dark.

The purpose of a light is the same as when man carried torches. Humans are visually-oriented creatures, especially during violent encounters where approximately 90 percent of our input about what is occurring is obtained through eyesight. Lights assist us in travelling through unfamiliar surroundings. You use light to locate, identify and if necessary engage threats. The light can be used as a communication tool, shining the light to let your partner know about an area of concern or the direction you want to move towards. A bright light in the eyes of the

The perfect location to mount a light is twelve o'clock, but this gets in the way of the sights. The next best choice is an eleven or one o'clock position. This way as you work around cover or clear corners the light is where is needs to be to get maximum penetration into the environment.

Having the light mounted in the right place is the key to being able to work cover or clear corners.

threat can disrupt their night vision, or buy you time to move off line of the attack. Handheld lights can be used as impact weapons, striking with the hard light instead of your soft hand. There are a lot of uses for the light.

All carbines should have weapon-mounted lights. There's no reason not to have a light on there. Normally you want the light to be mounted at an eleven or one o'clock position. The perfect location is twelve o'clock, but this gets in the way of the sights, unless you have a small light. With a weapon that's capable of being used at longer distances, though, you'll probably need a larger light to reach out there. Having the light at eleven or one o'clock means when you lean out the left or right of cover the light is where it needs to be.

Even though you have a light on your carbine you still must know how to use handheld lights. Depending on anticipated use of the firearm, a light attached to the weapon is good, but it is not the end-all solution to the variety of problems you may face. For instance, having only the one light attached to my weapon makes it difficult to maintain a ready position on a threat while scanning with the light to check for additional bad guys, cover or an exit. There is no guarantee you'll be fighting with your weapon. Without additional lights, or only practicing with the weapon-mounted light, sooner or later you'll find yourself in trouble.

Guidelines for selecting combat lights are similar to choosing what weapon to carry. The light should match your hand size and be something you are willing and able to carry. A large flashlight left at home is worthless. You should have a handheld flashlight on you all the time.

There is a wide variety of lights available. The only way to determine what works best for you is to test and experiment.

Additionally, it is a good idea to equip yourself with multiple lights. Low-powered lights are good for administrative duties, which don't require blinding white light, allowing you to conserve the burn time of your combative light for life threatening situations. No matter what type or brand combative light you carry, parts break and batteries expire. Fights rarely offer time to go home or back to your vehicle to retrieve a spare flashlight.

To be proficient at low-light fighting is more complicated than just selecting a light, choosing a single technique to employ light and AR, and shooting small groups onto a target. To be prepared for the realities of combat you must train with a variety of techniques. (For purposes of this chapter, the procedures discussed are limited to those utilizing a light with a pressure-activated switch on the tail cap.)

When using a handheld light you'll need a few different techniques. When working to the right side of cover, or clearing a left corner, the light needs to be on the right side of the AR. The support hand is holding the light on the right side of the handguard and the elbow should be high with the wrist bent upward. This creates a cradle for the handguard to rest in.

The light will need to be on the left side of the AR when working to the left of cover or a right-hand corner. For this technique you bring the support elbow low, underneath the handguard, and bend the wrist so the handguard can rest on the heel of the support hand.

Positioning the light on the correct side limits the amount of your body exposed, allows the light to penetrate into the environment and reduces the amount of light that reflects or bounces off the

When working to the right of cover, or clearing a left-turn corner, the light should be on the right side of the AR.

Light is on the left side of the AR to work left of cover, or a right-turn corner.

For scanning – keeping the AR pointing in one direction and using the light to check other areas – we use a variation of the old F.B.I. technique.

cover, which not only illuminates you, allowing the threat to see you more clearly, but also disturbs your night vision.

A variation of the old "F.B.I." technique works well for scanning. The support hand comes off the handguard and you scan as needed, keeping the muzzle pointing in a safe direction, toward the last known threat or where you last saw danger.

When it's necessary to manipulate the weapon, think about what to do with the handheld light. Having a lanyard ring on the light allows you to flip it out of the way, perform your manipulations, and then flip the light back into the hand ready for use. Or you can secure it underneath the strong side arm, clamping it under the armpit.

You use the light as little as possible or as much as necessary. There may be enough ambient light in the environment to leave the flashlight off until you locate a possible threat. The environment may be so dark that you have to use the light in order to move and ensure you don't expose yourself to an unexpected threat. One thing is for sure, if you turn the light on and someone starts shooting at you, turn the light off and move. After engaging a threat, you may need to turn the light off and move to avoid being targeted by additional threats, or it may be necessary to hold on the downed threat ensuring it no longer represents a danger.

Also practice working on low-light skills and transitions. There are a variety of different techniques, blending your normal low-light skills into transition drills. For example, you don't have the AR slung, so you transition as normally, clamping it in the support side elbow, while still using the light in the support hand.

It may be necessary to transition to the handgun, yet still use the light on the AR. By slipping the AR underneath the support arm and clamping it to the

Having a lanyard allows you to manipulate the AR while still keeping the light close. Here the light is flipped to the backside of the hand during manipulations, then flipped back into position for use.

Here the shooter has clamped the AR between the support arm and body so he can still use the handheld light while working with the pistol.

> Slipping the AR underneath the support arm and clamping it against the body allows you to use the AR's light while working with the pistol in the strong hand.

Something as simple as pressing the light's button can be complicated if you don't practice in advance.

body, you can still use its light while working the pistol with the other hand.

Obviously you can practice these techniques in the daytime, and I actually recommend it in the beginning to become familiar with them before doing it in the dark. At some point you'll need to work in some live-fire drills in low-light environments to discover how the shadows affect what you see. In the dark, you begin to really notice the amount of smoke created during live fire. The particles in the air start reflecting the light, which is like trying to drive when it's really foggy.

What it boils down to is that you'll likely employ several techniques to solve one problem. When you use the light and for how long, and when and

Using a dummy weapon – this is an old "rubber duck" training AR – allows you to practice your techniques.

Practice using the light on the left side of the AR. Notice how the elbow is low, so the hand is underneath the handguard, providing support.

where you need to move, is dictated by the situation. Fighting in the dark is a true art, and takes a lot of practice to become proficient.

Becoming adept at fighting in low-light conditions requires plenty of work, yet a large number of people only practice this when they attend a training class. All the schooling in the world won't help if you fail to practice. The most common excuse for not practicing low-light techniques is that very few outdoor ranges allow you to shoot at night, and most indoor ranges restrict your ability, either through rules and regulations or the structural environment itself, to move, shoot, use cover and engage multiple targets. Dry fire is the answer to all these issues. Using a dummy weapon – mine are made from old wood stocks with wood dowels for barrels – you can practice all the necessary skills in your home, garage or back yard without firing a shot. Then, go to the range and confirm that when you press the trigger you're getting good hits. •

DRILLS

1. **DRY OR LIVE FIRE:** From ready position come on target, turn the light on to identify and then engage. Finger off the trigger and "follow" the threat down. Engage the safety. From this point, work on scanning and moving. Sometimes you leave the light on while moving. Vary your practice by turning the light off, moving, and then scanning some more. Practice moving after every time you have the light on.

2. **LIGHT UP THE TARGET:** You identify it as a threat ready to attack, so you turn the light off immediately, move laterally one step, and then light up the target to engage. Follow the threat down and work on scanning and moving.

3. **SET UP MULTIPLE TARGETS** and use a decal or picture of a gun stuck on them, so they can be armed or unarmed. Your partner sets up the drill so you have to turn the light on, locate, identify and engage the threats.

Drills should be performed with both weapon and handheld lights. Practice flowing from one to the other. For example, you fire a couple of shots using the weapon-mounted light, then turn it off and transition to the handheld light, simulating that the weapon mounted-light has failed. Or transition to the handheld light to scan, while keeping your weapon on the last known threat. There are numerous variations of these drills.

Also practice manipulations, such as reloading and clearing malfunctions. Manipulating the weapon is a lot different when it's dark. Setting up the various manipulations required and running them while using handheld light is a little more difficult, and again practice is the key.

At some point you have to work in the actual dark to determine how to operate the light and deal with things like smoke, reflection and shadows.

CHAPTER 21

TRANSITION TO HANDGUN

FOR DEFENSIVE SITUATIONS when the AR stops working, regardless of whether it's empty or has a stoppage, the quickest way to put hits on the threat is to transition to the handgun – as long as you're within handgun distance.

The Combat Triad, established by Jeff Cooper, consists of mindset, marksmanship and gun handling. Marksmanship is the ability to hit your target. Gun handling includes reloads and malfunction clearances, which hopefully you practice until these tasks become subconscious processes. The weapon runs empty or a malfunction occurs, the conscious mind acknowledges this and initiates the reloading or clearing process, and the subconscious takes over to complete the procedure. Our conscious mind also determines when clearing a malfunction or reloading are not options due to time. I'm talking about those situations where, if you don't send rounds downrange immediately, you will die. When the rifle ceases to function under these conditions, regardless of the cause, the ability to transition to your secondary weapon is essential to survival.

Transitions, just like most things in life, are best when kept simple. Complicated actions consume additional time, increase opportunities for you to make a mistake, and are difficult to practice and apply. However, to prepare for the realities of combat you need several transition techniques.

Transitions with a tactical sling are fairly simple, but there may be times when you won't have a chance to strap into the sling. Daylight transitions will be different from low light actions. Maybe the only light you have is the one mounted on your rifle. Then there is no guarantee you'll even be fighting with your rifle. The conditions and situation will determine your best response.

First, let's look at the transition when you don't have a tactical sling or you don't have time to loop it around your body. The easiest way to transition from rifle to pistol is to just drop the rifle, using both hands to employ the pistol, but there are several reasons you might not want to ditch the rifle. Predicting exactly what it will take to stop the fight, and how long the fight will last, is impossible. You may have an opportunity to get the rifle back into action. During the fight, you may move to create distance, get to cover or just to make yourself a more difficult target for the threat to engage. Dropping your rifle pretty much guarantees that, if you have a chance to get it back into the fight, you won't be anywhere near where you dropped it. Then there is always the possibility your opponents could retrieve the rifle, get it operating, and employ it against you.

For these reasons I like transition techniques that include maintaining possession of the AR. The simplest technique is to use the primary hand to lower the rifle's stock down while the secondary hand, grasping the handguards, pulls the rifle tight against the center of your chest with barrel pointing up.

As soon as the secondary hand has control of the rifle, the primary hand presents the pistol. Pulling the rifle in tight against the body makes it easier to control, since it's not hanging out in front an away from the body, and it's also a plus in the retention department. Let the muzzle point up so the majority of the AR's weight is lower than where you're holding it on the handguard. Pointing the muzzle

When you don't have the sling looped around the body, the support hand holds the AR, pulling it into the body, and the strong hand presents the pistol.

Holding the AR with the support hand while using the strong hand to fire the pistol allows you to retain the AR in case you have an opportunity to get it running again.

down requires either twisting the support hand into an uncomfortable position, and having the weight of the rifle above our holding point, which means the AR wants to flip around, following gravity. Or you have to reposition the support hand on the weapon, adding a step into the sequence. Remember simple is best.

Maintaining the support hand's original grip on the rifle also reduces the actions required when it comes time to transition back to the rifle. Yes, you could continue the fight with the pistol, but the AR is much better at stopping threats. As soon as possible you want to transition back to the AR and get it running again.

You can also use the sling during the transition process. With a simple carry sling there are a couple of options, but keep in mind these techniques add steps to the transition sequence, which means additional time. The support hand can loop the sling over your neck into the scramble carry, as described in the section on carry modes. This allows you to use both hands to deploy the pistol, and with the sling adjusted properly you can leave it looped around the neck using it in the same manner as a tactical sling. With a tactical sling you simply lower the rifle with the support hand while the primary hand presents the pistol.

Low-light transitions when using a handheld light are basically the same, with only slight modifications. For example, the first technique described, where the rifle is pulled into the body with the support hand, works if we trap the rifle's handguard in the elbow of the support arm and clamp the rifle against our body.

The support hand operates the light and the primary hand is freed up to present the pistol. As mentioned previously, this technique works best with rifle muzzle pointing up. The sling techniques described above can also be employed, only instead of having both hands on the pistol the support hand holds the flashlight.

To employ weapon-mounted lights in conjunction with the sidearm we need techniques that will

With the sling looped around the body you can lower the AR using the support hand while the strong hand draws the pistol. Now you can use both hands on the pistol.

This series shows the transition in steps, with the rifle slung on the body. The rifle doesn't fire. The support hand lowers the rifle and the strong hand acquires the grip on the pistol, bringing it up. Now both hands can work the pistol, with the rifle hanging on the body.

keep the light of the rifle indexed on the threat. One option is to shift the AR over to the support side of the body, tucking and clamping it underneath the arm. The support hand maintains its original grip on the handguards where it can index the muzzle on target and operate the light. This frees up the strong hand to present the pistol. Although this technique takes slightly more time to shift the rifle from shoulder to side, it provides a good stable hold on the rifle that could be maintained for extended periods of time.

In the beginning your AR and pistol training are separate. Eventually you need to start working with both weapons together, combining them into a seamless package. Practice transitioning from rifle to pistol, from pistol to rifle, and even from pistol to knife. Ideally you want to flow smoothly from one weapon system to another without any gaps. To achieve this level of proficiency you must also unify your mind and body. As always, the mental aspects are the most important, and working with two weapons requires three or four times more thought. The mind must be prepared to make quick assessments and decisions, and the body trained to perform the physical actins required without delay or hesitation. It is essential to be able to flow from one weapon to another, and even more important that mind and body function as one unit. •

DRILLS

Using dummy weapons is the best way to begin your practice, getting the motions down so everything is done safely and efficiently. You start with the dummy rifle, then transition to the dummy pistol. Work these drills with and without the AR slung around your body so you get used to all the techniques. Remember, there may not be time to sling your tactical sling around the body, so you need to be familiar with all options.

On the range, for live fire practice, I have students load the AR then remove the magazine. They fire the shot, and then press the trigger again, which results in a "click" instead of a "bang." Now they can safely transition to the pistol, using the appropriate technique to control or maintain the AR according to how it is slung, or not slung. Eventually you can short-load your AR mags with just a few rounds. When the AR runs empty, transition to the handgun. When you have the chance, which means you have scanned and you're behind cover, holster the pistol, go back to the AR and get it running. Once you've reloaded the AR or cleared the malfunction, make sure to engage the safety. These drills are best performed using the Coach/Shooter mode, so you have someone watching to ensure you're doing everything safely. Also, by watching your shooter you'll learn through observation.

Once the basics are working well, add the transitions into your work with cover and low light with movement. The more skills you can combine the better, just keep in mind in the beginning start out slow, and then step by step work your way up into more complicated drills.

CHAPTER 22
CLEANING

CLEANING CAN BE divided into two categories – field cleaning and cleaning in your shop or at home. In the field, you need compact gear that you can carry easily. At home or in your shop, you want to use the proper gear to prevent excessive wear to the chamber and barrel of your AR.

During cleaning, or any time you're working on the AR, wear eye protection to keep solvents and debris out of your eyes. I also wear gloves to keep the solvents, oils or lead residue from getting on my hands. After cleaning the rifle, it's time to clean your body, washing your hands and face to ensure this stuff is not absorbed by your skin.

Cleaning begins with confirming the AR is unloaded. Use the proper techniques, ensuring you're consistently working the AR the same way every time. Next you'll need to field-strip the AR, removing the charging handle and removing the bolt from the carrier.

There are a lot of choices when it comes to field cleaning kits. Otis (www.otistec.com) has small compact kits specifically designed for the AR. There are "bore-snakes," which are lengths of fiber that you pull through the barrel to clean. You can also use the original G.I.-style rods, which are segmented and assemble to form a long rod. It's not a bad idea to have one of these on hand at all times, as they work well if you have to punch a stuck case out of the chamber. Remember, these

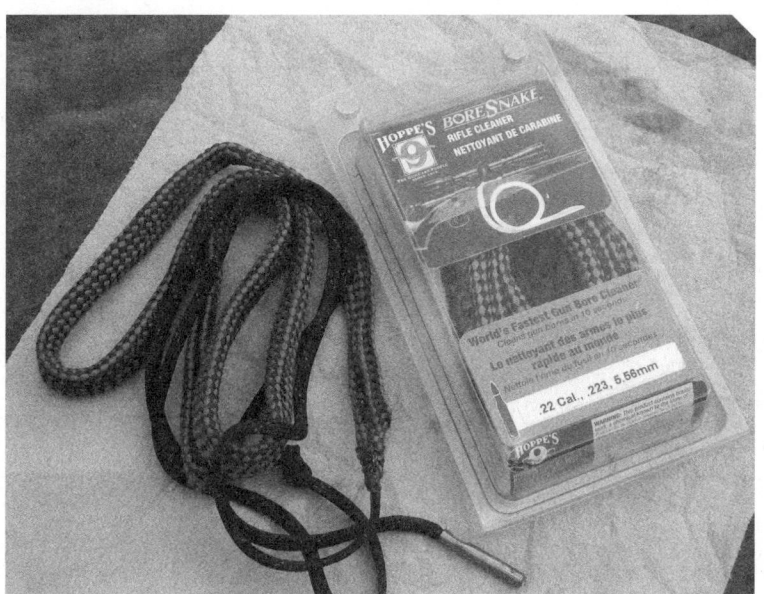

TOP: A bore snake is easy to pack in your gear and perfect for cleaning in the field. BOTTOM: Military-style cleaning kits also work well for field use, especially if you need to punch out a case that has stuck in the chamber.

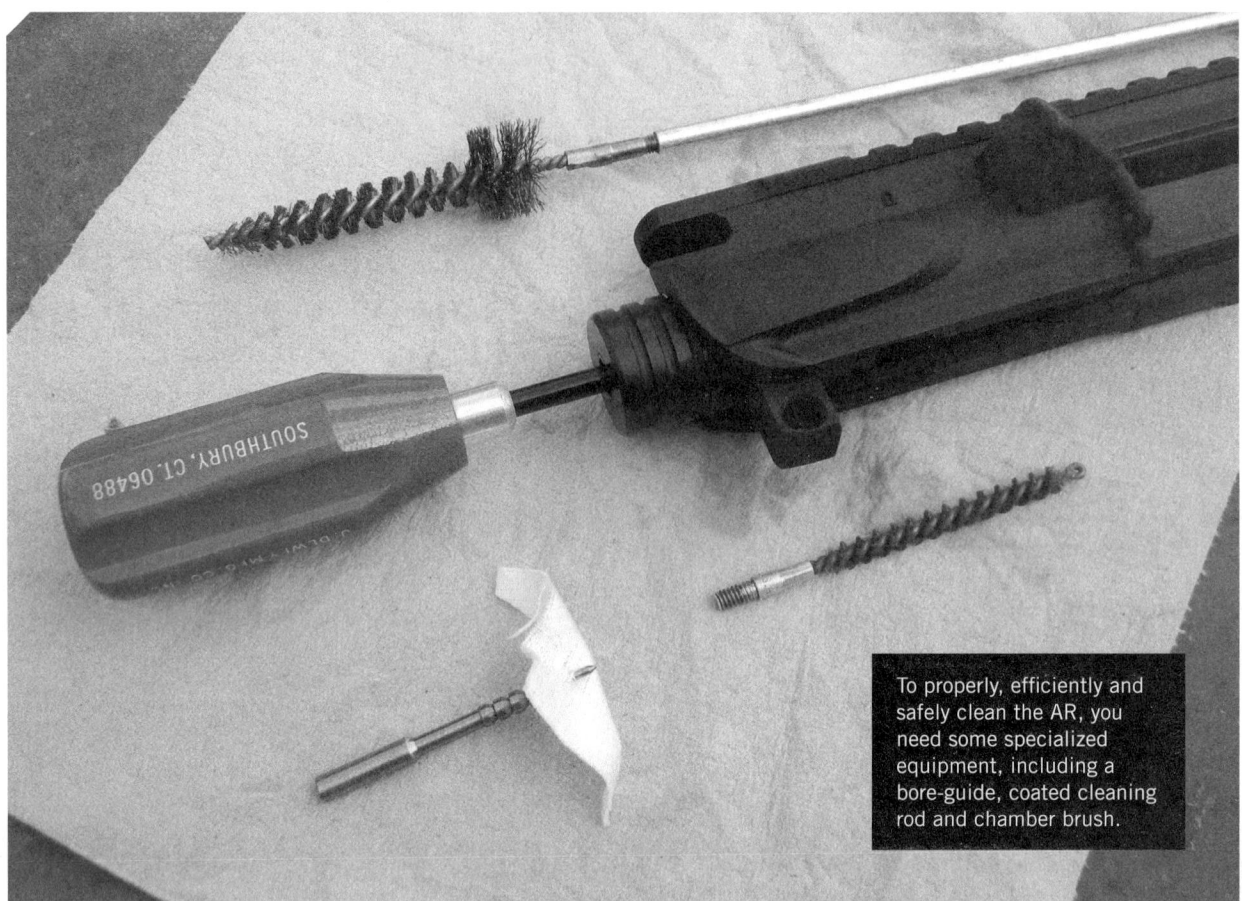

To properly, efficiently and safely clean the AR, you need some specialized equipment, including a bore-guide, coated cleaning rod and chamber brush.

tools are for field use only. The snakes or steel rods become impregnated with carbon, copper and other matter; regular use of them can cause premature wear and tear on the chamber and barrel.

Regular cleaning should be done with coated rods, a chamber or bore guide, and jags as opposed to a loop for your patches. A coated rod prevents abrasive material from getting embedded into the rod. After every pass through the barrel, wipe it off. The bore guide keeps everything in line and prevents the rod from wearing on the chamber and throat, where the bullet enters the barrel. With a cleaning jag, the patch surrounds the jag, preventing it from contacting the barrel. A loop, shaped like a large sewing needle, will probably rub against the barrel at some point. With a little use this isn't a problem, but extended cleaning like this will cause wear. You'll also need a chamber brush, which is specifically designed to clean out the barrel lugs and chamber.

There are different schools of thought when it comes to cleaning barrels. Also, it depends on whether you're cleaning one that's going into the gun safe for a long period of time or cleaning a carbine that sees regular carry or use.

One thing to remember is to always clean the chamber prior to cleaning the barrel. Cleaning the chamber after the barrel will cause a lot of crud to go into the barrel. This is where the chamber brush comes into play. It is specifically designed to clean the chamber and the lugs on the barrel extension where the bolt locks in. You'll probably want to use different type cleaning swabs and tips to get to all the various recesses and areas that need to be thoroughly cleaned.

To thoroughly clean the barrel – for example

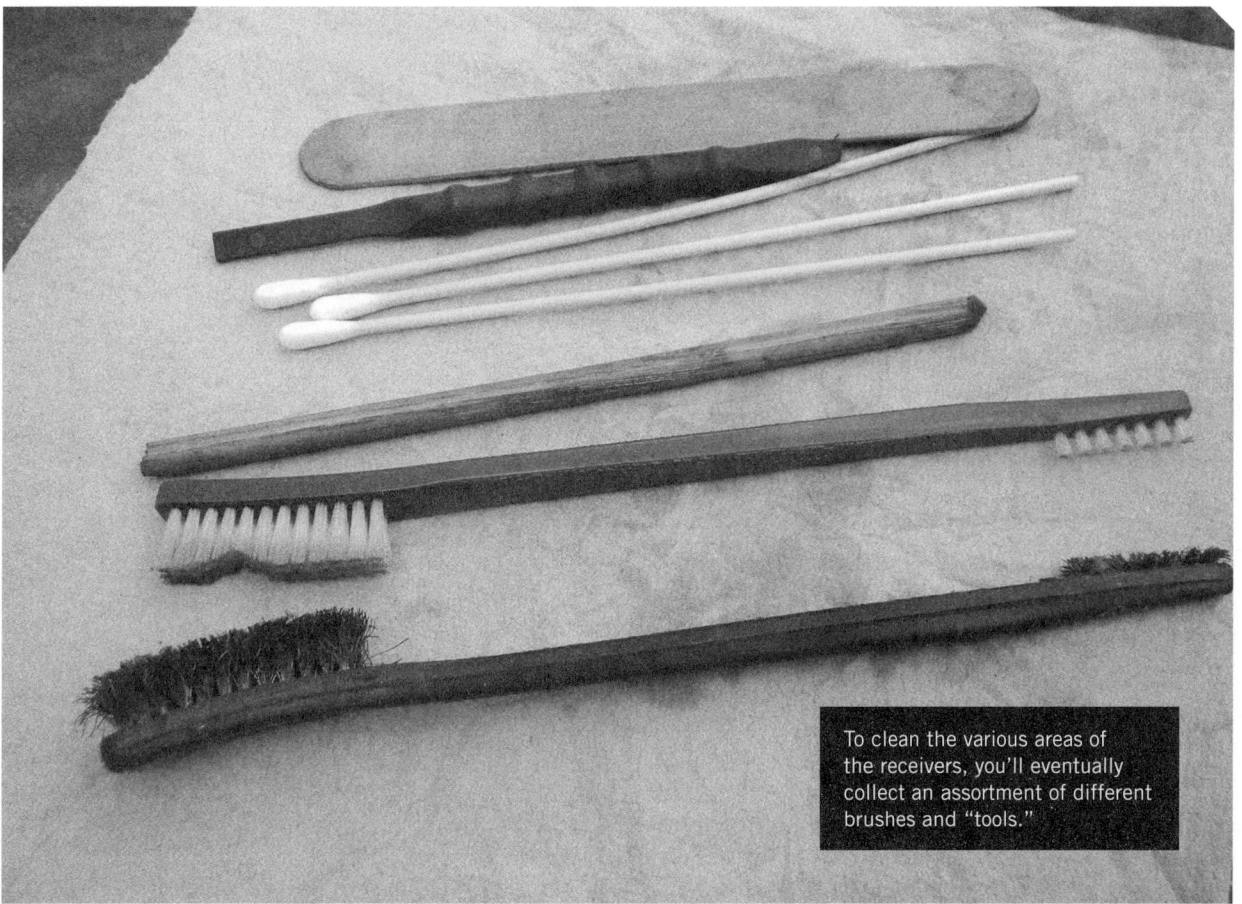

To clean the various areas of the receivers, you'll eventually collect an assortment of different brushes and "tools."

prior to storage – you'll need solvent that removes everything, including the copper from the bullet's jacket that builds up in the rifling. For this deep cleaning, use brushes to "scrub" the barrel clean. After using the brushes, you start working on it with patches.

For my carry carbine, which sees a lot of use, I don't use any copper cleaning solvent or brushes. The barrel has small pores in it. When shooting, copper from the bullets fills in these small pores, smoothing out the barrel. If you remove all this buildup, then when you start firing again it has to fill these pores in again. For cleaning the barrel of my carry AR I use CLP, on patches, which removes all the powder and carbon residue, but leaves the copper. After cleaning with CLP, using patches, I run a patch with oil through the barrel, then a dry patch to soak up any of the leftover oil, leaving a light coat of lubricant in the barrel.

Use the bore guide while cleaning to prevent damage to the chamber, and constantly wipe the rod down to remove the carbon and other grime that will be on it. After the barrel is clean it needs to be lubed in order to prevent rusting. A lubed-up patch run down the barrel will coat it well. For lubricating the barrel I use SLIP 2000 EWL or CLP. These are quality oils that are proven to work well.

The upper receiver needs to be cleaned; there will be a lot of buildup that needs to be removed. You can buy upper receiver cleaning kits, with rods and brushes specifically sized to clean the receiver. You'll also end up using different "tools" to get into the tight areas. Things like tongue depressors, small wooden dowels with a sharp point, or other tools that you can put a patch on help you work into the corners and other areas. Don't use anything that is

To release the hammer, in order to clean and lube the receiver and trigger group, hold the hammer back, press the trigger, and slowly let the hammer forward. Do not let it strike the receiver with full spring pressure.

steel or any material that is harder than the aluminum of the receiver. This will only scratch and damage the receiver.

For cleaning the receivers I don't use any solvent. Many of them have chemicals that can damage other parts on the receiver such as the stock or grip. The receivers don't need to be lubed, aluminum won't rust, and any oil or solvent left over will only attract residue and dirt.

The same procedure is applied to the lower receiver. Remember to release the hammer for cleaning the receiver. Hold the hammer back, press the trigger and slowly release the hammer forward. Pressing the trigger and letting the hammer strike the receiver can result in a broken or cracked receiver.

Compressed air is great for cleaning and blowing out the debris found in the receivers. When using air, be sure to wear eye protection to keep that stuff out of your eyes.

Pay close attention to the bolt and bolt carrier. These parts will have a lot of residue and carbon built up due to the AR's gas impingement system, especially the tail end of the bolt and the area where this seats in the bolt carrier. There are tools made for cleaning these areas and I highly recommend using them. They make cleaning these areas much easier. Brushes with brass bristles will help for scrubbing the outer surfaces.

Another area you need to clean is the extension or buffer tube. Remove the buffer and spring by depressing the detent. Wipe the buffer and spring off, and use a rod with a towel or rag to clean out the tube. There's a lot of friction here; every time the AR is fired the buffer goes back and forth. Eventually you can get enough residue built up in the tube and on the spring that it can retard the action, slowing the movement enough to create problems. After cleaning everything, put a light coat of oil on the buffer and spring and reinstall them.

Wipe down all the external surfaces that are steel to prevent rusting. A light coat of oil on the barrel, dust cover and all the pins and safety will do.

As mentioned, there are a lot of sources for detailed information on cleaning the AR. Eventually you'll figure out "your" way of cleaning, and the tools you need to help with the task.

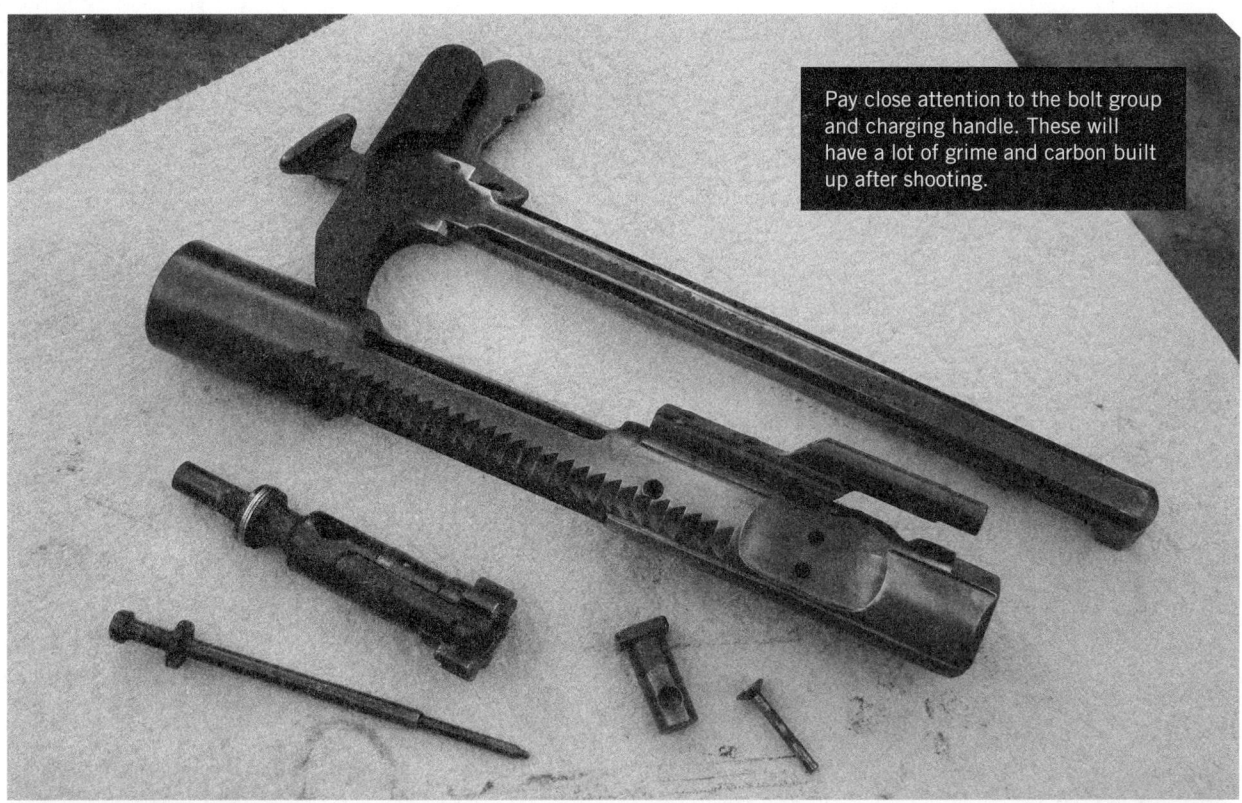

Pay close attention to the bolt group and charging handle. These will have a lot of grime and carbon built up after shooting.

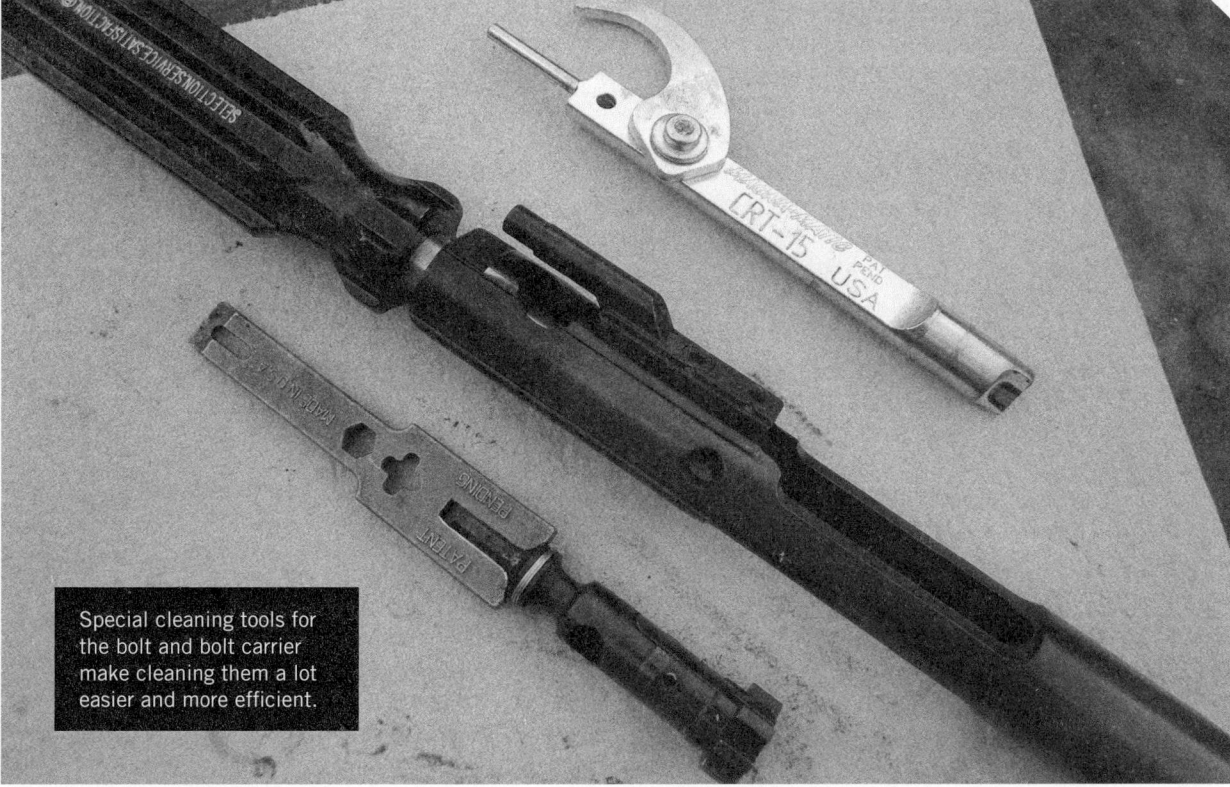

Special cleaning tools for the bolt and bolt carrier make cleaning them a lot easier and more efficient.

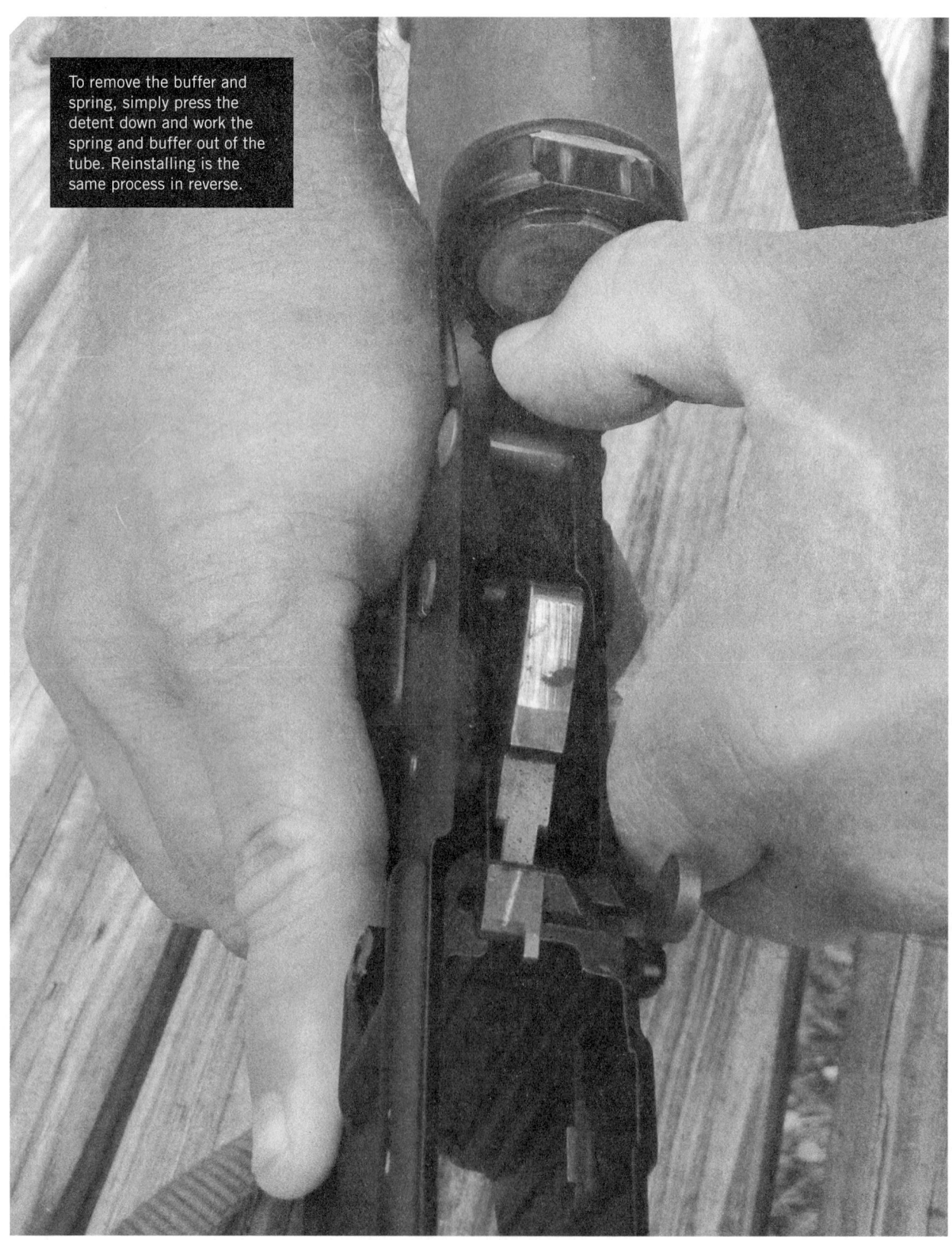

To remove the buffer and spring, simply press the detent down and work the spring and buffer out of the tube. Reinstalling is the same process in reverse.

LUBRICATION

One big misconception about the AR is that it won't run dirty. We have one AR Katana that has over 20,000 rounds through it without cleaning. It's always well-lubed, but has never been cleaned and so far we haven't had a problem with it.

Think about the AR as an internal combustion engine. The AR creates a lot of heat and friction when firing. Just like a car engine it will run dirty, but if it's not lubed you'll have a lot of problems.

The main areas that need lubrication are the bolt, bolt carrier and charging handle. The buffer spring also needs to be lubed, as discussed in the previous section. There are many ideas about the right way to lube the AR, and what lubes to use. We've found that a combination of grease and oil works best.

Oil is good, but after time it evaporates and gravity causes it to wick, or flow downward. Grease is good, but after time it can start to solidify, or under extreme cold conditions it can gum up. Using a combination of grease and oil works well. Put the two together and each compensates for the other's deficiency.

I really like using TW-25B grease, by Mil-Comm, and SLIP 2000's EWL oil, which was designed for fully automatic weapons. For most parts I apply a coat of the grease, then go over that with the SLIP oil.

The bolt carrier sees a lot of friction, and it is steel riding in an aluminum receiver, so lubrication is necessary to prevent wear and stoppages. Looking at the carrier will show you where it needs lube.

There are many ways to lube the AR, and techniques to use these lubricants. I've found that a combination of grease and oil work best.

There are rails on each side, at the top and bottom of the carrier, and the lower part of the carrier that resets the hammer. Apply a coat of grease to these areas, and work it in thoroughly. These are the areas that actually come into contact with the receiver or the hammer. The rest of the carrier needs a light coat of oil to prevent rusting, but since it's not for friction or wear it should be a very light coat.

The bolt needs lubrication. Put grease on the lugs and the tail of the bolt, then oil on top of that, including the gas rings. The same thing applies to the cam pin and firing pin.

The same combination is applied to the charging handle. Apply the grease, work it in well, then add a coat of oil. This is one place you want to actually be able to see a film of oil. The charging handle is aluminum and the receiver is aluminum. Without lubrication you'll quickly get galling, causing wear and making it difficult to cycle the handle.

Remember that any lubricant can be used in a pinch. Motor oil or transmission fluid from a car, bearing grease or anything else that will reduce friction and withstand heat will work.

For the trigger group all you want is a drop of oil on each side of the hammer and trigger springs. One drop is plenty, and it will migrate into the areas that need lube. You don't want too much lube, as this will only attract carbon and powder residue and other gunk you don't want building up.

SYSTEMS CHECK

Always give the bolt group a good inspection. The extractor and ejector springs on the AR should require a lot of pressure to move. Set the bolt in the carrier, turn it upside down and set it down. If the

Here you can see the shiny areas where the bolt carrier rides in the receiver. These areas must be well-lubricated for the AR to function properly.

carrier's weight causes it to collapse down on the bolt, the gas rings are worn or broken. (I've seen ARs run with two broken gas rings, but as soon as you remove the bolt they fall apart and need replacing.) Make sure the cam pin and bolt, which both have big holes in the center of them, aren't cracked or misshapen. Check the hammer and trigger springs to be sure they aren't broken, causing light strikes, and that the pins, including the firing pin, are good and straight.

How often do you clean your AR? This depends on how much you shoot it, the weather conditions, the quality of ammo you're firing and a lot of other factors. My "work" AR gets cleaned every so often. I'll take the bolt group out, wipe it off and lube it and the charging handle; it's rare that I do a complete cleaning. A weapon that's going into the safe for a long period should be well cleaned, regardless of how many rounds you've fired.

Eventually everyone decides how often they'll clean their AR, and the way to go about it. Like most other things you have to get started in the general direction to find out what works for you. For example, if you have access to compressed air it's great for blowing out the receivers. Just remember to wear that eye protection. Some people like to use ultrasonic cleaning tanks to clean their bolts and carriers. I lean toward "old school" methods, which give me time to inspect each part as I clean and lube it. Thoroughly cleaning an AR normally takes me about an hour or more.

To sum it up: Think about cleaning in the field, using the least amount of gear necessary. In your shop you have all the "proper" tools to thoroughly clean. Regardless of how it's cleaned, lubrication is the key to keeping your AR running and reliable. •

The bolt, lugs and gas rings should be lubed as well. I use a combination of grease with oil on top of that.

CHAPTER 23
PRACTICE TOOLS

THERE IS A world of difference between shooting and fighting. To fight effectively you need a lot of training and practice, way beyond just shooting targets on the range. In a fight we need to move, communicate, shoot if necessary and use cover whenever possible. To develop these skills, you'll need a few training aids like target stands, barricades to represent cover, moving targets and dummy weapons. You could go out and buy all these things, but in my world I relate everything to "ammo bucks." Building your own targets, barricades, and other training aids deposits more bucks into your ammo bucks account. This is a good thing, especially with the cost of ammunition today.

When I first started teaching I worked with various clubs and commercial ranges, booking their ranges to run my classes. Often the ranges were very primitive. I spent a lot of time on the road, and what I needed were training fixtures that were lightweight and would fit into the back of a car or truck. So I came up with a variety of items that are easy to construct, affordable and easy to transport. These range aids will greatly improve the quality of practice.

To train for defensive use of the AR you'll need some range equipment, including target stands, barricades – to use for cover – and other materials to create realistic drills.

Lightweight, portable target stands can be made using PVC pipe, which is easy to work with.

TARGET STANDS

If you're equipping your personal range or making use of a club range, it's important to have target stands that can be positioned at various locations and distances. In real life the bad guys are rarely all lined up in a row in front of you like they are on most ranges. My original target stands, which I still use, are lightweight, portable and work for both indoor and outdoor ranges. The stand is assembled from PVC tubing, which is easy to work with, affordable and available almost anywhere.

With a few sticks of PVC pipe, some "elbow" and "T" joints, and a little time, you've got a portable stand. I use two types of PVC for the stand. The high-pressure pipe (Schedule 40) is thicker and heavier, so it's used for the bottom part of the stand. For the upright portions of the stand, where the targets are attached, I use the thinner pipe (Schedule 30), which actually holds up to bullets better – it's more flexible and doesn't shatter when a bullet strikes it. End caps on the uprights keep them from filling with water, or even worse, a nasty wasp nest.

For each stand you'll need the following:

- **3 brace sections – 2 thick and 1 thin section (The width of these sections depends on the width of target. Allow for the distance the joints will take up.)**
- **4 base sections – thick pipe, 18 inches long**
- **4 uprights – thin pipe, 24 inches long, or longer for taller targets**
- **4 90-degree joints**
- **4 "T" joints**
- **2 end caps**

Once you have all your parts it's an easy process to cut the pipe sections to length and then stick everything together. When assembling the stands I normally don't glue them together. This way you can disassemble them for storage or transporting,

Making target stands easy. If you don't have a saw, get a friend to cut your pipes to the right lengths.

and it makes it easy to replace sections damaged during training. To attach my targets, normally cardboard ISPC targets, I use masking or duct tape. Since these stands are easy and cheap to build, you can assemble several of them. Now you can set up a variety of scenarios, placing targets at different angles and distances, and positioning shoot/no-shoot targets as needed. When you're setting up different drills, think safety. Always check your angle of fire to ensure there is no chance of any rounds missing the backstops.

I normally use standard cardboard targets, but I prefer having my students shooting armed attackers who aren't responding to verbal commands. It's also important to shoot based on the anatomy of the threat, especially for headshots. I use a stencil, made from a target and cutting out a hand holding a weapon, the eyes, nose and mouth for the face, and a two-inch square diamond for marksmanship drills. Using this stencil I paint my cardboard targets.

The cool thing about the stencil is that you can change the type or location of the weapon and reposition the facial features. Another easy way to modify your targets and make them more realistic is to take some pictures of friends' faces, enlarge them to actual size, and then attach these to the head of the cardboard backers. These small changes help prevent you from developing a range mentality, which is easy to do, especially if all you're doing is shooting at the same old target over and over.

BARRICADES

Unless you're fighting in the middle of the desert, there will be objects in your environment that can be used for cover. Your practice needs to represent reality, so you need barricades that are lightweight and portable to serve as cover. I use plywood, cut into various shapes and joined together with hinges to form a barricade. When opened they are self-supporting, and you can fold them flat for storage or transporting. Another advantage of using plywood is that, if anyone does fire a round that hits the "cover," the rounds don't bounce back, injuring the shooter. Repairing any holes or damage is easily accomplished with "bondo," used to repair automobile bodies, or by just cutting off the damaged area.

Although these barricades are too large to fit into a car trunk, they will easily fit into the bed of a pickup truck. You can build taller barricades, which allows you to set up various configurations replicating corners and hallways. Now you can work clearing techniques on a square range without having an actual clearing-house.

For our barricades we use 3/4-

Making a stencil allows you to mark your targets in various ways. Here there's a diamond, for marksmanship, the eyes, nose and mouth, for headshots and the threat is armed with a pistol.

inch pressure-treated plywood, which is durable and withstands the weather. But, you can use thinner plywood, especially if it'll be stored inside and protected. One sheet of plywood will make one short barricade, or use two sheets to build taller sections. I normally cut the bottom edge of the barricades so that, when assembled, they are taller in the center, leaning slightly inward. This angling creates a tripod effect, a little extra stability; it isn't as easily blown over by the wind.

On the range, set up your cover in various configurations, again trying to create a realistic environment. For example, the fight starts. You move to cover. After engaging the threat and scanning you notice cover behind you and to the right. Tactically you withdraw, putting more distance and better cover between you and the threat. The variety of scenarios you can set up is endless, just remember to keep it realistic and safe.

MOVING TARGETS

In a real fight everyone is moving. To develop the skills needed to shoot moving threats you need moving targets. There are expensive moving targets available, but with a little work and imagination you can construct your own. The easiest moving target to build is to simply add wheels to the stationary PVC stand described above, and use a rope and pulley system to move it. The stand will be bouncing around the ground as you pull it, so you will either need to glue the stand together, use small screws to hold it, or a combination of both to create a rigid stand. You could also build the frame out of wood, such as 2x4s, or if you're handy with a welder or have a friend who'll assist with the task you can construct it from metal.

I use lawnmower wheels, which can be purchased at almost any hardware store. A long bolt fits inside the wheel and attaches it to the stand. Use washers between the wheel and the frame for spacing so the wheel doesn't rub the stand. I construct it so the nuts are tight, but loose enough to roll, and they won't come loose or tighten up on you during use.

A couple of eyebolts provide a place to tie your ropes, and two pulleys mounted on stakes provide the target with movement. For use on an indoor range, you can secure the pulleys by using weights set on the floor. With a little imagination you can make one stand that will work for lateral movement or as a charging target that advances on the shooter.

Fighting a moving threat adds a completely different aspect to your practice. You're behind cover when the threat moves. You adjust your position in order to keep cover between you and the threat. You shoot until the threat stops moving, and then stay plugged in because they may decide to get

Constructing a rope-operated target stand is an easy job, and it can be made out of almost any materials.

back into the fight. There are bystanders between you and the threat, which forces you to concentrate on where the muzzle is pointing and when you shoot. It's very much like in real life.

DUMMY WEAPONS

Dummy weapons, or "blue" guns, are mandatory part of your training kit. Using a dummy weapon you can practice at home moving, using cover and the other skills that you can't normally practice on a range. You can also use them to practice disarming or retention techniques, something you definitely do not want to do with an actual firearm. Yes, you can buy dummy ARs, but you can also build your own.

To build a dummy AR carbine, find an old wood or synthetic stock. Use a piece of wood dowel, about one inch diameter, and glue and screw it to the stock for a barrel. Attach a section of nylon webbing for a sling, and you can even screw on a short section of picitinny rail for mounting a flashlight.

Another area of practice where dummy weapons come in handy is dry work on complicated drills before running them live. Any drills that contain completed movements, especially team tactics, can be run safely without the dangers involved when using live weapons. The key is to treat the dummy weapons just like you would live ones, consistently applying good gun-handling habits. Plus, even though the dummy weapons don't have any moving parts you can still perform the actions necessary to reload or clear malfunctions. The important thing is to handlie it like you would you're real AR, flipping the safety off and on and taking your finger on and off the trigger, adding as much realism to your practice as possible. The mental aspects make the big difference between just spending time practicing vs. actually improving your skills.

Dummy ammunition should also be considered part of your training gear. With the dummy round

Having dummy weapons to practice with is mandatory. This way you can practice the majority of your skills safely at home. Just remember to treat them like live, loaded weapons; otherwise you could develop unsafe habits.

you can practice the administrative actions, such as loading and unloading, plus the functional manipulations, reloading and clearing malfunctions. When you work dry, make sure there is no live ammo anywhere in the vicinity and that you have a backstop that would stop or trap a round if you were to make a mistake. The golden rule for dry fire practice: Once you're done, you're done. Stop then and there. Most of the negligent discharges you hear about with dry practice occur when someone stops, gets distracted or disrupted, and then decides to perform one more drill. I normally do all my dry practice, using an actual AR, on the range, and only use the dummy weapons inside the home. This helps ensure that nothing bad happens.

.22 CALIBER

With the variety of offerings, there's no reason not to have a .22 caliber AR to practice with. It's affordable and much cheaper to shoot than using .223/5.56 ammo. The .22s are lightweight, making it easier to spend more time handling the weapon without fatigue. Their operation is almost exactly the same as your standard AR, so all your manipulations are the same. For beginning or younger shooters, the .22s are a great way to get started. And with the parts available, you can set up a .22 caliber AR that is an exact match to your full-caliber AR.

The idea with all of these training aids is to get your practice as close to reality as possible. Shooting small groups is good for working on the fundamentals of marksmanship, but to fight effectively we need to move, communicate, use cover, and shoot as needed. Make your practice realistic and safe. Inspect your angles of fire to insure they are clear, that your range will contain all rounds fired, and that everyone on the range is accounted for at all times. The goal is to make your training interesting, realistic, and challenging without endangering anyone. •

There are a lot of advantages to having a .22 caliber AR, and with the parts available to modify them you can set one up just like your full-caliber AR. Plus, they are just plain fun to shoot, and great for beginners. The top rifle is a MHT Katana, while the bottom rifle is a S&W 15-22 in .22 lr that has been customized to match the Katana.

CHAPTER 24
VESTS, CHEST RIGS & PACKS

FOR SELF-DEFENSE OR law enforcement, you want to think about response to danger as a series of levels or layers. My first level of response is what I have on me every day – pistols, spare ammunition, knives and flashlights. The next level of response is going to the carbine, with time to shove a spare AR magazine in my rear pocket. For self defense, anything that requires going beyond that means you're in for really bad times. While this is unlikely, it is possible there may be times that going beyond the first two layers is necessary. For those situations, you'll be thinking about additional layers.

My next level is the addition of a chest rig, which has additional magazines (both pistol and carbine), flashlights and a basic trauma kit. I like the chest rig because it's quick to put on and quick to shed if necessary. Being a "chest" rig, it should be adjusted so it's actually chest high and doesn't get in the way of firing positions such as kneeling or prone. With it worn up high, I can still get to anything on my belt.

My final layer is throwing on a backpack. This has enough gear and equipment to survive for a few days. There are a lot of things you may need.

I like chest rigs, which are easy to put on, quick to take off, and when adjusted properly you can still get to the gear that's on your belt. It has spare mags, a trauma kit and flashlights.

GunDigest.com

The next level is a backpack, which has additional gear such as a poncho and liner, water, food, batteries and other items necessary to survive for a couple of days.

Each person's requirements will be a little different, especially if you consider the environment. A hot, wet area requires a different kit than a hot, dry environment. Try to think about gear that will work for a variety of different applications. For example, a military poncho and liner can be used for staying dry in the rain, sleeping, cover, shelter and camouflage, or to build a litter to carry out an injured team member.

Being prepared for a variety of different responses requires practice. Work with the bare essentials, as mentioned above, a magazine or two in your back pocket. If you anticipate using a vest or chest rig in response to a threat, you should practice with that equipment. Using this equipment takes some getting used to, especially when working from different firing positions.

You need to seriously consider your real-world application. In other words, consider what you might actually be involved in and the equipment necessary for that situation. It would be really unusual to need to gear up like a soldier in Afghanistan would. If you had that much time to get equipped, then your best option is to avoid and escape the situation. However, there might be times when you would need extra gear. During one of the times when we had serious tornadoes here, the power was out for almost two weeks. There was looting and shootings were taking place nearby, and during this time we did wear and carry extra gear until things settled down.

Ultimately you'll need to experiment, using and testing different gear until you discover what will work best for you. This means testing under all conditions. You'll need to work from a variety of firing positions, kneeling, sitting, prone and others. Practice in a variety of weather conditions. Adding bulky clothing and/or gloves will change how you handle equipment. For example, simply wearing a jacket with a hood will restrict your field of vision.

Additional gear is going to add to your body's profile, so you need to practice working in tight, restricted conditions in order to compensate for the additional gear.

When you're wearing vests or chest rigs, you're positions are going to be a little different. Plus, you need to practice acquiring magazines and such, which means practicing with the gear you might be wearing.

You never know what the situation may call for. While normally your best response is avoidance and escape, there may be times when you need more gear with you.

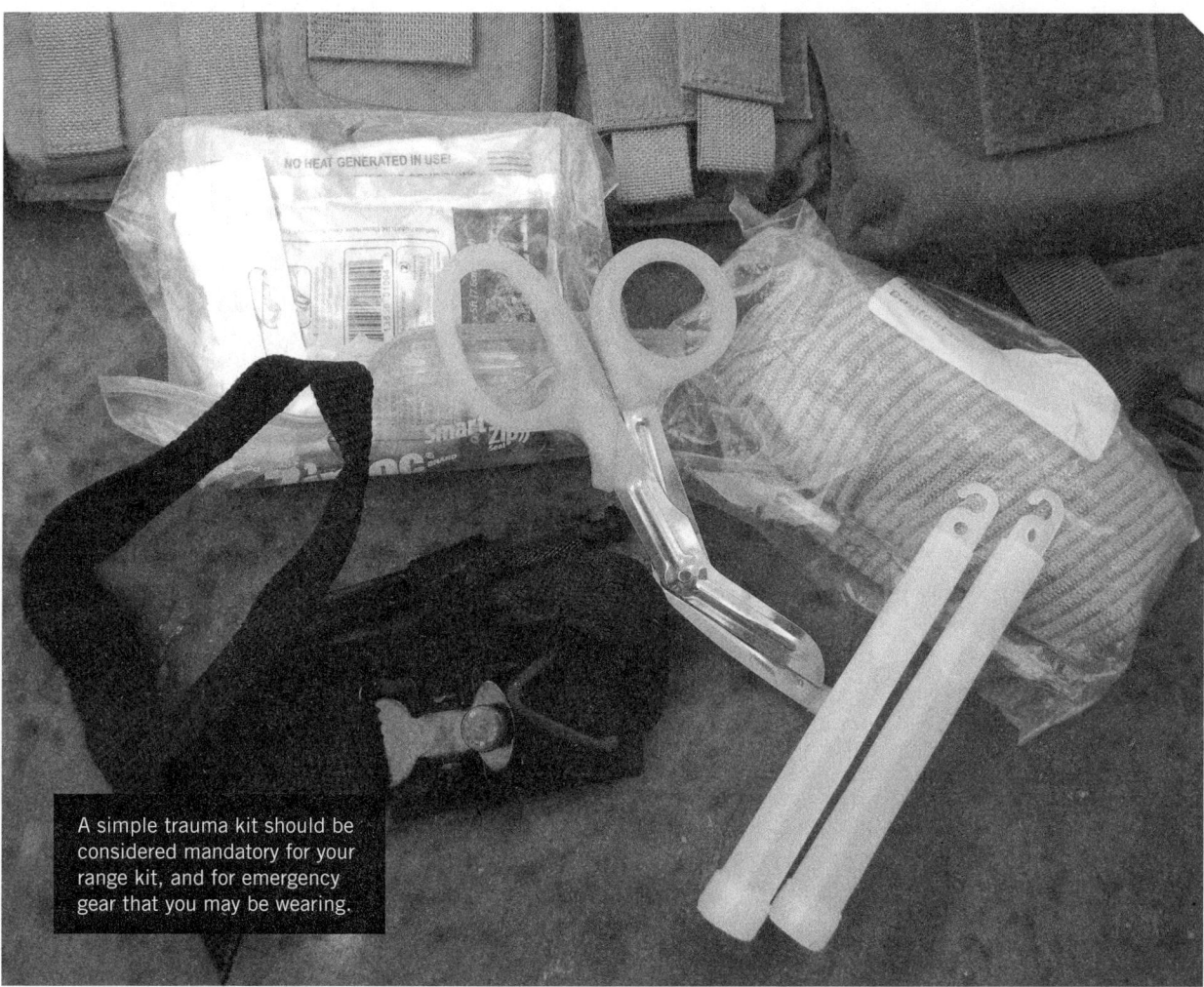

A simple trauma kit should be considered mandatory for your range kit, and for emergency gear that you may be wearing.

This requires you to move the head more by shifting the body around. Wearing gloves diminishes your ability to "feel" and your dexterity.

A mandatory part of your gear should equip you to deal with trauma or serious wounds. A tourniquet is mandatory. You also want an "Israeli" or "H" battle bandage. You don't want to use your sharp tactical knife to cut clothes off someone, so get a set of trauma shears, which are strong enough to cut through thick clothing or belts. I'm also a big fan of clotting agents, and have both powder and gauze, which has the clotting agent embedded in it. Glow-sticks are a good idea. They put out light in 360 degrees, and you can hold it in your mouth while working.

By experimenting, you discover what works for you. Then you need to practice with that gear, becoming familiar with it before it's necessary to use it. You can never predict when, where or the conditions under which trouble will come. Train, practice and test different equipment until you discover what works under various conditions. This is a never-ending process, and your kit is always evolving as you check out new gear. If it works better, use it, but don't be afraid to stick with the "old" until you discover something that is actually an improvement. •

LETHAL FORCE LAW: Get the Facts

Massad Ayoob's first book on the use of deadly force by the private citizen in defense of self and others, *In the Gravest Extreme*, is considered the authoritative text in its field. *Deadly Force* is the follow-up to this groundbreaking guide, incorporating Ayoob's thirty extra years of experience, during which he's been an expert witness in weapons cases, chair of the Firearms Committee of the American Society of Law Enforcement Trainers, and much more.

This guide will help you understand any legal and ethical issues concerning the use of lethal force by private citizens. You'll also learn about the social and psychological issues surrounding the use of lethal force for self-defense or in defense of others. In addition to exploring these issues, Ayoob also discusses the steps a responsible armed citizen can and should take in order to properly prepare for or help mitigate a lethal force situation.

Retail: $21.99 • ISBN: 9781440240614

Get our *LOWEST* prices online at
GunDigestStore.com
or call 855.840.5120 (M-F 7am-6pm MT)